Religion and Space

Also available from Bloomsbury

Sikhs Across Borders, edited by Knut A. Jacobsen and Kristina Myrvold
Religion, Postcolonialism and Globalization: A Sourcebook, Jennifer Reid
The Sacred in the City, edited by Liliana Gómez and Walter Van Herck

Religion and Space

Competition, Conflict and Violence in the Contemporary World

Lily Kong and Orlando Woods

Bloomsbury Academic
An imprint of Bloomsbury Publishing Plc

B L O O M S B U R Y

LONDON · OXFORD · NEW YORK · NEW DELHI · SYDNEY

Bloomsbury Academic

An imprint of Bloomsbury Publishing Plc

50 Bedford Square	1385 Broadway
London	New York
WC1B 3DP	NY 10018
UK	USA

www.bloomsbury.com

BLOOMSBURY and the Diana logo are trademarks of Bloomsbury Publishing Plc

First published 2016
Paperback edition first published 2017

British Library Cataloguing-in-Publication Data
A catalogue record for this book is available from the British Library.

ISBN: HB: 978-1-4742-5740-4
PB: 978-1-3500-4434-0
ePDF: 978-1-4742-5741-1
ePub: 978-1-4742-5742-8

Library of Congress Cataloging-in-Publication Data
Kong, Lily.
Religion and space: competition, conflict, and violence in the contemporary world / by Lily
Kong And Orlando Woods.
pages cm
Includes bibliographical references.
ISBN 978-1-4742-5740-4 (hb) – ISBN 978-1-4742-5742-8 (epub) – ISBN 978-1-4742-5741-1
(epdf) 1. Religion and geography. 2. Sacred space. 3. Religions–Relations. I. Title.
BL65.G4K66 2016
201'.691–dc23
2015033417

Typeset by Newgen Knowledge Works (P) Ltd., Chennai, India

Contents

Boxes

Religious Competition and Space

Religious competition in pluralistic societies

Religious competition is a common feature of religiously pluralistic societies. Religious organizations compete with one another and with secular groups for scarce resources such as adherents, funds, spaces for religious practice and religious privileges (in the form of tax exemptions, subsidies, rights to express their religious identity in public through clothing and custom and so forth). More abstractly, they compete for a hegemonic status in the social life of individuals. Religious competition has the potential to augment social welfare in a variety of ways, including, but not limited to, the expansion of religious choice available to individuals; increased provision of psychological and social support services through religious networks; the development of lean and efficient religious organizations; and the erection of organic bulwarks against religious fundamentalism.

Notwithstanding the above positive consequences, religious competition also has a tendency to degenerate into disruptive conflict and destabilizing violence. In its most extreme form, religious competition can escalate into the uncompromising desire for one religious group to 'overcome, eliminate, or convert the other to extinction' (Bouma 2007, 190; see also Lincoln 2003). Such desires are inherently political, and can have wide-ranging consequences that infringe upon both religious and civil liberties. In such instances, religious violence can implicate and affect religious and secular groups. Most importantly, it can compromise the authority of the state by challenging one of the central characteristics of statehood: the monopoly over the use of legitimate force/ violence. In addition, conflict and violence are economically costly; they reduce productivity, give rise to a more risky investment climate and impose considerable burdens on state resources by increasing the need for policing, surveillance and rehabilitation costs. Therefore, in order to allow religious competition and yet contain it from escalating into conflict/violence, public policy regarding religion needs to be informed by an understanding of the nature and forms of religious competition and the social, political, economic and technological circumstances under which competition might spiral out of control.

An understanding of religious competition needs to take into account who the competitors are. Broadly speaking, religious competition occurs between four different groups. The first – *inter-religious competition* – occurs between one religious group and another, often a hegemonic religious group and one or more minority groups. The second – *intra-religious competition* – occurs within a religious group, between denominations and sects in that group. The third – *religion-secular competition* – occurs between religious group(s) and secular organizations and imperatives. The fourth – *religion-state competition* – occurs between religious group(s) and the (secular or anti-religious) state or between secular group(s) and a religious state. In this book, we demonstrate how each of the above forms of competition varies in terms of its object; what combination of social, political, economic and regulatory environments precipitates competition; and the degree to which each of the above forms of competition might escalate into conflict.

Space as cause, conduit and effect

One of the core aims of this book is to develop an understanding and appreciation of how religiously motivated competition – which may result in conflict and violence – intersects with 'space'. In other words, this book aims to develop an understanding of how 'space' can be a cause, a conduit and an effect of religious competition, conflict and violence. As Hassner (2003, 3) argues, such a focus is both timely and important: 'given the prevalence of disputes over sacred space and their grave consequences, it is surprising that the causes and characteristics of conflict over sacred space remain understudied'. Among other things, space serves to ground religious practices and beliefs; it 'concretizes religion, giving it an earth-bound, material facet' (Hassner 2003, 8). By giving religion a visible and material presence, space makes religion tangible and, therefore, something that can be owned, developed, changed and fought over. Apart from sacred or religious space, religious competition, conflict and violence can also occur in secular space, with equally grave consequences. Space is, in other words, a viable and yet often overlooked analytical lens that can be used to classify and understand the processes and outcomes of religious competition, conflict and violence. In fact, we argue that space is a critical analytical lens that cannot be overlooked.

Space is the arena within which much of religious competition, conflict and violence unfold. A focus on spaces – both religious and secular – reveals otherwise hidden patterns of religious activity and structures of power and control. Depending on who claims, produces or contests it, space can play an agentic role that helps to either disguise or assert religious presence. Drawing on Foucault's (1984) understanding of heterotopia, Vasquez (2008, 163) argues that 'religion is heterotopic: it generates multiple overlapping spaces, but often conflict-ridden, spaces'. Religion and space share multiple layers of meaning and understanding, often more than surface appearances reveal. Space is therefore integral to the 'ever-shifting social geometry of power and signification in which the material and ideological are co-constitutive' (Jazeel and Brun 2009, 4). Religious groups often fill space with meaning, using it to promote an agenda or achieve an objective. Religious competition is subtle, and religious conflict is everywhere. In light of this, there is a need to identify and understand how 'power works through the various levels, realms and conceptions of space, in and through religious processes' (McAlister 2005, 249). An analytical focus on the spaces of religious competition and conflict stands to yield greater understandings of religious power, control and subversion.

The occupation and management of space is frequently heavily political. Often such occupation and management is 'inseparable from their [religious groups'] ability to impose their presence on a given territory' (Hervieu-Leger 2002, 101). 'Presence' may be physical and measured in terms of territorial conquest as Hervieu-Leger suggests (such as the opening of a new religious building, street evangelization and other public forms of religious praxis), or more abstract and measured in terms of changing social networks and identities, cultural interaction or religious acceptance. It can also be agentic insofar as it enables religious groups to exert and extend power and control over both people and territory. Whatever form 'space' entails, the fact remains that the religious occupation of space invariably involves the negotiation of 'hierarchical power relations of domination and subordination, inclusion and exclusion, appropriation and dispossession' (Chidester and Linenthal 1995, 17). It is, in other words, intimately bound up with assertions of and challenges to the power of religious groups. As Edward Said (1993, 7) argued:

> Just as none of us is outside or beyond geography, none of us is completely free from the struggle over geography. That struggle is complex and interesting

because it is not only about soldiers and cannons but also about ideas, about forms, about images and imaginings.

While Said's explicit concern is with 'geography', integral to geographical analysis and understanding is space. His argument may thus be read as nobody being outside or beyond space or completely free from the struggle over space, given that all human action is both constitutive of and enacted through space. Developing this line of thought further, Knott (2005a) argues that because space reflects and (re)produces the goals and achievements of religious actors and organizations, it should be seen as a medium, a methodology, and an outcome of religious activity. We return to these ideas repeatedly throughout the book.

Over the past few decades, theorizations of sacred space have developed along two distinct axes: the 'insider' or 'substantial' standpoint propounded by Eliade (1959; see also Lane 1988), and the 'outsider' or 'situational' standpoint propounded by social constructionists (see Smith 1978). These two approaches to the theorization of sacred space have important ramifications for how space religious and non-religious actors perceive and behave in relation to space.

Sacred space

Eliade (1991) draws a clear distinction between 'sacred' and 'profane' spaces. In his view, they represent two distinct forms of experience, and each is qualitatively different from the other. Eliade's axioms of sacred and profane space are based on the premise that the sacred erupts in certain places, called hierophanies. As sites of interaction between the human and superhuman realms of the cosmos, hierophanies provide believers with direct proof of the divine, and are distinct from the natural, profane world. The most paradigmatic hierophanies are termed *axis mundi* which, by providing a point of existential orientation for religious adherents, are 'a place that is sacred above all' (Eliade 1991, 39). Accordingly, Eliadian thought stipulates that sacred space is one-dimensional – it is a 'religious center at which the heavenly and earthly meet, a means of access between the human and the divine world' (Hassner 2003, 5; after Eliade 1958). More specifically, Hassner (2003) identifies three characteristics that are unique to sacred places. First, they are places wherein adherents can communicate with divinity through prayer, movement or other forms of worship. Second, they are places wherein divinity is believed to be present; as such, they often come with promises of healing, intervention or salvation. Third, they are places that provide meaning to their adherents by metaphorically reflecting and revealing the underlying order of the world to them.

When experienced in tandem, these three characteristics turn sacred spaces into sanctified centres – both spiritually and geographically – for the believer. Such spaces can take a variety of physical forms such as buildings, mountains, rivers, rocks and trees. Mount Meru for Hindus, Temple Mount for Jews and Mecca for Muslims are all examples of 'historical, spiritual and cosmological centers, places at which creation took place, at which space and time began and will eventually end, axes connecting heaven and earth around which the world revolves' (Hassner 2003, 5). Accordingly, this leads to a clear separation between sacred and profane spaces, with each representing a distinct modality of experience. As Brereton (1987, 526) argued:

> Objectively, and not only subjectively, a sacred place is different from the surrounding area, for it is not a place of wholly human creation or choice. Rather, its significance is grounded in its unique character, a character that no purely human action can confer on it.

Sacredness is therefore believed to be an intrinsic characteristic of sacred spaces; it is an embedded and wholly integrated quality, and cannot be changed or removed. That said, while the 'unique character' of sacred spaces may be recognized by the adherents of a given religion, such recognition does not necessarily extend to other religious or secular groups. For such groups, it is likely that such spaces will simply be interpreted as 'religious spaces' instead. This distinction is important, and will be discussed in more detail later in the chapter. Criticism of the essentialism upon which the insider standpoint is based has given rise to the social constructionist paradigm, and the associated shift from an ontological conception of sacred space to a 'critical interrogation of the human processes involved in making space "sacred"' (Knott 2005a, 169). We refer to this as the 'outsider' standpoint, and consider it in more detail below.

Religious space

Theoretical understandings of space have been influenced in recent years by the social constructionist turn in the social sciences. Accordingly, space has been theorized as something that is claimed, produced and negotiated by groups advancing specific interests. Social constructionist thought stipulates that 'nothing is inherently sacred' (Chidester and Linenthal 1995, 6), and that the presence of religion in space is a result of human agency. Much attention has been paid to the complexity and ambiguity associated with the construction, use and manipulation of space, and how such constructions, uses and manipulations can contribute to feelings of exclusion (or inclusion), marginalization and/or empowerment. Rather than being inherently sacred, place is believed to be imbued with meaning through various processes of sacralization – selection, demarcation, design, orientation, ritualization and so on (Hecht 1994). Such processes contribute to the ongoing construction and management of a place-bound form of sacredness. They are therefore needed to maintain a distinction between sacred and profane space, a 'purification involving practices of sacralization and desacralization, with various supporting mechanisms and ongoing maintenance to keep this separation [from the secular world] in place' (Ivakhiv 2006, 172). Without such processes of sacralization, place is meaningless, and the sacred is an empty signifier.

For example, Mazumdar and Mazumdar (1993) show how religious identity and attachment to sacred space are strengthened through processes of ritual and the ongoing sanctification of the Hindu house. They show how the sanctification of the house includes the purification of the outside (e.g. harmonizing the house with the outside environment), sacralization of the inside (e.g. *poojas*, lighting of sacred fire, anointing), and sacred learning in space (e.g. imparting norms of appropriate behaviour upon children). More recently, in Berlin, Germany, plans to build a 'House of One' – an integrated religious space that includes a church, mosque and synagogue in one site – provides a clear example of social constructionist thought (BBC News, 21 June 2014). Having three prominent monotheistic religions worship at one prominent site – Petriplatz in central Berlin – shows how a religious space can be constructed in order to promote inter-religious cooperation and understanding. Examples such as these show how religious space can be as much a result of extrinsic (or outsider) constructions of sacredness as they are the intrinsic revelations propounded by Eliade.

The value of social constructionist perspectives is that they sensitize discourse to the fact that space is always becoming; it is never 'complete'. Space is dynamic and ever-changing, just as religion is not a fixed set of elements but an ever-evolving web of shared meanings and understandings that is used in different ways by different people (Gardner 1995). In line with the evolution of social constructionist thought, over the past decade or so (since Kong's 2001a call for research to go beyond the 'officially' sacred), the scope of analysis of religious spaces has expanded dramatically. While the 'officially' sacred comprises 'churches, temples, synagogues, mosques and such places of worship that are commonly identified as "religious places"', the 'unofficially' sacred comprises 'other [ostensibly secular] types of place which reinforce religious identity and facilitate religious practice' (Kong 2002, 1573; see also Kong 2010, 756–7 for an overview of the proliferation of work on the 'unofficially' sacred sites of religious activity). Such a refocus has served to expand scholarly understandings of the relationship(s) between religious groups and space, and has involved more in-depth explorations of the secular and quasi-secular spaces of religious activity. These themes are examined in more detail in Chapter 3.

Henri Lefebvre and *The Production of Space*

Social constructionist thought has been heavily influenced and guided by Henri Lefebvre's (1991) work on *The Production of Space*. Specifically, Lefebvre's distinction between spaces of representation, representations of space and spatial practices provides a useful framework for understanding the relationships between power and space. Spaces of representation are lived spaces while representations of space are conceptualized space. Spatial practices embrace 'production and reproduction, and the particular locations and spatial sets characteristic of each social formation' (Lefebvre 1991, 33). Given Bourdieu's (1989) assertion that violence is inextricably entwined with the production of space, sensitivity to the spatial claims, constructions and contestations of both minority and majority groups will contribute to an understanding of how violent outcomes intersect with the spatial practices of different religious groups.

Spaces of representation are those associated with minority religious groups, or religious groups that strive to resist the controlling influence of secular agencies. In doing so, they typically 'mak[e] imaginative and symbolic use of physical space in order to realise the possibility of resisting the power of a dominant order, regime or discourse' (Knott 2005b, 165). Such groups create spaces that enable them to establish a presence within a given territory, as has been done so successfully in Latin America where (once minority) Pentecostal groups have 'single-handedly created religious and social space where Latin Americans from the popular classes are free not to be Catholic' (Chesnut 2003, 39). Eking out such a space requires the spatial strategies of minority groups to be 'explicitly reflexive, deliberately focussing on the preservation of group identity or defending against the effects of assimilation or discrimination' (Stump 2008, 231). As shown in the ensuing chapters, doing so often involves disguising religious motivations and presence by engaging with society and other religious groups in a variety of non-religious (i.e. secular) ways, and by characteristically operating in and through secular spaces. While this creates competitive advantages for minority groups, it can also be a source of conflict with dominant religious and secular agencies.

Conversely, representations of space are hegemonic, ideological spaces that are (re)produced by dominant (i.e. majority) agencies that try to exert power and control over a given territory. The control that dominant groups have over secular spaces and landscapes is widespread, and often formalized through social institutions or naturalized as part of the prevailing sociocultural habitus. Characteristics such as these dictate the ongoing production of society, space and culture, creating an ongoing form of spatial politics that marginal groups must continually contend with. Nationalistic religious groups and institutionalized religions are commonly associated with representations of space. These are explored in more detail in Chapter 2. In the most extreme cases, the representations of space articulated by majority groups may overwhelm minority religious groups, nullifying their agency and facilitating the razing, closure or relocation of their religious spaces.

Box 1.1: Distinguishing between *religious* and *sacred* spaces

Conceptually, there are subtle yet important differences between the terms 'religious' and 'sacred' when referring to space. Such differences are contingent upon the perspective and religious position of the user of the space. 'Religious spaces' exemplify the perspective of an outsider – they are believed to be socially constructed, and more claims-based. Conversely, 'sacred spaces' exemplify the perspective of an insider – they are more essentialized (or intrinsically sacred), and are typically belief-based. Sacred spaces are, in other words, closer in understanding and interpretation to Eliade's *axis mundi* than religious spaces, which are more likely to be socially constructed.

The differences between insider and outsider perspectives are many. Insiders believe that sacred spaces 'allow communication with the divine and presence of the divine on earth' (Hassner 2003, 32), whereas outsiders would reason that religious spaces are little more than locations of ritual. Insiders are more likely to believe that the sanctity of a sacred space is communicated in a top-down fashion (i.e. from the gods). Such communications could either be via some sort of symbolism or signage (e.g. Mount Sinai – the place where Moses received the Ten Commandments according to Christian tradition), because a significant religious event occurred there (e.g. the Viva Doloresa – a street in Jerusalem that Jesus is believed to have walked down carrying his cross, again according to the Christian tradition), or because of the presence of relics (e.g. the catacombs in Rome). Outsiders, on the other hand, are more likely to believe that space is imbued with religious meaning as a result of human processes of sanctification and cleansing.

Outsider perspectives often recognize the evidence of religious presence, but are considerably less likely to believe that it provides proof of the divine. As a result, they are less likely to accept the conditions of sanctity that insiders hold in such high regard. Such differences in the understanding and approach to sanctity can cause conflict over the desecration of sacred spaces by outsiders (including other religious and secular agencies), or competing claims to sacred space by different religious groups (see Box 2.1).

Although 'religious space' is used as the default means of classification throughout the book, readers should nevertheless be sensitive to the different interpretations of religious space according to insider or outsider standpoints.

Negotiating religious and secular claims to space

Religious competition, conflict and even violence have occupied academics for a long time, and certainly, exercise policymakers as well. A central challenge for religious policy in secular countries has been to balance individuals' rights to have religious beliefs and act according to those beliefs with the preservation of a secular and peaceful society. Attempts to strike such a balance have invariably invoked a division between religious and secular *spaces* in society, and generated space-specific regulations that govern what can or cannot be done in each of these spaces. In this regard, using space as a main conceptual frame for understanding religious competition, conflict and violence is not only desirable, but also essential.

In addition, using space as a way of categorizing the types and forms of religious competition is of particular relevance to land-scarce countries (such as Singapore), or land-scarce regions (such as cities). This is for two key reasons. First, in land-scarce countries or regions, the allocation of space between competing (religious or secular) uses is likely to be highly contentious. Second, in multi-ethnic/multi-religious societies, ethnically and religiously diverse communities either live in close proximity to one another or share the same physical spaces. As such, there is a significant potential for overlap between group-specific religious spaces and between religious and secular spaces. There is ample historical evidence to suggest that such overlaps in 'spaces' have been the sites of particularly violent episodes of religious conflict.

Consequently, it is clear that there is significant potential for religious conflict in a secular space when competing claim(s) to the (religious) use of that space are made by competing religious groups. Equally, however, religious conflicts might arise when secular groups, including the state, make claims over religious spaces. Such claims may take the form of *ownership claims* (e.g. when a religious space, or more generally, a religious resource, is redesignated as a secular space or resource) or *authority claims* (e.g. when secular groups, especially the state, attempt(s) to influence or regulate religious praxis within religious spaces).[1] Finally, in some cases, a particular religious space itself can be a source of religious conflict when there are competing claims to its ownership by different religious groups. Even though such instances are relatively rare, they are also the source of the most violent and virulent forms of religious conflict.

The changing roles of religion over time

The dynamics between religious groups, and between religious and secular groups, is ever-shifting because religious processes and practices are embedded within and influenced by broader, macro-scale social, cultural, political and economic drivers. Religion is not an a priori category, and an analysis of religious practice, leave alone religious competition and conflict, cannot therefore be divorced from the context in which it occurs.

In the post-World War II period, there have been two broad-based (and inter-related) shifts that have significantly influenced and altered the production and consumption of religion throughout the world. The first is modernity – and processes of modernization – which has caused the societal function of religion to change. In many postsecular, Western contexts, it has caused religious groups to adopt more of a secular role in society. Second, processes of globalization have caused more religious groups to come into contact with one another, which in turn has dramatically increased the potential for inter-religious competition and conflict. While each shift will be more or less relevant to a given context, when combined, they have transformed the way that religion is perceived, experienced and negotiated.

Religion in a modern world

To many, it might appear anachronistic that religious competition and conflict continue to remain prominent landmarks in the sociopolitical landscapes of many secular countries. Sociological theories in the post-war period predicted the waning of religious influence on the lives of individuals, societies and nations (see, e.g. Berger 1967; also Deutsch 1953; Anderson 1983; Gellner 1983). The secularization thesis was developed in order to explain the perceived decline of religion (and its withdrawal from public life) in the modern world. Developed on the basis of observations of modern European contexts, secularization theory focuses primarily on the evacuation of Christian churches from areas of civil society that were previously under their influence and control. Rather than being in a position of de facto authority, religious groups must now compete against other (implicitly secular) institutions for such authority. Casanova (1994) has disaggregated the secularization thesis into three constituent parts: a decline in individual religious belief and practice; the privatization of religious belief and practice; and the institutional differentiation of social, political and economic systems such as the state, the economy, education and religion. In sum, the secularization thesis attempts to account for the withdrawal of religion from non-religious aspects of public life (Bruce 2002).

In recent years, however, a growing body of empirical and symbolic evidence against the 'secularisation of the world' has been so compelling that the secularization thesis has now been discredited (see, e.g. Habermas 2006; also Megoran 2004), not least for being a 'legitimizing ideology for European hegemony' (Wilford 2010, 329; see also van der Veer 2001; Asad 2003). Now it is generally accepted that religious consciousness continues to thrive and, in many cases, grow in spite of the modernization of many societies and cultures. Modernization has not, in other words, led to a decline in the social significance of religion in everyday life; on the contrary, in many instances it has galvanized religion. This is particularly true with regard to the emergence in various Western contexts of alternative spiritualities (Heelas and Woodhead 2005) and postsecular societies (Taylor 2007). Indeed, the responses of religious groups to modernization has led to a re-theorization of the relationship between religion and modernity. More specifically, it has been argued that modernization has led to structural shifts in both religious orientation and praxis.

In terms of religious orientation, modernization is associated with a shift towards more rational thought and action (Weber 1956). Such a shift has been seen to favour world religions (e.g. Christianity, Islam, Buddhism) over their traditional counterparts (e.g. animism, ancestral worship) (see Hefner 1993; van der Veer 1996). More specifically, the ethical, emotional and intellectual challenges of everyday life that are associated with modern living (and rational thinking) are believed to be better addressed by a 'transcendental realm vastly superior to that of everyday reality' (Hefner 1993, 8). Such a shift is clearly evinced in Singapore, where the 'intellectualization' (Tong 2007, 4) of the population is believed to have contributed to the significant growth of Christianity in recent decades. In addition to the rationalization of society, some of the consequences of modernization (e.g. urbanization, industrialization and globalization) are also believed to explain a reorientation towards world religions. Such consequences include socio-economic (or 'relative') deprivation (D'Epinay 1969, Parker 1996), social disorganization (Talmon 1962) and changing sociocultural contexts (Yang 1998; Smilde 2007). In these instances, religious groups that are best able to meet the felt – and implicitly more rational – needs of a modernizing population are the most competitive, and the most likely to grow at the expense of their more traditional counterparts.

Modernization has also contributed to religious revivalism and the re-emergence of religion within the public and secular domains. According to Beaumont (2010, 8), such a dynamic has proven to be 'one of the defining features of the 21st century'. Indeed, it is clear that religious identities continue to shape peoples' world views, their moral paradigms and their behaviour in a globalized world, as strongly as they have ever done in the past. In light of this, religious groups, individuals and organizations face an ever-evolving array of challenges and opportunities when it comes to establishing and growing a presence in space. While it may have been proven and generally accepted that religion has not withdrawn from the public domain, the public nature of religious presence has changed. It has become more intermixed with the secular. As Emile Durkheim (1984 [1894], 169) observed in the late nineteenth century:

> Originally, it [religion] pervades everything; everything social is religious; the two words are synonymous. Then, little by little, political, economic, scientific functions free themselves from the religious function, constitute themselves apart and take on a more and more acknowledged temporal character. God, who was at first present in all human relations, progressively withdraws from them; he abandons the world to men and their disputes.

While Durkheim's depiction of God withdrawing from human relations and 'abandon[ing] the world to men and his disputes' may be allegorical, it also draws attention to the politics of religion in the modern world. It emphasizes how manifestations of religion – religious symbols, identities, spaces and ideas – are closely linked to the exertion and contestation of power. To control its influence, religious expression is constantly being shaped by more secular forces, and by competing religious groups. As Rorive (2008, 2670) rightly asserts, 'National political cultures and social histories weight [*sic*] heavily on the construction of concepts framing the scope of freedom of religion, such as secularism or public order.' Religious freedom and expression is manifested through the filtering effect of 'concepts' that are defined by politics, culture and social history. Different religions are granted different degrees of precedence according to the parameters of the contexts and frameworks that they operate within. It is when religious groups start to operate outside of such parameters that competition is heightened and conflict can ensue.

Importantly, these parameters also influence how religious groups operate in and through space. Religious belief can provide potent justification for claims to space and to feelings of spatial belonging, and it is the assertion of such claims that drives much competition and conflict. Nowhere is this more true than the recent scholarly focus on the 'postsecular' city (cf. Cox 1965; see Molendijk et al. 2010; Wilford 2010; Baker and Beaumont 2011a; Cloke and Beaumont 2013). Associated almost exclusively with Western cities, the postsecular city has been defined as 'a public space which continues to be shaped by ongoing dynamics of secularization and secularism . . . while negotiating and making space for the re-emergence of public expression of religion and spirituality' (Baker and Beaumont 2011b, 33). In addition, the urban environment is often the epicentre of religious pluralism and competition. Rapid industrialization causes urbanization, physical dislocation from family and community support networks and feelings of anomie. As a result, urban environments are often sites of religious experimentation and switching; a dynamic that has been fuelled by the activities of faith-based organizations (FBOs).

Of particular interest is how various FBOs meet the needs of poor and underprivileged communities as the state and secular agencies retreat from the public domain. Such a dynamic is most pronounced in urban environments, which are typically sites of multiple degradations (e.g. social, familial, moral, capitalist) and polarizations. The ensuing void creates a 'gap' (see Chapter 3) that religious groups have started to fill as their secular counterparts (including the state) have started to retreat. More than anything else, this shows how religious engagement with society (and, by extension, competitiveness in both the religious and secular domains) is dictated not just by the ability to meet people's spiritual needs, but their socio-economic needs as well. The most successful religious organizations in the contemporary world – that is, those that are best able to attract, retain and energize adherents – are those that are able to 'maximally fill the limited space (both geographic and social) available for plausible and relevant enchantment of the modern world' (Wilford 2010, 335). They are, in other words, those that are sensitive to the dynamics of geographic and social space, and have the means to use it to their advantage.

Religion in a globalized world

Ironically, globalization and related phenomena, rather than hindering, have abetted the maintenance, proliferation and deepening of religious consciousness in several ways. First, at a psychological level, globalization has sponsored widespread anomie by disrupting traditional modes of production and being. By its commitment to a material-secular ethic, it has contributed to demystifying peoples' lives and denuding it of transcendental meaning. Many argue that religious revivalism is a reaction against such anomic processes and pressures (e.g. Quah and Tong 1998).

Second, the increased mobility of people across national borders has resulted in a significantly more plural religious demography in many parts of the world. As Levitt (2001a, 3) recognizes, 'social, economic and political life increasingly transcend national borders and the constraints of national culture. Individuals sustain multiple identities and loyalties and create culture using elements from a variety of settings'. In other words, when people migrate, they often do so along with their cultural and religious identities. This has the potential of bringing 'alien' religious traditions and practices into contact with an unreceptive 'native' community and can engender religious antagonisms. Migration and its associated outcomes (e.g. religious and cultural pluralism) can legitimize the political aspirations of established religious groups who seek to prevent their religious sovereignty or dominance from being diluted by minority religious groups (see Robertson and Chirico 1985). Exacerbating this is the fact that migration, over time, gives rise to diasporic communities that are often defined by the desire to preserve a distinct identity that, to varying degrees, differs from the host society. Accordingly, significant pockets of religious minorities develop, which intensify religious competition for access to state and social resources.

Third, technological advancements that precede and accompany globalization have greatly augmented the ability of religious groups and religious elites to disseminate religious messages and religious content across national and, even, continental boundaries. This has promoted the growth of transnational religious communities. Whereas a transnational community is one constructed by immigrants 'forg[ing] and sustain[ing] multi-stranded social relations that link together their societies of origin and settlement' (Basch et al. 1994, 7), a transnational *religious* community is one whereby religious affiliation supercedes citizenship considerations as the primary marker of individual and group identity. To this end, transnational religious communities are defined by religious (and social) fields that cross geographic, cultural and political borders.

Accordingly, they are often defined by religious associations and affiliations that are multifaceted and hybridized in nature.

The ways in which such transnational dynamics contribute to religious competition and conflict are manifold. With the presence and impact of transnational religious communities becoming widespread, it is clear that religious competition and conflict are no longer spatially isolated; rather, (local) conflict in one part of the world can be easily globalized (i.e. imported into other countries and regions). There is a significant amount of evidence to suggest that local religious elites often appeal to instances of religious conflict/persecution in other parts of the world to legitimize local religious conflict. In addition, technological developments have also facilitated the ability of religious groups to mobilize human and financial resources for religious purposes more efficiently. This ability has particularly boosted the capacity of new religious movements to be resilient against state and social sanction.

Finally, the ease of access to religious doctrine on the World Wide Web and the new-found ability to engage in religious praxis/ritual in a 'virtual' space has significantly lowered the costs of religious participation for individuals. Lower costs naturally translate into a greater ease in maintaining religious identities in the face of increasingly time-intensive secular-economic demands on individuals and protect religious commitment from erosion. At the same time, these 'new' practices have challenged traditional authority structures within religious organizations and given rise to debates over their authenticity.

A note on book structure

This book is organized as follows. Chapter 2 examines the potential for *religious spaces* to be sites for religious competition and conflict, and ways in which they have been embroiled in some competition and conflict. Chapter 3 investigates how religious competition and conflict might take place (has taken place) in *secular spaces*. The study of competition and conflict in secular spaces is further subdivided into three categories: educational, civic and political spaces. Chapter 4 looks at how globalization has generated new forms of religious competition and influenced the scope and scale of traditional forms of religious competition. Finally, Chapter 5 examines the relationship between religion and social resilience, focusing specifically on how religious groups can help develop a capacity for social resilience amongtheir adherents, how religious groups react to situations that require social resilience, and how in some contexts social resilience is used as a form of religious regulation.

In each of the chapters, the discussion will be informed by the contemporary (post–World War II) experiences of various countries with respect to religious competition, conflict and sometimes violence. Where necessary, some historical (pre–World War II) examples will be used in order to provide more background information that is relevant to present-day understandings. Extended case studies are presented in boxes for ease of reference.

Religious Space: Competition, Conflict and Violence

Introducing religious space: 'A space distinguished from other spaces'

Religious space is a space where the primary purpose of activity is to achieve a religious objective (e.g. where people worship and perform rituals, whether individually or communally, and where religious knowledge is disseminated or acquired). Religious space is also where the protocols of personal and social behaviour are derived from religious authority, which override secular authority. Examples of spaces that are clearly 'religious' include places of worship (such as temples, mosques, churches), places of religious instruction (such as *madrasah*s, seminaries), and places exclusively designed for the performance of specific religious rituals (such as burial grounds, cemeteries). Religious spaces exist at various scales. In some cases, a religious space is contained within particular premises such as in a church or mosque, but sometimes, the extent of religious space is much wider and not premise-dependent, for example, 'holy' cities (such as the Vatican City) or cities that are sites of pilgrimage (such as Santiago de Compostela and Mecca). In even more extreme conceptions, a whole nation-state can constitute a religious space (e.g. a theocratic state such as Saudi Arabia). At the other end of the scale, the individual body can be treated as a religious space. Mainstream and alternative religions alike prescribe the body as a site of religious ritual (e.g. circumcision) and regulate what can or cannot be done to the body (e.g. injunctions against suicide or abortion). In a later section, we return to explore in more detail how religious spaces exist at various scales.

Religious spaces typically constitute 'a space distinguished from other spaces' (Brereton 1987, 526). Such distinctions mean that religious spaces are demarcated, marked out in such a way that the perimeter forms an important gateway to the sacred. Boundaries emphasize the dichotomy between religious and secular spaces, a distinction that enables space to be conceived of as either sacred or profane. This distinction, according to Emile Durkheim (1965, 55), is the very basis of all religious belief 'since the idea of the sacred is always and everywhere separated from the idea of the profane in the thought of men, and since we picture a sort of logical chasm between the two, the mind irresistibly refuses to allow the two corresponding things to be confounded, or even put in contact with each other'. As far as possible, therefore, the boundaries of sacred space need to be well-defined and easily recognizable. They need to be unambiguous.

Despite clear demarcations and definitions, religious spaces remain malleable. Indeed, the source of religious competition lies in attempts by religious groups to expand the extent of group-specific religious spaces. If we are to believe Hassner's (2003, 3) assertion that sacred spaces are inherently 'indivisible' (i.e. there is no 'sharing, dividing or finding substitutes for contested sacred places'), then it is clear that problems arise when religious spaces are 'claimed, owned, and operated by people advancing specific interests' (Chidester and Linenthal 1995, 15). Empirical evidence from various sociocultural contexts and religious traditions around the world shows how 'disputes have erupted over the ownership of sacred sites, the desecration or construction of tombs, temples, churches, mosques and shrines, or over demands for free exercise of controversial rituals on pilgrim routes or burial grounds' (Hassner 2003, 5). This has resulted in them being contested in their essence, causing them to become the loci of both inter- and intra-religious tension and competition.

Religious space: From competition to conflict and violence

Conceptually, competition related to religious space may be said to take place in two distinct but related dimensions – ownership and autonomy. Ownership-related religious competition takes place when religious groups attempt to acquire new or retain existing religious spaces. Autonomy-related religious competition takes place when religious groups attempt to retain their freedom to interpret religious doctrine, engage in religious rituals and practices, disseminate religious knowledge and regulate individual and social behaviour *within* existing group-specific religious spaces without interference by other groups. In this chapter, we will elaborate on such ownership- and autonomy-related religious competition (and conflict) as related to religious space, drawing examples and case studies from around the world.

While ownership- or autonomy-related claims are sources of competition, the likelihood of competition degenerating into conflict is often determined by the *centrality* and the *exclusivity* of the religious space under question. Broadly speaking, these two parameters 'indicate the attachment of a group to a sacred site and the price it attaches to maintenance or change in its status quo' (Hassner 2003, 7). Centrality refers to the proximity of a given space to the divine and, therefore, its degree of primacy within the spiritual landscape of a religious tradition. For example, shrines within Japanese homes, or the trees and rocks within which local deities are believed to reside, are much less 'central' than Ise, the central shrine at which the Sun Goddess Amaterasu – the guardian of Japan – resides (Reader 1994). It goes without saying that the more central a religious space is, the greater symbolic value it holds and, therefore, the greater the need for its protection and preservation.

Exclusivity refers to the degree to which access to a religious space (and behaviours within it) are circumscribed, monitored, sanctioned and enforced by a religious leadership. The sacredness of religious spaces is something that is (re)produced through such access and behaviours. Gestures are often performed at the perimeter of the religious space, and often emphasize the transition from secular (or profane) to religious (or sacred) space. Such gestures may include covering or revealing the head (in Judaism and Sikhism), making the sign of the cross (in Catholicism), removing shoes (Islam) or washing the mouth (Shintoism). Moreover, within the religious space, religious codes often dictate dress and behaviours. Failure to comply with such regulations (whether intentionally or not) can be interpreted as a form of desecration. As with centrality, the more exclusive the site, the 'greater the risk that foreign presence or conduct will be interpreted as an offensive act' (Hassner 2003, 8).

While centrality and exclusivity are likely to cause religious competition to degenerate into religious conflict, it is the concept of *indivisibility* that makes reconciliation so problematic. According to Hassner (2003, 14), the central premise behind indivisibility is that 'the total structure [of a religious system] cannot be divided, separated into subcomponents or parceled out without being deprived of its sacred function.' It is this characteristic that is unique to sacred space that provides a 'combustible combination: territory of supreme value, disputed and indivisible' (Hassner 2003, 24). Hassner identifies three criteria that, if all present at once, make a religious space indivisible: first, it is perfectly cohesive; second, it has unambiguous boundaries; and third, it cannot be substituted or exchanged. Another layer of intransigence is added when religious and ethnic identities are combined, causing any dispute that arises to almost certainly be indivisible, thus making resolution a seemingly impossible outcome (see Licklider 1993).

The problems associated with dividing religious space is highlighted by the example of the Tomb of the Patriarchs in Hebron, Palestine. Following the Israeli conquest of the Tomb in 1967, the large prayer hall was partitioned into separate Jewish and Muslim prayer areas. Despite elaborate prayer schedules designed to keep the two parties apart, the Tomb soon became a locus of Jewish–Muslim violence. Such violence was the outcome of prolonged antagonism by both parties – Jewish worshippers refused to remove their shoes when entering the prayer area (as is Muslim custom), while the amplified *azan* (the Muslim call to prayer) was often issued during Jewish prayer times. Congregations were separated by head-high aluminium barricades, would pray under twenty-four-hour camera surveillance, and would keep their sacred texts in fire-proof safes for fear of desecration. Despite a strong military presence – one that rendered the Tomb 'the only house of worship anywhere with its own army commander' (*Los Angeles Times*, 29 March 1986) – dozens of worshippers have since been killed or injured in knife and gun attacks and bombings. The violence culminated in the execution of thirty-nine Palestinians by a Jewish gunman during Muslim prayers in February 1994; an attack that caused another sixteen people to die in subsequent waves of violence, and the stalling of the Arab-Israeli peace process by months (*New York Times*, 25 February 1994).

The next two sections of this chapter analyse in detail both ownership- and autonomy-related religious competition and conflicts that take place within and over religious spaces. Implicit in this analysis is the fact that such religious competition takes place at a variety of scales, and so, the subsequent section of the chapter focuses the reader specifically on how religious competition and conflict takes place across different scales, and how religious competition and conflict over religious space at one scale can escalate to other scales. The chapter concludes with ways in which conflict over religious spaces may be resolved.

Ownership-related competition and conflict

Inter-religious competition and conflict

Competition and conflict over religious spaces between religious groups can arise when different religious groups stake exclusive ownership claims over the same religious space, or when a religious group tries to 'enter' a religious space 'occupied' by another religious group. Depending on the source of inter-religious competition, the larger socio-economic political environment, the centrality of these religious spaces and the exclusivity of these spaces, there are different propensities for the competition to escalate into conflict or violence. Conceptually, such inter-religious competition and conflict may occur under three types of conditions: between two or more different religious groups, each with strong following and deep claims over religious space; between dominant and minority groups with uneven power relations; and between incumbent-entrant religions.

In the first type of religious competition and conflict, two or more different religious groups claim that a particular religious space (often a place of worship) belongs exclusively to them. Both sets of claims have a historical-mythical basis, therefore the religious space over which competition takes place is a compelling religious symbol for all groups involved. In addition, due to this symbolism, it is easy for religious and religious-minded political leaders to rally popular support behind their exclusive ownership claims. Such claims may arise when a religious group splits into rival factions, thus creating competition over a common (previously shared) religious space (Hassner 2003). Here, competition is often a result of the emergence of irreconcilable rifts in religious groups, which may arise from disagreements over theology or group leadership. Staking claims to a religious space that may have once united the group, 'each rival asserts its claim as inheritor of the true faith' (Hassner 2003, 16). For example, in Missouri, United States, two rival churches – the Reorganized Church of Jesus Christ of Latter Day Saints and the Church of Christ (Temple Lot) fought a legal battle over an empty lot in the city of Independence. Both churches seceded from the Church of Jesus Christ of Latter Day Saints. Mormon revelation suggests that the lot was the site of the garden of Eden, and will be the future Temple of Christ during his Second Coming. While the Church of Christ is now in possession of the lot, the Reorganized Church of Jesus Christ of Latter Day Saints has established its headquarters and world conference auditorium on lots that are adjacent to the lot under dispute (Ostling and Ostling 2000).

Often, inter-religious competition over the same religious space is characterized by a long history of unresolved conflict over the disputed religious space, which hinders current attempts at reconciliation. This leads to a paradoxical situation: while the status quo, vis-à-vis the ownership of the space is unacceptable to the competing groups, any slight deviation from the status quo also has the potential to provoke religious conflict and violence. Further, the scope for political or civic resolution of the dispute is low. This is because religious/political elites from either group risk losing credibility with the masses – given their role in constructing and sustaining the conflict – by making concessions or diluting their ownership claims.

High profile examples of this type of competition include the Jewish–Islamic conflict over the Temple Mount in the Old City of Jerusalem (Box 2.1) and the Hindu–Islamic conflict over a mosque in the northern India state of Uttar Pradesh, the Babri Masjid (Box 2.2). While the former highlights how the violence associated with ownership claims over a sacred space can become (internationally) virulent, the latter provides a complete history of competition degenerating into violence. As such, these two case studies illustrate the systemic weaknesses and governance failures that can often result in communal violence.

Box 2.1: Conflicting claims to the Temple Mount/Haram el-Sharif and the globalization of violence

Jerusalem is a sacred city that is claimed by both Israeli Jews and Palestinian Muslims. The old city of Jerusalem is home to a sacred site – trapezoidal in shape and amounting to approximately 35 acres – known as 'Temple Mount' to Jews and 'Haram el-Sharif' to Muslims. The site contains relics that are deemed holy by both groups – the Jewish Temple, the Dome of the Rock and the Al Aksa Mosque respectively. The failure of the Camp David Summit in July 2000 – a series of meetings between US president Bill Clinton, Israeli prime minister Ehud Barak and Palestinian Authority chairman Yasser Arafat that aimed to end the Israeli–Palestinian conflict – has been primarily attributed to the inability of Israelis and Palestinians to agree on the status of the sacred site. Following the negotiations, in September 2000, Israeli opposition leader Ariel Sharon attempted to assert Jewish sovereignty over the Temple Mount by visiting Jerusalem. Such a move was deemed to be unnecessarily provocative by Palestinians. It marked the beginnings of the Palestinian uprising (named Al Aksa Intifada, in honour of the Mosque in Haram el-Sharif), the collapse of the Israeli–Palestinian peace process, and inter-religious violence of a scale and intensity not seen before. Such violence was enacted primarily through the desecration of various religious spaces.

More specifically, one week after Sharon's visit to Jerusalem, Palestinians attacked a sacred Jewish tomb in nearby Nablus, razing a seminary located at the site, desecrating the library and painting the tomb green to symbolize its conversion into a mosque. In Jericho, a seventh-century synagogue was also razed. Jewish retaliations led to the vandalism of three mosques in Tiberias and Jaffa, which in turn resulted in the firebombing of synagogues in Jaffa, Haifa, Ramla and Shfaram, the defacement of Jewish tombs in Galilee, and the spray-painting of a Jewish settlement synagogue with swastikas and anti-Semitic remarks (*Jerusalem Post*, 29 October 2000). Thereafter such isolated acts of vandalism evolved into a full-scale armed conflict between Israeli and Palestinian forces, claiming nearly 4,000 lives by March 2004 (*Sunday Herald Sun*, 21 March 2004).

One of the most interesting aspects of this example is the international virulence of violence stemming from competing claims on religious space. Beyond the Middle East, there was a noticeable increase in anti-Semitic violence. By October 2000 (one month after Sharon's provocative visit), seventy-seven synagogues around the world were reported to have been vandalized; a 400 per cent increase compared to previous months that year. By 2001, the figure exceeded 130, spanning various countries, from Australia, to Brazil, Russia and Sweden (Hassner 2003). As this example illustrates, local competition over claims to sacred space can have not just violent effects, but virulent effects that affect religious communities and spaces located in territorially dispersed (and often seemingly unconnected) locations. The irresolution of conflict is largely attributable to the indivisibility of the Temple Mount/Haram el-Sharif (see Albin 1991).

Box 2.2: The Babri Masjid conflict: The perils of disturbing the status quo and weak governance

The Babri Mosque is located in Ayodhya in the Northern Indian state of Uttar Pradesh. Ayodhya is a site of special religious significance for Hindus, as the birthplace of Rama, a deified figure in the Hindu religious tradition. (Especially, right wing) Hindus allege that the Babri Mosque is located on the site of an ancient temple for Rama, one that was replaced by a mosque by the Mughal patriarch Babar (hence, the name of the mosque). Excavations conducted by the Archaeological Survey of India on the site have been inconclusive about the early history of the Babri Mosque (*The Times of India*, 2 October 2010). However, the ownership of the site remained keenly contested between Hindus and Muslims till 1992 when a Hindu mob, under a right-wing Hindu leadership, demolished the mosque; the incident sparked large-scale and widespread communal riots throughout the country in which an estimated 1,000 and more people were killed (*India Today*, 5 December 2011).

This case study highlights the perils of disturbing the status quo in ownership of disputed religious spaces, as well as of the state's inability to contain religious competition from becoming violent. A new dimension to the age-old conflict was added in 1949 when idols of Rama were smuggled and installed inside the mosque (BBC News, 30 September 2010). While the Indian Prime Minister at the time regarded this encroachment as setting a dangerous precedent, no government action was taken to remove the idols in the face of potential violent opposition from Hindu religionists. The symbolism involved in the idol installation *altered the status quo* of the identity of the disputed structure, opening the doors for further conflict in the future. Then again, in the 1980s, yet another dangerous precedent was set when the national government decided to allow Hindus to offer worship to the idols within the mosque which muddled the question of the identity/ownership of the religious site further (BBC News, 30 September 2010).

Both government inaction (to remove the smuggled idols) and action (to allow worship) can be seen to have contributed to emboldening the Hindu right wing's claim to ownership of the mosque. The final governance failure occurred in 1992 when both the federal and the provincial governments failed to protect the structure from demolition.

A second type of inter-religious competition and conflict involves a dominant group asserting its power over a minority religion. This is most stark where religious nationalism is involved. While nationalism provides a way of 'identifying oneself and others, of constructing sameness and difference, and of situating and placing oneself in relation to others' (Brubaker 2012, 4), religious nationalism emerges when religion is either superimposed on or becomes an intrinsic part of nationalism. The potential for discrimination and persecution increases significantly under the circumstances: religious nationalists make primordial claims to territory, and often seek to regulate, control or subdue minority religious groups that make competing claims.

Religious nationalisms become hegemonic when they become overtly exclusivist, or when they seek to strengthen the self (the dominant religion) at the expense of the other (minority religion/s). In contexts where religious nationalism is strong, hegemonic actions prevail and the propensity for inter-religious conflict increases. For example, in regions such as South and Southeast Asia, the Balkans and the Middle East, where political and religious boundaries coincide, disputes over space have been the catalyst for inter-ethnic riots and armed confrontation. Such disputes typically draw on a base of fear or insecurity in order to legitimate claims to religious authority (see Springer 2011). One topical example of the exclusionary effect of religious nationalism is the exodus of minority Rohingya Muslims from Buddhist-majority Myanmar (*The Economist*, 20 May 2015; see also Parnini 2013). Rohingya Muslims are a minority ethno-religious group based in Rakhine State in Myanmar. They have been described as one of the most persecuted minority groups in the world: they are not officially recognized by the government, and are denied citizenship and all legal rights. They have also been subject to sporadic violence and ethnic cleansing on behalf of Buddhist nationalists based in Rakhine. The government, ruling in the name of a Buddhist nation, is seen to support such anti-Muslim sentiment through its policy of non-intervention. In doing so, it provides a clear example of the exclusionary effects of hegemonic religious nationalism.

Mapping religion onto the space of the nation is, however, in danger of being weakened or erased by secular modernity (see Vasquez 2008). Secular processes of globalization play an important role in disrupting such associations between religion and nation, and have caused nationalist religious groups – especially those situated in postcolonial societies – to become more hegemonic as a result. It is within these societies that 'militant "fundamentalist" or neo-traditionalist, puritanical-primitivist' (Robbins 2003, 73) movements emerge, posing a political threat to religious minorities and a moral threat to religious freedom. Such movements often react by embracing and combining traditions such as nationalist and culturalist ideals, religiously oriented hegemony, anticolonialism and civilizational struggle (Hall 2003).

More pervasive is the 'antiglobalisation' stance adopted by many nationalist religious groups. Juergensmeyer (2007, 13), for example, shows how Muslim activists throughout the Middle East 'reject the intervention of outsiders and their ideologies and, at the risk of being intolerant, pander to their indigenous cultural bases and enforce traditional social boundaries'. Such movements are frequently exclusivist, confrontational, and sometimes violent in opposition to the competitive actions of other (often more globally expansionist) religious groups. Such opposition underscores Tambiah's (1986, 139) warning that Theravada Buddhists in Sri Lanka, Myanmar and Thailand are pursuing increasingly political agendas that openly resist modern multicultural society. Instead, they have adopted a 'religio-complex' that fuels the construction of a 'heady collective identity and a fury of displaced and misplaced anger against the alien others, the minorities, who are seen as a challenge to their chauvinistic manhood'. As the abovementioned example of the Rohingya Muslims in Myanmar attests, it is clear that the strengthening of religious nationalisms often has the effect of depressing religious pluralism.

Besides competition and conflict over religious space arising from the two types of circumstances addressed thus far (between two or more contesting religious groups with similar depth and history, and between dominant and minority groups with uneven power relations), a third type of religious competition and conflict may arise when an entrant religion meets the incumbent. This may also be viewed as a variant of the second circumstance discussed above. Often, this is exemplified by 'new' religious groups trying to 'enter' religious spaces occupied by another religious group. These attempts to capture religious market share from an existing religious monopoly can take the form of establishing a place of worship or any other type of religious institution in an area where a large majority of residents belong to a different religious group. In addition, a new (or, 'foreign') religious group may also try to gain market share by undertaking aggressive 'evangelical' campaigns – that combine missionary and intense proselytization activities – among followers of the established, majority religion.

Entrant groups may also seek to 'enter' religious spaces occupied by another religious group because of historical conquest. As Hassner (2003, 16–17) argues, 'because sanctity rests in location, as well as in the structure that marks the location as sacred, the physical destruction of sacred structures does not diminish the sanctity or centrality of sacred sites'. Over the course of history, therefore, conquerors have sought to integrate such sites into their own religious traditions. The purpose of this is twofold: to displace the local tradition and to assert their claim to it; and to leverage the convenience of having a ready-made focal point that can be used to ground their own religious practices. As a result, there are often 'competing claims to strata along the sacred axis, an archeological palimpsest of sorts, demanding different and often conflicting rites from members of opposed religious affiliations' (Hassner 2003, 17).

An example of this may be seen in Jerusalem, the Temple Mount or Haram el-Sharif (depending on Jewish or Islamic viewpoints) which is located atop various religious ruins – a reflection of the fact that each successive conqueror of the city weaved the site into its religious traditions. Accordingly, the site has been occupied by a Templar church, a temple for Zeus, a temple of Jupiter and a Jebusite shrine (see Lev 1989). The most recent conflict, however, stems from Jews identifying the site as being where Abraham had prepared to sacrifice Isaac, and from Muslims claiming that Muhammad visited the same site during his journey described in Surah 17 of the Qur'an (Hassner 2003). Both groups have commemorated the site through the construction of religious buildings, and both claim the space as their own (see Box 2.1 for more details).

Entrant-incumbent conflict not only results when incumbent religious groups react to new groups by mobilizing social, political or ideological resources to maintain their own hegemonic status, but also when the state passes or enforces legislation that seeks to discriminate against new and/or minority religious groups. In the UK, for example, planning law is designed to preserve the 'Britishness' of the built environment which, in some instances, has caused problems when minority Muslim, Hindu and Sikh groups try and obtain the permissions needed to build new places of worship. As McLoughlin (2005, 1047; see also Eade 1996; Werbner 1996) demonstrates, such legislative frameworks reflect how 'some members of the ethnic majority tend to read the re-inscription of "old" spaces with "new" cultural meanings in terms of an ever-expanding (Islamic) "threat" to "the English way of life"'. Such readings limit the potential for minority groups to develop and express their religious identities. This can, in turn, force them to use secular spaces for worship purposes instead, and can cause feelings of non-acceptance and otherness to become institutionally entrenched (see Box 2.21 on the important role of the mosque for diasporic Muslims living in Britain).

Religious conflict of this form almost always accompanies the phenomena of religious innovation (i.e., the setting up of new religious groups) and religious dispersal (i.e. the spread of religions beyond the countries or regions of their origin). As such, most countries with a plural religious demography have invariably witnessed such forms of competition and conflict throughout their history and continue to do so. A study of these histories suggests that entrant-incumbent competition can evolve over time into one of two distinct equilibria. In one equilibrium state, the society in question makes a harmonious transition into a more religiously plural society in which, the entrant religion becomes significantly large with clearly defined ownership rights over its religious spaces and autonomy over its religious practices. Inter-religious competition for religious market share is minimal, since each religious group manages to establish a stable niche in society. In the other equilibrium, early disputes over the entrant religion's religious space and practices endure over time, resulting also in a plural society, albeit one where the pluralism is a tenuous, continuously contested one. Such societies are likely to oscillate between periods of active and dormant conflict. In many instances, entrant-incumbent competition sustained over time morphs into majority–minority competition. They remain as inter-religious competition over religious spaces because the incumbent religions continue to claim a hegemonic position in the religious lives of individuals and societies. For example, the Hindu right wing in India thinks of the whole country as a Hindu religious space and Christian groups in many countries in the Western world view the countries primarily as Christian religious spaces.

In cases where entrant religions are closely and popularly associated with political acts, opposition to the establishment of new religious spaces can become more pronounced, as can the potential for conflict. This has clearly been the case in countries such as the United States and the UK post-9/11, when Islam became closely associated with terrorist acts in the public consciousness. In such countries, the construction of mosques has led to social, political and religious polarization. Nowhere has this been more pronounced – or more symbolically loaded – than in the Lower Manhattan area of New York City, with the proposed construction of an Islamic community and prayer centre on a parcel of land adjacent to Ground Zero; the site of the former World Trade Center that was destroyed in the 9/11 terrorist attacks (see Box 2.3).

Box 2.3: Opposition to the 'Ground Zero mosque' and the symbolic significance of religion in space

Since the 9/11 terrorist attacks against the United States in 2001, questions surrounding religious pluralism and the integration of Islam into mainstream American society have been at the forefront of public discourse and debate. Nowhere is this more apparent than in the Lower Manhattan area of New York City, where a parcel of land near the site of the former World Trade Center has been subject to intense scrutiny by the public and media. In 2009 the land was bought by Soho Properties – a Muslim-owned real-estate developer with close ties to the Cordoba Initiative (an Islamic foundation that aims to promote inter-faith dialogue and fight against extremism) and the American Society for Muslim Advancement. It was proposed that a thirteen-storey Islamic community centre and prayer hall be built on the site. The project was originally named 'Cordoba House' (in reference to the peaceful coexistence of Muslims, Christians and Jews in eight- and eleventh-century Cordoba, Spain), but was subsequently renamed 'Park51'. Informally, it has been referred to in the media and by opposition groups as the 'Ground Zero mosque'. Importantly, the site is not actually on Ground Zero. Neither did the developers intend for it to be designated as a mosque. The inaccuracy of the 'Ground Zero mosque' moniker reveals the intentional (and symbolic) misrepresentation of the project by oppositional groups to further their own agenda.

Since the land was acquired in 2009, the project has polarized public, political and religious opinion (see Dehghani et al. 2014). Supporters of the project claim that it could act as a beacon for moderate Islam in a location where the effect of Islamic extremism still resonates most strongly, and in doing so, it can also help facilitate the integration of Muslims into mainstream American society. Opponents claim that the project would become a sort of 'victory memorial' to Islam; it would offend the families of the victims of 9/11 and could be used as a front to promote Shariah law and other forms of extremist activity. In September 2011 – ten years after the 9/11 attacks – a temporary Islamic centre and prayer space opened in the renovated Park51 location. In August 2014, it was announced that the Park51 site will change its usage, becoming a museum of Islamic culture (which will still include a prayer space) and residential block spanning the original site plus neighbouring properties. The overarching opposition to the project brought about the change in land use, and brought to national attention issues surrounding the usage and symbolic nature of space for religious purposes. As such, the project has fuelled more widespread support for restrictions on mosque-building throughout America (*The Guardian*, 12 August 2010; *New York Times*, 7 August 2010).

The Ground Zero mosque case study brings to light three key issues that arise when minority religious groups make claims to space. The first concerns the symbolic nature of religious space. Ground Zero is the site of one of the most devastating terrorist attacks on American soil, while the Islamic centre represents the religion from which the attackers claimed allegiance and inspiration. While the spaces are separated by a few blocks, the conflicting meaning – not to mention the symbolic resonance – of each to the other has proven difficult to reconcile (Jia et al. 2011). The second is the confusion and distrust surrounding religious minorities. Oppositional sentiment was informed by the conflation of Islamic extremism with more moderate Islam, and the perceived conflict between conservative Islamic teachings and American democratic principles. The third raises the question of who decides the location and function of religious spaces. The plans for the Ground Zero mosque were privately funded, legally approved and constitutionally sanctioned by the First Amendment, yet it was society and the media that intervened and provoked the change in usage. Legal and political frameworks tend to play an abstracted role when it comes to the allocation and usage of space for religious purposes; often it is the community that yields greatest influence over such decisions. Overall it is clear that religious spaces are the most value-laden form of land use, not least because of the meanings and associations that they imbue, and the emotions they can evoke.

Whether a society makes a harmonious transition into a more religiously plural society or one in which early disputes over the entrant religion's religious space and practices endure over time, resulting in a fractious, continuously contested plural society, depends on the intensity and fractiousness of the early phases of the entrant-incumbent competition. The more fractious this early interaction is, the harder it is for the society to develop into a harmonious, religiously plural polity. In Chapter 5, we return to the issue of how fractiousness may be reduced and hence social resilience enhanced. Meanwhile, several case studies of India, Timor Leste, Taiwan and elsewhere (see Boxes 2.4, 2.5 and 2.7) demonstrate how entrant-incumbent competition might operate in ways that enhance the likelihood of inter-religious antagonisms to persist over time with the result that a religiously plural society on the surface might rest on religious fault lines that can be torn apart by slight tremors. An analysis of these cases is instrumental to drawing inferences about public policy interventions necessary to manage entrant-incumbent religious competition (and more generally, minority–majority relations) in a way that prevents religious resentment and conflict from becoming a permanent feature of modern religious societies.

Box 2.4: Religious conversion and conflict in India

As Josh (2009) states, the issue of religious conversions of non-Muslim and non-Christian populations in India to Islam and Christianity has been highly contentious since the early days of competition between the incumbent religion (Hinduism) and the entrants (Islam and Christianity). The conflict over conversions continues to resonate clearly in the political and social discourse of modern-day India and frequently erupts into violence. Christian religious elites, perhaps due to their higher profile as proselytizers, have borne much of the brunt of this sporadic, but steady, violence: incidents of priests being paraded naked or nuns being raped and murdered appear periodically in the Indian media (*Hindustan Times*, 27 June 2007). In 1999, in the Eastern Indian state of Orissa, Australian missionary Graham Staines, along with his two younger sons, was burnt to death in his car by a Hindu mob. The experience of India in this regard offers evidence that fractious entrant-incumbent competition can lead to a social equilibrium that might be religiously plural, but contains a high level of religious tension.

From a public policy perspective, the Indian example highlights how constitutional design, political architecture (federalism, for instance), governance failures and the expediency of multi-party electoral politics can sustain hostile and violent entrant-incumbent competition over time. It is instructive to examine some of these factors in greater detail (recognizing that other factors are at play which will be addressed in other sections of this book), paying particular attention to loopholes in the law that make the Indian states' attitudes towards religious conversion (and, by extension, towards inter-religious competition for religious market share) at best, ambivalent and, at worst, paradoxical. The lack of legal clarity has been repeatedly exploited by incumbent elites (the Hindu right wing) to escalate the competition for followers into, often violent, conflict.

When the Indian constitution formally took effect in 1950, it included the 'freedom of religion' as a fundamental right. Significantly, this freedom included the freedom to profess, practise and *propagate* religion. As Josh (2009) chronicles, 'propagate' was added on to the constitutional clause guaranteeing religious freedom after much wrangling: liberal members of the Constituent Assembly in charge of drafting the constitution argued that adherents of Islam and Christianity, essentially proselytizing religions, needed to be guaranteed the freedom to spread their religion. On the other hand, representatives of the Hindu right were fundamentally and vitriolically opposed to the idea of giving constitutional endorsement to religious conversion. The ability of this constitutional guarantee to engender circumstances for civic inter-religious competition was compromised by a further clause about religious conversion which stated, 'conversion from one religion to another brought about by coercion or undue influence shall not be recognised by law' (see Josh 2009, 100). This qualification has often been the basis on which right-wing Hindu groups have challenged the legitimacy of *all* conversions to Christianity, both ideologically and in courts of law.

Further, legally grounded disincentives for religious conversion operate. For example, 'lower caste' Christians are excluded from positive discrimination schemes such as reservations in public educational institutions and for public sector jobs. The positive discrimination schemes were initially earmarked for lower caste Hindus, but later expanded to include lower caste Sikhs and Buddhists; Christians have been excluded, in spite of repeated calls for inclusion, under the justification that 'converts' to Christianity have voluntarily opted out of the caste system (Josh 2009). Given that one of the primary sites of Christian evangelical activity is the lower caste population base, socio-economic discrimination biases the playing field for inter-religious competition; a key ingredient in producing fractious entrant-incumbent conflict.

Another example of a legally grounded disincentive is the creation of Hindu personal laws that disadvantage converts from Hinduism in marriage, divorce, guardianship of children and inheritance of family property. Josh (2009) highlights how the Hindu Marriage Act (1955) states that a partner ceasing to be a Hindu by converting to another religion gives legitimate ground for divorce. The Hindu Succession Act (1956) stipulates that although a convert retains the right to inherit, the children born to that person after conversion and their descendants are disqualified from inheriting the property of their Hindu relatives unless the children remain or become Hindus. The Hindu Minority and Guardianship Act (1956) disqualifies a convert from being the guardian of his own child. The

Hindu Adoptions and Maintenance Act (1956) states that a convert does not have any say over his/her partner adopting a child; one parent can give his/her child in adoption without the consent of the partner if he/she has converted.

A third example is the recent spate in the enactment of anti-conversion laws by various provinces. While Article 25 of the Indian Constitution (1947) grants all citizens the right to freely profess, practice and propagate their religion (so long as it does not disrupt public order), over the past five decades a series of 'Freedom of Religion Bills' have been passed at the state level in order to protect against religious conversion. Orissa was the first state to enact such legislation in 1967, followed by Madhya Pradesh in 1968 and Arunachal Pradesh in 1978; similar anti-conversion laws were more recently passed in the states of Chattisgarh in 2000, Gujarat in 2003, Himachal Pradesh in 2007 and Rajasthan in 2008. More recently, in 2013 the nationalist Hindu Bharatiya Janata Party (BJP) declared that it sought to enact such anti-conversion legislation on a nation-wide scale. While the BJP won the 2014 general election in India, such plans are yet to be enacted. Indeed, while such legislation is stated to mitigate against the risk of unethical conversion, it has also been viewed as evidence of increasing Hindu protectionism that is designed specifically to prevent conversion to Christianity, and to increase the surveillance of Christian communities in India and beyond, reflecting suspicion towards that religion.

All of the above indicate a failure to have a coherent and internally consistent set of legal principles and statutes that govern how entrant-incumbent competition is carried out. This sort of ambivalence generates confusion, increases uncertainty, makes law enforcement discretionary and fuels the potential for fractious inter-religious conflict for religious market share.

Box 2.5: Entrant-incumbent conflict in Catholic Timor Leste

Asia's newest country, Timor Leste, has an overwhelming Roman Catholic majority. Although Catholicism is not constitutionally credited as the official religion of the country, the Roman Catholic Church wields significant political influence. This influence is overt: the former president, Jose Ramos Horta, has been quoted in the Australian media as saying, 'only an idiot or an atheist would govern this country completely alienated from the church hierarchy and the church as a whole' (ABC Radio Australia, 17 October 2008).

Given this nexus between a dominant (incumbent) religion and the government, minority (entrant) religions' attempts to capture religious market share is almost always fractious, with representatives of the incumbent group responsible for the intimidation of, and violence against, new members of entrant religions (converts). This phenomenon is most clearly observed in the competition between the Catholic Church and several evangelical churches trying to gain a foothold in the country. Wright (2008) captures the hostility of competition by noting that converts to Protestantism are routinely intimidated by visits from nuns and death threats and are often beaten up. If such circumstances persist, it is highly likely that even if the country becomes a religiously plural society with significant religious minorities, the memories of violent entrant-incumbent competition will work against the establishment of religious harmony in the future.

Box 2.6: Anti-cultism and counter-cultism

One key aspect of religious revivalism in the late twentieth century has been the growth of new/alternate religious movements (NRMs). Several such movements are characterized by aggressive proselytization and, accordingly, provide fertile grounds for the study of entrant-incumbent inter-religious competition. Many such movements are designated as cults or sects,[1] although there is a wide variation in their lineage, doctrines, traditions, rituals, geographical spread and followership. That said, certain common characteristics of cult movements can be identified: they are small; they demand high religious commitment from their followers; they are aggressive in their competition for religious market share; they subscribe to a heterodox religious doctrine and an esoteric world view; and they have religious practices that are considered deviant by the society of the day.

Entrant-incumbent competition involving cults are likely to give rise to conflict and violence in the following two ways. First, cults might be the perpetrators of violent acts. This violence may be directed at society at large (e.g. in the Sarin subway attack by members of Aum Shinrikyo in Tokyo in 1995) or may be directed inwards (e.g. in the mass suicide committed by members of the Order of the Solar Temple in 1994 in Switzerland). However, while cults acting violently as a way of expressing religious identity provide an interesting area of study, these acts of violence are largely sporadic and unsystematic. In addition, they are unconnected to the issue of how entrant-incumbent competition can generate religious conflict. As such, this book concentrates on the second aspect of cult-related conflict. In this instance, precisely because of cults' tendencies to have heterodox doctrine and praxis, and pervasive perceptions of the queerness of their recruitment and indoctrination methods, they are viewed with suspicion by mainstream religious groups (and, even large sections of secular society). In many cases, the secretiveness of their practice and the imposed isolation on cult members from normal forms of social interaction – through communal living on cult premises – contributed further to the growing perception that cults constitute a grave danger to social stability. In the United States, it was commonly believed that cults and sects engaged in 'brainwashing' to attract and retain followers (Introvigne 2002). Similar perceptions of cults were also imported into Asian societies that experienced rapid growth in the post-war era, namely South Korea and Japan (Yoshihide 2010). Thus, in various parts of the world, mainstream religious groups have actively lobbied for systematic persecution of cults. A key goal of such efforts has been to disable cults from acquiring religious spaces. In addition to restrictions on the ownership of religious spaces, cults also face problems of loss of control (autonomy) over their religious practices. This aspect of entrant-incumbent competition and its potential to engender conflict are discussed subsequently in the chapter. Rather than disabling cults, their active persecution runs the risk of generating fundamental and perhaps permanently divisive conflict by producing a siege mentality among cult followers, which in turn produces stronger bonds among cult members. It also threatens to drive cult practices underground and thus renders them immune to objective criticisms and civic monitoring.

Mostly in the United States, but also in Japan and Korea, the way in which competition between cults and mainstream religious groups for members has taken place is especially capable of generating inter-religious conflict. In the 1960s through to the 1980s, members of mainstream religious groups growingly engaged in the practice of kidnapping cult members (often, at the behest of other non-cult members of the family) and subjecting them to 'deprogramming' processes that routinely involved forced seclusion and 'counselling' (Richardson and Stewart 2004). These kidnappings and deprogramming were thought to be necessary to counteract the impact of the 'brainwashing' that cults were alleged to use in acquiring and indoctrinating followers.[2] In response, cults filed cases against the disappearance of their members in courts of law, giving rise to inter-religious competition in an atmosphere that was highly acrimonious. This acrimony often spilled over into civic spaces in the form of violent clashes between cult and counter-cult movements. In Israel, for example, the Orthodox Jewish group *Yad L'Achim* has violently opposed the missionary activities of various cults since its inception in 1950. Such opposition was most pronounced in the late 1990s, when Jehovah's Witnesses were reported to have filed 120 complaints of harassment, assault, theft and vandalism against *Yad L'Achim* (US Department of State 1999).

Box 2.7: Christianity in Taiwan: A counterexample to fractious entrant-incumbent competition

Taiwan provides an interesting example of how an entrant religion (various denominations of Christianity) has competed amicably for religious market share with incumbent religions (mostly Buddhism and variations of Chinese traditional religions). Understanding the circumstances in which such competition has taken place provides an insight into why conversions to Christianity in Taiwan have not been met with the same degree of hostility as they have been in many other countries.

A key strategy adopted by the Church in Taiwan to pre-empt hostile reactions against conversions (and, converts) to Christianity has been to minimize the stress that conversion places on the traditional family structure. By accepting (and, in some cases, endorsing) a syncretic, culture-specific version of Christianity, the Church has enabled young Taiwanese converts to adopt a Christian identity and belief system, while adhering to time-honoured cultural traditions (such as performing traditional Chinese death rituals and engaging in ancestor worship) (Petersen 2009). Conflicts between traditional Chinese praxis and Christian doctrine have been reconciled via creative and more accommodating interpretations. As Petersen (2009, citing Bigelow) elaborates: 'Showing respect for and honoring our deceased loved ones is in complete harmony with gospel principles, but what to one person is religious and spiritual ritual to another is simply a way of showing respect to deceased ancestors, no more a religious ritual than the custom of placing flowers on a grave. For example, two people could be performing what appears to be the same rite of ancestor worship, each bowing reverently several times before a wooden tablet listing the names of deceased relatives. The one could easily be in harmony with the precepts of the gospel, while the other is in opposition to what the Lord has commanded.'

In addition, the Church in Taiwan (especially that of the Latter Day Saints) has collaborated with the government in developing and implementing initiatives to strengthen the family as the basic unit of Taiwanese society. Such initiatives have included the development and distribution of family promotion literature (both of religious and secular orientations), the organization of family strengthening programs and advisory services for the government (Petersen 2009). These measures have been instrumental in fostering the idea that the Church *does not* intend to destabilize local society by replacing family-based relationships/social networks with Church-based ones or asserting the primacy of obligations to the Church over obligations to the family. Consequently, public suspicion of the Church is minimized, its perception as a threat reduced and misgivings about conversions to Christianity are muted.

Overlapping religious spaces

Overlapping religious spaces are those that are characterized by different and overlapping layers of religious meaning or action that are found in a single space. They are inherently contradictory, often confusing – not least for the people that advertently or inadvertently occupy them – and often strategic in intent. In many Western contexts, for example, the demise of institutionalized religion has lead to the appropriation of church spaces for state-sponsored, multi-faith events (see Knott 2010). In such cases, it is clear that religious spaces are appropriated and enmeshed within the politics of the state.

Such spaces can, however, also be developed as a way by which minority religious groups may seek to align themselves with a dominant religious order. Such alignment could be for the purpose of protection or subversion (or both). For example, McGregor (2010) shows how in post-tsunami Aceh, Indonesia, some Christian NGOs helped to rebuild Islamic mosques and other infrastructure. Doing so reveals an awareness of the fact that 'if you want to have an impact here you have to do it through Islam' (cited in McGregor 2010, 741). Such actions give rise to quasi-religious spaces – those which, on the surface, may be strongly equated with one (often dominant) religion (Islam in this case), but are appropriated and used by other religious agencies (Christian in this case) to advance their own religious objectives. Similarly, Woods (2013a, 661) shows how in Colombo, Sri Lanka, evangelical groups helped to rebuild the perimeter wall of a Buddhist temple, the aim being to 'enable new forms of spatial understanding and new opportunities for the reframing, acceptance and growth of Christian groups'. In this instance, the fact that Christians were seen to work within a Buddhist space – and to reinforce the boundary of such a space as well – helped the local community to view Christianity in a more positive (and less threatening) light. While such activities may appear benign or charitable, they should not be looked upon uncritically as being divorced from their overarching religious motivations.

Box 2.8: Overlapping religious spaces and pre-school education in Sri Lanka

Evangelical Christian groups operating in Sri Lanka have developed innovative strategies of evangelization that avoid Buddhist surveillance (by operating through secular spaces) while enabling various forms of competition to prevail that result in Christian acceptance and growth. Beyond evangelizing through secular spaces, however, Woods (2013a) also shows how Christian groups evangelize through Buddhist spaces as well. Specifically, Christian pre-schools are sometimes established *within* the confines of Buddhist temple precincts. Doing so 'reflects an encroachment of Christian influence into the traditionally sacrosanct confines of Buddhist space; a process that enables multifaceted forms of competition to exist within the same spatial register' (Woods 2013a, 661). In other words, the presence and association of Christian pastors within everyday registers of Buddhist power and influence grants them a degree of acceptance among local communities. It also enables the obfuscation of evangelical space, and the obfuscation of evangelical intent. The overall effect is that processes of Christian influencing can occur in and through a variety of spaces: Christian, secular, and even Buddhist. This enables Christian groups to establish and develop competitive advantages through different types of space.

Religious-secular competition and conflict

Beyond inter-religious competition and conflict, competition between religious groups and (secular) states over the ownership of religious spaces has been growing in importance as a potential source of religious conflict. This phenomenon is particularly noticeable in land-poor, rapid industrializing countries and cities, where a growing economy and a growing population are constantly increasing the demand for secular-material uses of scarce land resources (such as the construction of public infrastructure). In these contexts, religious groups have come under increasing state pressure to cede ownership of their religious spaces to the state. In the interests of more efficient land use and more effective urban planning, the state has attempted to reduce the size of religious spaces; relocate religious spaces (especially places of worship) from urban centres to the fringes; take over religious spaces (such as graveyards and cemeteries) by discouraging or banning land-intensive religious ritual; and, encouraging the sharing of civic spaces by various religious groups for specific religious purposes (e.g. different church groups sharing hotel banquet halls, school halls, etc., for congregation and study purposes).

The competition between religious groups and secular states for religious space can be sources of religious conflict in two distinct ways. First, redesignation of religious spaces as secular spaces can be easily perceived by affected religious individuals and groups as an act of desecration and bring the material agenda of the state into direct conflict with their spiritual needs. Relatedly, these individuals/groups can find it harder to reconcile their twin loyalties to the state on the one hand and to God on the other. The perception of spiritual disenfranchisement can, in turn, prompt reactionary ideologies among religious groups that can trigger subversive, anti-state actions. Subversive acts, when countered with the state's use of force, can create circumstances for the escalation of conflict into violence. It should be noted that the risk of conflict and violence is greater when the state's actions with respect to the expropriation of religious spaces are perceived to be discriminatory towards a particular religious group. In Singapore, for example, government expropriation of the Bukit Brown and Bidadari Cemeteries in order to make way for new expressways and public housing estates has triggered a public debate about the sanctity of burial grounds. In Turkey, the government has repossessed numerous properties belonging to the minority Greek and Armenian Orthodox communities on the grounds that they were under-utilized; indeed, in past decades it has tacitly supported the destruction and desecration of such buildings by branches of the Turkish army (see Vryonis 2005).

Second, as the ownership of religious spaces by religious groups diminish, the performance of religious rituals (essential to maintain religious identity) gets driven out into secular spaces. In such cases, there is a clear potential for secular-religious tensions. Further, when several religious groups share the same space for the performance of religious ritual, inter-group tensions may also arise, which can trigger communal violence. Inter-group tensions in secular spaces is discussed in greater detail in the next chapter.

The preceding discussion on the mechanisms via which conflicts between religious groups and secular states over religious spaces can arise throws light on some key strategies to manage and contain conflict and minimize the potential for violence. These include, but are not limited to the following. First, if political leaders are able to forge a trans-religious consensus about the value and priority of secular-material goals for the betterment of society, the possibility is enhanced that religious groups will be able to 'sacrifice' their religious space for a larger good. Second, political leaders who are able to foster a strong trans-religious national identity which dominates religious identities, religious groups may then be able to accept that the needs of the 'nation' need to be prioritized over the needs of individual groups within. Third, where religious discourses may be harnessed to provide religiously grounded justification for the actions of the state and the obedience of its subjects (through the reinterpretation of religious narratives), acceptance of loss of religious space may result. Fourth, with the help of religious leaders, political leaders may seek to establish that certain land-intensive religious traditions/rituals are not essential to the maintenance of specific religious identities. Fifth, it is critical that political leaders and policymakers create and sustain the perception that state actions do not systematically discriminate against particular religious groups. Finally, devising clear, transparent, universally accepted and easily enforceable rules to govern religious behaviour that spills over from extant religious spaces into secular spaces is critical.

In one way or another, the effectiveness of all of the above strategies is dependent on the degree to which the state is able to co-opt the religious leadership of various religious groups in the formulation, dissemination and popularization of state goals. We offer two case studies to show how the complicity between the state and religious groups has mitigated the risk of religious-secular conflict despite large-scale state appropriation of religious space and the resulting restrictions on some space-intensive religious practices (see Boxes 2.9 and 2.10).

Box 2.9: Religious relocation, conflict and consensus-building in Singapore

Singapore, on account of its small size, rapid industrialization, and a state agenda committed to material secular goals, provides a rich ground for studying the conflict between religious groups and the secular state that arises from the relocation of religious spaces. In its short history, accelerating public infrastructure needs have contributed to a spate of state acquisition of places of worship belonging to various religious groups. In some instances, such acquisitions have been accompanied by the provision of alternative sites to religious groups for the dislocated religious spaces. Examples include:

- The relocation of Angullia Mosque, Ngee Ann Kongsi land, Bethesda Chapel, Chek Sian Teng Chinese Temple, Sri Sivan Temple and a Sikh Temple at Kirk Terrace to make way for the Mass Rapid Transit stations in the Orchard Road corridor.
- The acquisition of the Central Sikh Temple in 1978, which was located in Queen Street, and its subsequent relocation to Towner Road.
- The relocation of Sri Vairavimada Kaliamman Temple from Killiney Road to Orchard Road and then again to Somerset Road.
- The relocation of Kim Lan Beo Temple from Yan Kit Road to Kim Tian Road.
- The relocation of Jin Long Si Temple from Lorong How Sun to Tai Seng Avenue.

In all of the instances above, state acquisition of religious spaces has engendered feelings of resentment, albeit of various degrees of intensity, among affected religious groups. Resentment against loss of religious space has primarily been due to a usurpation of the sacred meaning invested in places of worship (Kong 1993a); to a large extent, peoples' sense of powerlessness in contesting state actions has also played a significant part in inflating this sense of resentment.[3]

However, while resentment of state acquisition of religious space has been pervasive, it has never escalated into a full blown conflict between state and religious groups. As such, it is instructive to identify the factors that have been instrumental in the containment of religious conflict. First, the state's land acquisition policy is universally acknowledged to have been non-discriminatory and fair to all religious groups (Kong 1993a). Second, the state has been successful in imposing its ideological hegemony over religious leaders.[4] Third, religious individuals have coped with the loss of their religious spaces through various forms of behavioural and emotional adaptation (Kong 1993a). In the absence of such coping mechanisms, there is a significantly greater risk of resentment manifesting itself as irreconcilable conflict. These adaptations have been crucial to sustaining the state's ideological hegemony over shaping collective or national goals, while maintaining the notions of the sacredness of religious spaces. Kong (1993a) reports that a key element of the emotional adaptation process for many religious individuals is to search for precepts in their own religious narratives that legitimize state actions. For example, Christians base their acceptance on scriptural injunctions to place common good over self-interest, or on assertions that demolition/relocation is part of the larger cosmic plan; Buddhists cite injunctions to be detached from world things, and so forth (see Kong 1993a for a comprehensive review). In addition, a considerable amount of reinvestiture of sacredness in other concepts takes place to compensate for the separation of sacredness from religious place. Sacredness is invested variously, in the self, in a community of believers, in sanctified religious paraphernalia carried on the person, and so forth (Kong 1993a).

Box 2.10: Changing death rituals in East Asia: Conflict and consensus

Many East Asian states, including South Korea, Hong Kong, Taiwan and China, have witnessed a gradual shift from the traditional practice of burial of the dead to cremation. By and large, this transformation has been peaceful. In all of the cases, the shift has been actively promoted by the state with an eye, primarily, towards reducing the demand for burial grounds. In addition, states have hoped that, by negating the ritualistic importance of burials, they would be able to divest burial grounds of their 'sacredness' and hence minimize religious opposition to using them for secular ends.

Given that death rituals are essential elements of religious praxis in most Asian (and, especially, East Asian) cultures, government projects encouraging 'innovation' have been invariably met with 'resistant cultures and cultures of resistance' (Kong 2012). In response, the states in question, in complicity with religious leaders, have attempted to manufacture a national consensus that adopting new funeral practices does not compromise one's identity as a Christian or a traditional Chinese religionist. We use South Korea as an example to show how the church adapted to, and implicitly supported, the government's pro-cremation propaganda. Hong Kong and Taiwan will tell the Confucianist side of the story.

South Korea has witnessed a rapid spread in Christianity after World War II, to the extent that the Church – Catholic and Protestant combined – is the single largest religious group with nearly 14 million followers. In 1993 and, then again in 1997, the South Korean government introduced similar bills in the National Assembly promoting a switch in funeral practices from burial to cremation. While the Catholic Church was unanimous in its support of the government policy, having lifted the 1886 ban on cremation since 1964, Protestant attitudes to the proposed switch were divided. Pro-cremation Protestant ministers fronted a campaign in 1998 by establishing the 'Christian Centre for Promoting Cremation' (Park 2009). Reconciling Protestantism with cremation for this group of protestants was based on identifying that many key aspects of Korean burial practices were 'unchristian' in nature to begin with, for example, in involving *feng shui* principles; asserting that the Church had a role to play in alleviating social problems associated with burial; and believing that a pro-cremation approach would enhance evangelical prospects. In addition, innovations such as exclusively Protestant columbaria and specific methods of treating Protestant remains have been initiated to maintain the 'Christian' identity of the deceased and those he is survived by, in spite of cremation.

On the other hand, a negative stance towards cremation within the Protestant Church is also strong. However, in the negative responses articulated – especially by the Presbyterian Church – although burial is promoted as the funeral method of choice, there is no proclamation that cremation is a fundamentally 'unchristian' way of dispersing the dead. Thus, as Park (2009) suggests, Christian anti-cremation discourses 'do not see governmental policy on cremation as a "persecution" of Christianity'. Consequently, conflict between the Church and the state has been avoided.

In Hong Kong and Taiwan, the reconciliation between the state and Chinese religious groups on the issue of transformation of traditional funeral practice has also taken place on the grounds that cremation does not compromise the maintenance of the Chinese identity, and does not jeopardize the status and condition of the deceased in the afterlife. Maintenance of identity despite changes in religious ritual (vis-à-vis funeral practices) are achieved through the continued performance of other commemorative rituals such as Qing Ming and Chong Yang (Kong 2012). By keeping the ritualized tradition intact, even though the site of performance of ritual shifts (from graveyards to columbaria and even to cyberspace), pro-cremation initiatives of the government are assimilated as a part of modern religious traditions without causing destabilizing religion-state conflict.

Distinct from the preceding discussions about competition between religious groups and (secular) states over the ownership of religious spaces so that the space may be used for secular developmental purposes, the control and use of sacred space is often also linked to underlying symbolic and political purposes. Both secular and religious leaders have long sought to dominate religious sites, the aim being to 'symbolize their control over the community, by virtue of the social, economic and political centrality of that space in the daily life of the community, or in order to exert influence on pilgrims that frequent the site' (Hassner 2003, 19). For example, in 1979, the Grand Mosque in Mecca, Saudi Arabia, was commandeered by armed gunmen and 1,000 pilgrims were held hostage for several days. The standoff ended with an assault on the mosque by Saudi forces that was sanctioned by a unique edict from the *ulema* – the Saudi religious elite. That such an assault took several days to effect is because the Saudi government struggled with the difficulties of sanctioning force inside Islam's holiest shrine (see Buchanan 1981). Such a shrine has repeatedly been a focus of (planned) terrorist attacks, including the apprehension of Iranian Revolutionary Guards – posing as pilgrims – trying to smuggle weapons into the Mosque in 1986, the shooting of 450 pilgrims by the Saudi National Guard following a demonstration by Iranian pilgrims in 1987, and the beheading of 16 Kuwaiti pilgrims following the explosion of two bombs within the vicinity of the Mosque in 1988 (Hassner 2003). The uncompromising responses on behalf of the Saudi government reflect the intolerance of any form of challenge to their control over, or sanctity of, the country's foremost religious space.

Autonomy-related competition and conflict

In addition to competition over the ownership of religious spaces, regulation of religious practices *within* religious spaces is also a potential source of religious conflict. As the state is the primary author of such regulation, the ensuing conflict can be seen as arising from competition between religious groups and the state for autonomy over deciding the types of religious activities that can be conducted in religious spaces, over how religious doctrine is to be interpreted, and what protocols should govern conduct within religious spaces.

The pursuit of autonomy is a never-ending goal for most religious groups. Irrespective of majority or minority status, autonomy is often mediated by various secular and religious agencies that seek to regulate and control religious presence and praxis. This is as true for Christianity in the East as it is for Islam in the West, which have received wide-ranging scholarly attention. In Europe, Islamic groups are recognized as being 'anchored in a social and symbolic milieu, a concrete geographical, geopolitical and "geo-religious" space which was not at first very favourable to it' (Allievo and Dassetto 1999, 244). Building on this observation, Metcalf (1996, 12) shows how Islamic groups in Europe and North America 'strain at being thus constrained', with resistance from majority (Christian, and secular) groups helping to shape and guide their patterns of action and presence in space. Put differently, 'geo-religious' space plays a deterministic role in how religious groups operate and compete on a day-to-day basis.

Indeed, as noted in the Introduction, the modern, secular nation–state can be thought of as consisting of two distinct spaces – religious and secular – which overlap to different degrees in different places. Generally, the state retains jurisdiction and control over secular spaces while ceding dominion over religious spaces to religious leaders. In many cases, the state exchanges a promise of non-interference in religious affairs, conducted within religious spaces, for a promise by religious groups to not subvert its authority in the secular sphere or challenge its secular goals. In equilibrium, this results in a clear division between secular and spiritual authority, each paramount in its own domain; religious groups accept minimal, administrative regulations such as registration, periodic financial book-keeping and so on, in return for state-sanctioned privileges such as tax exemptions and subsidies. Consequently, there is no autonomy-related competition.

Autonomy-related competition between state and religious groups may be thought of as a breakdown of this covenant between state and religious groups. This competition takes the form of attempts by the state to impose greater and/or more stringent regulations on religious spaces. Of course, competition can also take the form of attempts by religious groups to increase its own influence over secular spaces; this form of autonomy-related competition is discussed in the next chapter. Here, our focus is on how the state attempts to regulate religious spaces more and/or more stringently, which can result in conflict and even violence. These attempts take numerous forms deriving from varied motivations, as the case studies later in the chapter demonstrate. They may take shape in ideologically justified actions to increase its own sphere of influence. They may also be reprisals against religious groups for challenging state authority over secular spaces, (actually or potentially) subverting state authority/sovereignty, and (actually or potentially) subverting state goals. Further, state actions may be prompted by the perceived or real need to protect the interests of secular and other religious groups from infringement by a religious group. They may also be populist interventions (actions to appease popular sentiment for more regulations); or paternalistic interventions (actions to protect members of religious groups from self-inflicted harm).

Whatever motivations the state might have for regulating religious spaces, it invariably comes into conflict with religious leadership; this conflict can be self-perpetuating. Because any incursion by the state into religious spaces breaks the 'non-interference pact' between states and religious groups, it licenses (further) challenges by affected groups against the authority of the state over secular spaces, giving rise to a potentially violent, vicious cycle. In the extreme scenario, religious groups can completely reject state authority and develop and promote a separatist agenda.

It should also be noted that the incursions by state into religious spaces is not always clearly identifiable. This arises because the relationship(s) between the state and religious groups is often one of fluid boundaries and shifting understandings so that it is not a simple task to categorically say that the state has incurred into the boundaries of religious space. In China, for example, the state divides religions into two distinct groups: those that are officially sanctioned and those that are officially banned. Also in existence, however, are a vast number of religious groups that fit into neither category (e.g. Pentecostal churches), or defy 'religious' identification (e.g. groups that are not considered religions, but are engaged in spiritual or religious practices such as yoga, New Age occult or magic) (Yang 2006). Such ambiguity is true not just in China but takes shape in many other religious contexts around the world as well, making it an equivocal task to adjudicate when incursions into either boundaries have taken place.

Be that as it may, insofar as clarity is obtained about state-religious interaction and insofar as they can be managed, the discussions that follow will demonstrate how certain features of state-religious interaction might abet or inhibit autonomy-related conflict (over religious spaces) from resulting in a permanent social fracture. These include the ability to institute the state-desired changes in religious practice through consensus rather than through coercion; consulting religious leadership about proposed regulations rather than taking unilateral decisions and imposing them in a 'top-down' manner; enabling religious groups to adapt to the new regulations by providing a reasonable adjustment period; ensuring that proposed religious regulations are perceived as non-discriminatory; and resisting popular pressures to regulate the religious spaces belonging to particular religious groups, simply because group practices deviate from the social norm.

To demonstrate the numerous general principles and observations above, our discussion below is focused on different ways in which states attempt to regulate religious spaces and practices, and these are: regulations over religious practices in religious spaces, regulations of places of instruction, regulations of cults, regulations of religious conversion. Finally, as an extreme form of regulation, we draw attention to the armed occupation by state agencies of religious spaces.

Regulations over religious practices in religious spaces

When states try to regulate religious practices in religious spaces that do not challenge state authority or sovereignty, the justification for doing so is often grounded on the fact that the regulated practice encroaches into secular spaces and disrupts public peace. Affected religious groups contest the state's rights to regulate such practices by asserting that the practice occurs within a religious space, and that the practice is essential to maintaining religious identity. A clear example of this form of regulation, and the subsequent contestation by religious groups, is the regulation(s) restricting the use of loudspeakers in mosques (see Box 2.11).

Box 2.11: Loudspeakers in mosques and the call to prayer

The call to prayer, five times a day, by a *muezzin* at a mosque is a central part of Islamic religious practice. Since the invention of the loudspeaker, mosques have installed them as a way of broadcasting the traditional call to prayer. However, mosques have very often come into conflict with state agencies over this practice for two reasons. First, the use of loudspeakers for religious purposes infringes on secular interests by disturbing public peace and generating noise pollution (*The Telegraph*, 12 December 2011). Second, external loudspeakers in mosques have a history of being used to incite communal tension and riots in places as varied as Israel, India, Pakistan and Indonesia. Especially in the Western world, bans on the use of loudspeakers in mosques have received widespread public sympathy ranging from Bavaria and Cologne in Germany to Oxford in UK to Michigan in the United States (*Agence France-Presse*, 23 July 1997; *New York Times*, 5 May 2004; *New York Times*, 5 July 2007). Grassroots-level objections to the installation of loudspeakers in mosques have been based on their potential to disrupt peace and Islamize the locality. For example, Dr Alan Chapman, a resident of Oxford, who lives in the neighbourhood of a mosque that planned to apply for permission to broadcast the call to prayer, expressed his discomfort by saying 'the Muslim call is a theological statement' (*Daily Mail*, 14 January 2008).

Opponents of the ban, mostly Muslim religious groups and leaders, cite the freedom for religious expression as grounds for continued use of loudspeakers, while proponents (mostly secular individuals, members of other religious groups and state officials) point out that the use of loudspeakers is not central to Islamic practice, has no scriptural precedent and is an environmental problem (*The Telegraph*, 12 December 2011). Given that the regulation of religious activity of local religious spaces generally lies with local governments in most parts of Western Europe and the United States, bans on the use of loudspeakers are applied non-uniformly. In Pakistan, an Islamic state, mosques have been banned from using loudspeakers other than for the call to prayer (e.g. preaching or sermon delivery) (*Gulf News*, 11 June 2001). In India, however, proposed legislations to ban the use of loudspeakers in mosques has failed. Whether governments (either local, regional or national) want to or manage to regulate this religious practice, the issue is deeply divisive and routinely generates religion-state conflict over religious autonomy in religious spaces.

Regulation of places of religious instruction

Religious education is an integral part of religious practice. In most modern secular countries, religious and secular education are not mutually exclusive; rather, the former exists to supplement more comprehensive secular education programs. Although the marginalization of religious education has met with general opposition from religious groups, states have defended the regulations on paternalistic grounds by arguing that (even) religious individuals need minimal levels of secular education to participate fully in, and profit from, economic growth and development.

On the other hand, as the following case studies show, in many instances, religious groups' resentment of state interference in religious education has been amplified by a suspicion that state regulations are not *merely* grounded in paternalistic considerations. These religious groups (including Muslims in Europe, southern Thailand and China, and Tibetan Buddhists in China) see such regulations as discriminations against their community by the state. Accordingly, state restrictions on religious curricula, the appointment of religious teachers and the mobility of religious scholars within and between countries – enforced via constant monitoring – have proven to hold the potential to provoke religious conflict.

Box 2.12: Regulating *pondoks* in Thailand

Liow (2007, 163) reports that 'Islamic education has long been a potentially explosive issue in the politics of Southern Thailand.' The Islamic religious schools or *pondoks*, which provide such education, are central to the maintenance of the Malay-Muslim identity. The religious teachers or 'Tok Guru' not only command great respect from lay religious people, but also wield significant political influence.

Attempts by the Thai government to streamline and regulate the *pondok* curricula so that graduates from the Muslim education system are equipped to benefit from the modern economy, are met with resistance and have invariably failed. For example, a 2004 government exercise to register an estimated 500 *pondok* schools in Southern Thailand (by promising state support and funding for those that registered) elicited a very weak response (Liow 2007).

The government's failure to engage *pondoks* – and by implication, local Muslim communities – can be attributed to several factors. First, regulatory exercises such as the above have been attempted in an atmosphere of mutual suspicion and distrust. The state sees *pondoks* as sites of indoctrination into a separatist ideology and promotion of militancy, especially those receiving funding and scholarships from Middle Eastern charities (Liow 2007). Second, the state has a history of subjecting *pondoks* to surprise checks by gun-wielding soldiers (as opposed to bureaucrats and civilian state representatives) who, in the process, have manhandled the Tok Guru. As such, Muslim community leaders are sceptical about the paternalistic intentions of the state and are apprehensive that the registration with the state would lead to greater government intervention and more armed raids (Liow 2007). Third, *pondoks* have rarely benefitted from past promises of state financial support. Where funds have been allotted, the trickle down to the grassroots institutions has been meagre, on account of corruption. As such, the carrot of financial benefits fails to be a sufficiently lucrative stimulus for accepting regulation.

In Thailand, the state's failure to win the trust of local communities is compounded by the fact that coercive, top-down regulation has also proven to be ineffective; such attempts merely succeed in driving *pondoks* 'underground' and further out of reach of state regulation.

Box 2.13: Regulation of religious education in China

China's regulation of religious education is rooted in the anti-religious state philosophy, which rejects a division of authority between state and religious groups over secular and religious spaces respectively. Restrictions with regard to religious education are multi-layered (affecting curricula, examinations, clergy appointment and mobility of both students and teachers in places of religious instruction). For example, the 2010 International Religious Freedom Report on China states that: 'While the form, content, and frequency of "patriotic" education at monasteries varied widely, the conduct of such training was a routine part of monastic management. Increasingly "legal education" was a major theme of the training. Authorities often forced monks and nuns to denounce the Dalai Lama and study materials praising the leadership of the CCP and the socialist system. Authorities also pressured monks and nuns to express allegiance to the government-recognized eleventh Panchen Lama. Monks and nuns reported that patriotic education campaigns detracted from their religious studies, and some fled their monasteries and nunneries because they faced expulsion for refusing to comply with the education sessions. According to sources, the overall numbers of monks and nuns in monasteries and nunneries remained at significantly lower levels than before the riots in March 2008. Government-selected monks had primary responsibility for conducting patriotic education at each monastery. In some cases the government established "official working groups" at monasteries, and religious affairs and public security officials personally led the patriotic education' (US State Department 2010).

In regions such as Tibet, the Chinese state's attempts to regulate religious instruction have also been motivated by a desire to repress the dissemination and popularization of the separatist agenda. Regulation takes place at many levels and comprehensively. Some such measures, which have fuelled considerable disquiet among the Tibetan Buddhists, include: the mandatory requirement for monks and nuns to attend 'patriotic' and 'legal' education courses; the appointment of Lamas by the government, whose religious education is closely supervised; tighter enforcement of bans on a Tibetan traditional practice of sending young boys and girls to monasteries and nunneries to receive religious training; and restrictions on the movement of Tibetan monks in the Tibet Autonomous Region (TAR) to other monasteries in China (and, especially, to India, where the Dalai Lama lives in exile) and, vice versa, for receiving religious instruction or as religious teachers.

All of the above practices have contributed to a deepening schism between the state and, both the religious leadership within the TAR and the highly traditionally religious ordinary Tibetans. The growing perception of discrimination by the state has also contributed to an increasing sense of persecution and insecurity about religious identity, which can lead to a stronger rather than weaker separatist movement.

Box 2.14: *Madrasah* regulation in the UK?

State regulation of religious spaces in general, and places of religious instruction in particular, can be grounded in a desire to appease popular sentiment. When the state becomes a vehicle for perpetuating the 'tyranny of the majority', it contributes to the development of an inferiority complex among persecuted communities – that of being 'second class citizens'. Such complexes can fuel anti-state resentment, a greater sympathy for religious fundamentalism (loyalty to the state diminishes with a corresponding increase in loyalty to religion) and, in extreme cases, lead to an active, though covert, subversion of the state agenda. Since 2001, Muslim religious spaces have generally evoked public distrust, especially in Western countries. Muslim places of religious instruction, *madrasahs*, have come under public scrutiny for their potential involvement in breeding Islamic fundamentalism. Often, calls for more stringent control of *madrasah* activities have been made under the pretext of a secular concern (e.g. dissatisfaction about separation of older boys and girls into different classes for religious instruction). Thus governments, in responding to popular calls for greater regulation have to be scrupulously careful in 'not choosing sides' and acting within the ambit of existing legal codes.

In 2012, based on a BBC report about 400 allegations of physical abuse of children in UK *madrasahs*, the National Secular Society argued for stricter monitoring and regulation of *madrasahs* (National Secular Society, 26 January 2012). The state resisted calls for greater regulation, in spite of any secular merit in the demands. Key to the state's argument was that, under UK law at the time, corporal punishment was legal in religious settings; hence regulation of *madrasahs* in this regard should succeed an amendment in the larger law. In addition, the then children and families minister said that it was not practicable for the government to implement a national register of *all* supplementary schools (*madrasahs* in the UK are classified as supplementary schools) and so, focusing only on *madrasahs* would appear discriminatory and reinforce unhelpful stereotypes.

Regulation of cults

State regulations of cult (especially, radical cult) practices traditionally have either been a reflection of popular misgivings about the goals and methods of cults, or have been reprisals against cult subversion of state authority or agenda. The regulation of cult activity is surprisingly easy and often achieved through an apparently benign mechanism – registration. While it is a common practice in many countries in the world to require religious groups to register themselves in return for state sanctioned economic benefits (such as tax exemptions and subsidies), the requirement of registration (and re-registration) combined with the attendant bureaucratic difficulties in doing so, helps states to control access to the valued tag 'religious group' and concomitant constitutional guarantees of protection. With respect to cults, a failure in acquiring official status as a religious group – on account of failure to register or re-register, or due to a state ban – significantly endangers their ability to survive in a hostile public environment. As noted in a previous section, cults without official status as religious groups can face difficulties in acquiring religious spaces, which by default, is a serious infraction of their autonomy over religious practice.

State regulation of cults is pervasive simply because it is a notoriously easy thing to do. More often than not, cults are insignificant minorities and conflict arising out of their regulation is, at first sight, easy to contain or suppress. However, states have to be mindful of the fact that regulating cult activity (especially though the denial of official status as a religious group) has the potential to drive cult activity underground, where it is potentially immune from state surveillance and (further) state regulation. Further, given that some cults have historically evolved into global religions, state regulation of cults may engender an anti-state sentiment that might be detrimental to state interests when the cult grows large enough to establish itself as an alternative power centre. Whatever the outcome, it is important to understand why states seek to regulate cults; the case studies in this section focus attention on this.

Box 2.15: Anti-cult regulations as state reprisals

In countries with a policy of compulsory military service, Jehovah's Witnesses, a Christian cult, has invariably fallen foul of the law. Owing to their doctrinal opposition to armed violence, they have routinely refused to participate in a state-imposed national obligation (a contestation of state authority over secular spaces), which has led them to be banned and deregistered as a 'religious group'. For example, Singapore, Russia and Israel are some countries which have either banned the religious group entirely or have made it difficult for them to obtain official status in the country (US State Department, 2010).

In Japan, following the Sarin gas attack in Tokyo's subway network, the Aum organization has faced intense regulation by state authorities. In the immediate aftermath of the event, Aum's status as a 'religious corporation' was revoked and in the face of mounting claims for compensation from victims and survivors, Aum was declared bankrupt and its assets were frozen (Mullins 2001). Further, to keep the organization and followers in check, the Japanese government initiated and passed legislation in 2001 that allowed Aum to be continuously surveilled for the next three years. This bill required Aum to submit information on its members and activities every three months and allowed security officials to enter its premises for inspection (Mullins 2001).

Box 2.16: Anti-cult regulation as appeasement of popular sentiment

In the case of Aum discussed above, although state regulation can be thought of as a reprisal for the gas attack, these regulations had widespread resonance among the population in general. Watanabe (2001) identifies this pervasive public antipathy to Aum as a key factor in the ease with which the government was able to institute new regulations governing religious practices.

Similarly, in France following the Solar Temple mass suicides, there was an overwhelming public distrust of radical cults. In order to appease popular sentiment, the government created an 'observatory on sects/cults' in 1996, which was later reorganized as the 'Interministerial Mission of Vigilance and Combat against Sectarian Aberrations' (MIVILUDES) in 2002. Laws were passed making dissolution of cults easier and MIVILUDES published a guide for public servants and local authorities on how to identify and combat cults (Grim and Finke 2011). Despite all this, there was no attempt at disambiguating what a 'cult' was; the vagueness in definition potentially enable a selective and discriminatory application of anti-cult laws at the local level by local authorities.

Box 2.17: Ahmadiyya Muslims in Pakistan: Anti-cult regulations in a religious state

Ahmadiyyas, a minority Islamic sect in Pakistan, have been confronted with heavy state interference in their religious practices and in the management of their religious spaces. Much of the regulation (with antecedents dating back to the early 1970s) has been based on a denial of their religious identity as Muslims in a Muslim state. Ahmadiyyas are followers of a late nineteenth-century religious reformer, Ghulam Mohammed, who described himself as the second prophet. This assertion can be considered blasphemous in Islam, owing to the orthodox view that Muhammad is the final prophet (Valentine 2008). Ganguly (2007) provides a list of such regulations and attempts that have targeted the Ahmadiyya community's autonomy over religious performance over the past three decades. These include the inclusion of Ahmadis as non-Muslim citizens; the prosecution of Ahmadis for carrying the Quran or uttering Islamic confession of faith; and impositions of bans on Ahmadis' participation in Friday prayers. Further and more recent restrictions on Ahmadiyyas in Pakistan have included bans on preaching and on pilgrimages (especially to Saudi Arabia for the Haj).

This is an illustration of a case where public violence against a religious sect follows government curtailment of the sect's religious autonomy, and is in contrast with the cases where government regulation follows the lead of popular sentiment, described in the previous case study. The Pakistan state's disregard for the religious autonomy of the Ahmadis is justified by categorizing them as the 'other', the non-Muslim in a Muslim state and has had the effect of fanning public grievances against the community. Orthodox Muslims have interpreted state actions to sanction public violence against the Ahmadis, leading to genocide, destruction or desecration of their places of worship and public incitation, by fundamentalist religious groups to further violence.

Regulation of religious conversion

Religious conversion has been defined as 'processes of movement and change that affect individuals, communities, organizations and localities, yet they are also embedded within, and influence, interreligious and religious-secular relations at the macro-scale' (Woods 2012a, 441). Religious conversion is implicitly associated with – and a driver of – religious competition and conflict. Religious conversion is not just a matter of religious concern for the individual, but is both informed by and contributes to a myriad of otherwise secular discourses surrounding the nation and community, the provision of aid and charity, and the appropriation and use of space. In what follows, we discuss religious conversion in terms of the conversion of people and the conversion of space.

Converting into a new religion reflects the numerical strengthening of one group and a weakening of another. The processes that lead to religious conversion – evangelization, for example – reveal the competitive (in)efficacy and (dis)advantages of religious groups. The conversion of people can be analysed from various scalar viewpoints. At the macro-scale, a number of structural shifts associated with modernization have been held accountable for religious revivalism in the post-war period. Such shifts have caused large-scale religious switching (to, e.g. Christianity), and include the side effects of modernization, such as urbanization, industrialization and the shift towards more rational thought and action (see Chapter 1). At the micro-scale, attempts have been made to understand the individual human processes that are embroiled in religious switching (see, e.g. Beckford 1978; Rambo 1989, 1993; Richardson 1985). Beyond the obvious psychological bias associated with unravelling human choice, discourse has also considered the role of social networks (between friends, family and colleagues for example) in influencing conversion patterns and behaviours. For example, Lofland and Stark (1965, 871) were among the first to show how cults, and other small religious groups that are typically more aggressive in their growth, develop strong affective bonds with potential converts, concluding that 'conversion [i]s coming to accept the opinions of one's friends'. The most competitive religious groups are attuned to these factors, and often use them to their advantage.

Specifically, conversion is often as much a political act as it is a religious one, with 'much nationalism and imperialism hav[ing] found purpose and justification in religious difference and in proselytizing' (Agnew 2006, 185). Such 'purpose and justification' are felt most acutely in postcolonial contexts, where the contemporary spread of evangelical Christianity (in particular) provides a potent reminder of missionization during colonial rule. Attempts to control conversion out of a dominant religion have seen authoritarian regimes prescribing punishments for members who contravene such controls, as seen most recently in the cases of a Sudanese woman being sentenced to death (but subsequently acquitted) for renouncing Islam and converting to Christianity (BBC News, 24 June 2014), and a Nigerian man being imprisoned for renouncing Islam in favour of atheism (*The Guardian*, 25 June 2014). To this end, religious conversion often stimulates residual feelings of resentment and insecurity, and can provide a foundation for the regulation and persecution of proselytizing religious groups.

In some instances, however, religious conversion is also associated with exploitation. As global inequality in wealth increases, so does the potential for relatively wealthy religious organizations to focus their evangelistic and social upliftment activities on countries, regions and population cohorts that are sites – or victims – of environmental (e.g. tsunami, drought), social (inequality, lack of education), political (war, corruption) and economic (poverty) degradation and upheaval. Converting under such circumstances can reflect a sort of shallow opportunism that fuel discussions about the number, type and quality of 'real' converts. Indeed, the focus on 'gap-filling' (see Chapter 3) and other activities related to the distribution of aid and other forms of charity has sparked debate about how 'evangelical practices discourage and disrupt vulnerable and not yet 'awakened' individuals' from developing the spiritual aptitudes that can enable them to discern the true worth of a religion' (Mahadev 2014, 213). Accordingly, there has been a growing focus on the spaces wherein conversion practices and processes occur, and the politics of conversion are embroiled. Box 2.18 outlines one attempt to regulate against 'unethical' conversions in Sri Lanka.

Box 2.18: Regulating against 'unethical' conversions in Sri Lanka

In Sri Lanka, the practices of evangelical Christian groups pose a competitive threat to the dominance of Sri Lankan Buddhism. Such practices date back to colonial-era missionary endeavours that attempted to disrupt Buddhist practices and lifestyles. In the postcolonial era, the dominant Sinhala-Buddhist population has sought various ways to assert and protect their ethno-religious primacy. For example, the writing of the Sri Lankan constitution of 1972 enshrined the central role of Buddhism by conferring it 'the foremost place' with the state being responsible for 'protect[ing] and foster[ing] the Buddha *Sasana* [the teaching of the Buddha]' (Article 9). In 2004, riding on the wave of anti-Christian sentiment that followed the death of a revered Buddhist nationalist monk – Venerable Soma Thero – the Jathika Hela Urumaya (JHU) was elected to the Sri Lankan Parliament. The JHU is an ultranationalist political party comprised entirely of Buddhist monks.

Since 2004 the JHU has drafted and lobbied a Prohibition of Forcible Conversion Bill (PFCB) that seeks to outlaw religious conversion by 'unethical' means. This parallels measures taken by other countries around the world. In 2002, seventy-seven countries restricted proselytizing activity (especially that of foreign missionaries), twenty-nine of which prevent conversion away from the dominant religion (Fox 2009). Proposed by the JHU in July 2004 and Ministry of Buddha *Sasana* Affairs in June 2005, the respectively titled 'Prohibition of Forcible Conversion (Private Member's Bill)' and 'Freedom of Religion Bill' seek to contain the perceived threat to Buddhism posed by minority religions. The Prohibition of Forcible Conversion Bill seeks to criminalize the conversion of Buddhists to other faiths by persuasion or fraud, which underpins the fact that conversion is a key driver of religious tension in Sri Lanka (Owens 2007). If passed, anyone caught aiding or abetting such activity will be liable for imprisonment of between five and seven years and a fine of between Rs. 150,000 and Rs. 500,000. Significantly the higher sentence and fine are for those accused of converting 'samurdhi [welfare] beneficiaries, prison, rehabilitation and detention centre inmates, physically and mentally handicapped persons, members of the armed forces, the police, students, the inmates of refugee camps and minors' (*The Sunday Times*, 8 February 2009). While still being debated in parliament, the PFCB has been widely criticized, given its potential for manipulation that could result in curbs to – rather than protection of – religious freedoms. The Sri Lankan case shows how religious nationalists attempt to harness the power of the state in a bid to impose sanctions on minority groups that pose a threat to their authority and control.

Woods (2012a) suggests that delineating between 'legitimate' and 'illegitimate' spaces of conversion is a first step towards filtering and sharpening the focus on how religious groups (mis)use space in their attempts to compete and grow. Existing understandings of religious conversion often fail to take into consideration the fact that religious conversion occurs in and through space, with space often having a deterministic influence on conversion processes and outcomes. Conversely, conversion is not only a process that is performed within space, but is also a process of spatial change and transformation. It is to these spatial questions that we now turn.

The conversion of space entails a change in the meaning, use and sometimes form of space, from secular to religious (or vice versa), or religious to religious. The conversion of space can be temporary (i.e. a church service in a house that may last for one or more hours), semi-permanent (the weekly rental of a hotel function room for worship services) or permanent (a legal change of land use from secular to religious, or vice versa). Like the conversion of people, the conversion of space is a politicized act that symbolizes the strengthening of a religious group. Such strengthening can either be vis-à-vis other religious groups, or against secular agencies such as the state. The conversion of space can hold strategic value for minority religious groups looking to establish and grow their presence, with the ensuing spaces often being characterized by 'ambiguous meanings, flexible uses and an overarching commitment to [religious] growth' (Woods 2013a, 660). Given that the codification of physical space is often heavily invested with symbolism and meaning, the conversion of space provides a tangible and visible reminder of religious power and control (see Chivallon 2001).

The conversion of space can occur at various scales. At the macro-scale is the carving up and (re)mapping of territory into new political jurisdictions. One of the most contested examples of the delineation of territory along religious lines is the conversion of Palestine into the Jewish settlement of Israel in 1948. Since then, both sides have claimed and fought over their right to the land through processes such as the renaming of physical spaces and landmarks, and the mapping and counter-mapping of territory (see Azaryahu and Golan 2001; Gorlizki 2000). More recently, the rebel group Islamic State (IS) has captured large swathes of territory in Iraq and Syria, where it has imposed a self-styled caliphate. The name of the group has evolved repeatedly since its inception in 1999. Recently, it has been reported in the media as either Islamic State (IS), Islamic State of Iraq and Syria (ISIS), Islamic State of Iraq and the Levant (ISIL) or *Da'ish* – an acronym of the group's Arabic name. The caliphate has overruled the political authority of the governments of Iraq and Syria, instead imparting and enforcing its own extremist Islamic worldview and judicial code on the people and territory under its control (*The Independent*, 15 March 2015). It has garnered widespread media attention and political condemnation for its brutal strategies of religious, ethnic and cultural cleansing. Given that the group's motto is *Baqiyah wa-Tatamaddad* ('Remaining and Expanding'), it is apparent that the seizing and conversion of territory is the primary way by which the group justifies its claims to – and assertions of – Islamic power (ABC News Australia, 3 July 2014; *New York Times*, 10 August 2014).

At the micro-scale is the conversion of buildings into spaces of new meaning or purpose. Woods (2013b), for example, explores how evangelical Christian groups operating in Sri Lanka convert the domestic space of a house into the sacred space of a church in order to avoid Buddhist surveillance and to introduce Christianity to communities in a non-threatening way (see Box 3.19). While such acts are highly informal and used to circumvent complex and bureaucratic (and often prejudiced) regulatory frameworks, in other contexts, converting a house (or other secular building) into a religious space is a more formal process that is a cheaper alternative to building a new place of religious worship. Since the 1970s, Britain's growing Muslim community has, for example, converted a range of nineteenth-century terraced houses, laundries, lorry and brush factories, schools, banks, photography studios, betting shops, caravans, taverns and, interestingly, churches, into mosques.

One prominent example highlighted by McLoughlin (2005; see also McLoughlin 1998) is that of the 'York Road' mosque in Bradford. In 1985 a group of three Muslim men wanted religious instruction to be made available to Muslim children within close proximity of their homes. They obtained support from a local Anglican vicar, who volunteered his under-used church hall to be used for teaching. In 1989, the hall was sold to the Muslim group and formally converted into a mosque with plans to develop it over time into a multi-functional centre that could serve the diverse needs of the local Muslim community. While the origins of the mosque are clearly a result of inter-religious co-operation, it has since evolved into a space wherein 'one of its main functions would seem to be to maintain ethnic and other boundaries' (McLoughlin 2005, 1061). It can, in other words, be seen as a space of dissimilation that provides cultural resonance with the homeland at the expense of integration with the hostland. Such spaces fuel debate in the UK (and elsewhere) about the 'Islamisation of public space', which often reflect 'majority fears about the erosion of a "British way of life" in an age of global migration and ethnic pluralism' (McLoughlin 2005, 1046). In parts of the United Kingdom with sufficiently large diasporic communities from South Asia, there has been much criticism and concern about public expressions of Muslim identity. Consequently, there have been attempts to restrict the number and size of mosques being built (or established) – a bid to reduce the symbolic encroachment of Islam into British public space.

The conversion of space is closely monitored and often highly regulated. In land scarce Singapore, for example, religious – usually Christian – groups commonly use secular spaces (e.g. hotel and other function rooms, houses, schools, auditoria) to conduct religious activities on a temporary or semi-permanent (or even permanent but unofficial) basis. In 2010, however, new guidelines were introduced to limit the use of secular spaces, and the frequency at which they are converted into sites of religious activity, in order to protect their secularity (Woods 2012a). Specifically, the guidelines are designed to ensure that buildings are used non-exclusively for religious purposes: that only part of a building is used for religious activity, that religious activities are only conducted on designated days of the week, that there is no permanent religious signage outside and no religious ornamentation inside the building, and that the conducting of religious activities causes minimal disturbance to the public (in the form of traffic, noise or parking). The justification for such measures is to ensure that the primary function and character of each building – whether commercial, industrial or public – is preserved. More directly, majority groups can also assert power through the conversion of minority religious spaces back into secular space or, in some instance, majority religious space. In the Indian state of Gujarat, for example, Jenkins (2007) shows how evangelical churches have been overcome by nationalist groups and converted into Hindu places of worship. The conversion of space is clearly a geopolitical process, one that can reflect, challenge and enforce prevailing systems of power and control.

The case study presented earlier in Box 2.2 is a clear example of a majority religious group converting the spaces of minority groups in order to assert control or dominance over territory. The conflict over the Babri Masjid originated from the belief that the Muslim Emperor Babar had destroyed a Hindu temple that marked the birthplace of Rama in order to build a mosque at the same location. Throughout the era of the Mughal Empire (1526–1857), rulers frequently constructed mosques in place of Hindu shrines, often going so far as to incorporate building materials from the destroyed shrines in order to construct the mosques (Pannikar 1991). Consequently, Hindu nationalists have more recently started to claim the right to conduct Hindu rituals within at least four mosques (the Krishna Janmasthan in Mathura, the Kashi Vishwanath temple/Gyanvapi mosque in Varanasi, Quwwat-ul-Islam mosque in New Delhi and the Babri Masjid in Ayodhya), their rationale being that they lie on top of desecrated Hindu temples. The Quwwat-u-Islam mosque in New Delhi, for example, is believed to be built using the ruins of twenty-seven Jain and Hindu temples (*Hindustan Times*, 14 December 2000; see also Hassner 2003). These examples show how religious conquest can be accompanied by the appropriation of the sacred sites of the vanquished, a process that causes sacred spaces to become layered, stratified, claimed and contested.

Armed occupation by state agencies of religious spaces

Competition between religious groups and the state for autonomy over religious spaces is often at its most intense following the armed occupation of a religious space, however temporary, by state agencies such as the military and the police. Realizing this, states in general have only engaged in this form of interference as a last resort, when state sovereignty or its ability to maintain public order is critically challenged. Affected religious groups see such armed intrusions as acts of desecration and, where they have the capacity to protest, the ensuing protests often have a violent character.

Box 2.19: Armed occupation of religious spaces in India, Pakistan and Thailand

In 1984, Indian army personnel entered the Golden Temple, located in Amritsar, Punjab, and considered to be the holiest of Sikh shrines, in an effort (codenamed Operation Bluestar) to flush out members of the Khalistan separatist movement who had taken refuge in the shrine. The holy place was thus turned into a battle ground and provoked deep resentment among the Sikh community (*New York*

Times, 3 September 1984). In protest, a Sikh bodyguard assassinated the Indian Prime Minister, Indira Gandhi, who ordered the attack (BBC News, 31 October 1984). The assassination, in turn, mobilized deep public resentment against the Sikh community, who were systematically targeted by Hindu mobs in widespread communal riots throughout the country (BBC News, 1 November 1984).

Similarly, a Pakistan army operation to remove suspected militants from the Lal Masjid (Red Mosque) in Islamabad (codenamed Operation Sunrise) in 2007 provoked widespread uproar among the Muslim religious leadership, which resulted in intense anti-state propaganda that sought to portray the state as un-Islamic (MSNBC, 7 December 2007). The Pakistan example shows how, even in religious space, the religious majority can come into open conflict with the state over the question of autonomy of religious spaces.

In southern Thailand, growing separatist activity has led to a militarization of Buddhist religious spaces like monasteries. Such militarization has been defended on the grounds of a need to protect Buddhist religious spaces, its leaders and its relics from Islamic separatist violence (Jerryson 2010). However paternalistic the state's intentions might be, the occupation of Buddhist religious spaces by armed agencies of the state has provoked resentment among Buddhist religious leadership. The concerns about desecration of religious space have been exacerbated by scepticism about the state's intentions (many religious leaders argue that military encampment of Buddhist religious places is motivated by the fact that these spaces are strategically located and provide the armed forces with an advantage over separatist soldiers), and the conduct of the armed personnel within the premises of the monasteries (many instances of soldiers and policemen drinking alcohol and engaging in rowdy behaviour in monasteries such as Wat Nirotsangkaham and Wat Chang Hai in Pattani, Thailand (Jerryson 2010, 196). Concerns about soldiers' behaviour are compounded by the fact that barracks within the monasteries are located next to the quarters of novices.

Religious spaces and scale

Scale is an important consideration when exploring any spatial activity, as a change in scale necessitates a reframing of spatial dynamics and understanding. Importantly, the genesis and effect of religious conflict can occur at multiple scales. This has mainly been implicit in all our preceding discussions and occasionally explicit. In this section, we turn dedicated attention to religious spaces and the range and types of competition and conflicts at various scales.

One noticeable characteristic of religiously motivated conflict and violence is the speed at which it can escalate from a relatively small-scale (and spatially contained) infraction to widespread (and spatially dispersed) devastation and loss of life. In 1964, for example, the theft of a relic from the Hazratbal mosque in Srinagar, Kashmir, led to Hindu–Muslim riots and, within six days, to 160 deaths, 600 injuries and the exodus of 700,000 refugees into India. It has also been identified as a causal factor in the outbreak of the Indo-Pakistani war (see Ganguly 2001). In a similar manner, in 1998 the destruction of the holy Temple of the Tooth shrine by Tamil separatists sparked outrage among Sri Lanka's Buddhist community, leading to violent military reprisals against Sri Lanka's Hindu population and the termination of negotiations to end fifteen years of civil war (*Financial Times*, 3 February 1998). As these two examples indicate, the disproportionate responses to the initial actions reveal the symbolic potency of religiously claimed and owned spaces, and highlight the need for appreciation of how they are used, negotiated and contested by different religious and secular agencies at various scales of analysis and understanding.

Religious groups must constantly negotiate various scales of understanding, of operation and of action. Communalist religions such as Christianity and Islam, for example, ideologically integrate their adherents into a global community of like-minded churches and believers, while operating on a day-to-day level within a given area or locality. Oftentimes, negotiating 'the dialectical relationship between macroscale ideology and microscale praxis' (Woods 2013b, 1072) can be a source of tension and conflict for both the individual and religious group. As Hassner (2003, 24) argues: 'because disputes about sacred space involve religious ideals, divine presence, absolute and transcendent values, there is no room for compromise and no substitute for the disputed space'. As such, when macroscale religious ideals or ideology start to play a determinative role in the opinions and choices of religious actors, claims to space become exclusive, and conflict inevitable.

In recent decades, one of the biggest changes to an understanding of religion and scale has been the impact of globalization. Global processes have, to a large extent, deterritorialized religious understanding and praxis, and have caused religious issues to become a matter of concern for territorially detached communities of religious adherents. Migrants, for example, must often simultaneously negotiate multiple religious attachments at various scales of analysis – from the local place of worship, to the diasporic community to which they belong, to the global community of believers with which they share a common identity. In particular, the globalization of Pentecostal churches such as the Assemblies of God has provided numerous opportunities for spaces of attachment that exist at multiple scales, with many adherents worshipping locally but thinking globally and often supporting cross-border church planting efforts. In light of this, it is clear that the 'globalization of religion produces a climate that encourages transnational religious connections and creates elements needed for their enactment' (Levitt 2001a, 19).

Transnational religious actors and communities intersect with religious spaces in various ways and at various scales of interpretation. Vasquez (2008, 157), for example, has documented how the rapid and large-scale influx of migrants from Latin America, Asia and Africa to the United States has resulted in changes to the American religious landscape. Such changes are often transnational in character, given that 'global processes tend to be de-linked from specific national territories while transnational processes are anchored in and transcend one or more nation-states' (Levitt 2001b, 202). Beyond the country-level, however, he also draws attention to the fact that the new religious practices associated with such migrants are often more performative in nature. They tend to 'involve the body and operate by primarily carving out new sacred spaces through ritual action and the transposition of spatio-temporal tropes in the diasporic imagination' (see also Orsi 1999). In this example, four scales of analysis are evident: the international movement of people, the national-level religious context within which they become embedded, the diasporic community of which they are constitutive and their own bodies that are integral to their religious practices. At each scale, there arises possibilities for competition and conflict. This means that whenever a space of religion is examined, it should be recognized as being part of a multi-layered system that can be re-interpreted at a more macro- or micro-scale of analysis. Some of the most common scales of understanding religious space are covered in more detail below – from the religious mapping of the world, to the religious body and embodied religion.

The religious mapping of the world

Religious groups are distributed unevenly across the world, with each occupying spaces of relative dominance and subordination. Academic theories of religious growth and decline (which draw attention to the competitive (dis)advantages of religious groups) are similarly uneven in their explanatory potential. For example, the secularization theory applies largely to Western Europe and North America (Bruce 2002; see also Dobbelaere 1981), as do theories of religious economy (Woods 2012b) and postsecularism, but have doubtful value elsewhere.

Sensitivity to the religious mapping of the world not only helps to reveal the shortcomings of such universalist approaches to theory, but also the systems of religious power and control that exist within different geographical contexts.

There are two ways to approach the religious mapping of the world. The first is to examine how religions are mapped across space. This involves an 'outside-in' examination of the distribution of religious groups around the world (and, on a more micro-scale, within regions, countries, cities or towns – see Stump 2008), and to explore where each is in a position of relative strength or weakness and the effect of such positioning on religious praxis. The second is to examine how religious groups map space. This involves an 'inside-out' exploration of how religious groups view the spaces they occupy (or want to occupy), and how such views may come into competition and conflict with the views of other religious groups, or of secular agencies such as the state. The religious mapping of space is often conflict-ridden, given that 'religious belief and doctrine provide potent justification for claims to territory' (Woods 2012a, 447). An exposition of such claims can 'shed visible light on the strains and stresses in community self-identification' (Viswanathan 1998, 90), and can lead to various types of identity politics. Each approach is explored in more detail below.

The first approach focuses attention on the fact that the mapping of religions across space is not equal. World religions such as Christianity, Islam, Hinduism and Buddhism occupy much larger – and more geographically entrenched – territories than smaller-scale sects and cults. Christianity, for example, is typically associated with (and yields greatest influence in) Europe, the Americas and the Levant, whereas Islam is commonly equated with the Arabian Peninsula and parts of south and southeast Asia. Not only do the encampments of religious groups vary across space, but the relative growth (and decline) of each is context-dependent as well. For example, since the 1980s Pentecostalism has grown 700 per cent, to approximately 500 million adherents worldwide (Anderson et al. 2010). Such an explosive rate of growth has been labelled as one of the greatest 'success' stories in the current era of cultural globalization (Robbins 2004), and has re-shaped the religious landscapes of much of Africa, Latin America, and some parts of Asia (see Martin 1990). Growth has, however, been much more muted in Northern Africa, the Middle East and much of Asia (Woods 2013a). Clearly, some spaces are more or less resistant to evangelical activity than others. This underscores the importance of understanding spatial patterns of growth, and why some spaces are more amenable to the presence and growth of new and/or different religious groups than others. In order to illustrate the spatial variance in religious supply and demand on a global scale, Box 2.20 below examines Christian evangelism in the '10/40 Window'.

Box 2.20: Spiritual warfare and Christian
evangelism in the '10/40 Window'

A much-publicized focus of global evangelism has been the '10/40 Window' –
a belt of territory that spans 10 to 40 degrees north, and includes Northern
Africa, the Middle East and much of Asia. The territories that comprise the
10/40 Window have provided a focus for evangelical Christian (especially
Pentecostal) expansionism. Given the large and dominant encampments of
Islamic, Hindu and Buddhist religious groups in many of the countries found
within these territories, evangelical Christian groups have, however, found
it 'difficult to secure a base and avoid moves to contain and isolate [them]'
(Martin 2005, 28). Despite this, evangelical groups view such territories as
being in need of salvation, and have become some of the most fertile sites of
evangelical activity in the world (see Gerhardt 2008). Evangelical expansion
into the 10/40 Window is often articulated in terms of 'spiritual warfare', and
the associated desire to create a Christian space in non-Christian contexts. The
effect of creating such a space is that Christian groups are able to convert and
'release' their adherents from the religio-cultural traditions into which they
were born. Established religious groups often find such practices antagonistic,
and a driver of conflict.

The second approach is concerned with spatial identity and outlook. Given
its claims to ultimate authority and universal and timeless 'truths', religion
provides 'a powerful framework for imagining community and a set of schemas,
templates and metaphors for making sense of the social world' (Brubaker 2012,
4; see also Chen 2002). It can shape and determine outlooks or worldviews, as
can be seen in the various Islamist movements that draw upon a pre-political
entity centred on the *umma* (the global community of Muslims) to justify claims
to an autonomous state or caliphate (Friedland 2002). Another example is the
role of the Pope for Catholics – a 'high priest of a new universal civil religion
of humanity and the first citizen of a global civil society' (Casanova 1994, 130).
Being Catholic, recognizing the global sovereignty of the Pope, and being part
of 'a new universal civil religion' can be both empowering and emancipatory; it
can elevate the individual above and beyond local or national concerns, and can
shape their worldview accordingly. Religious belief can influence and determine
perceptions of the world, with such perceptions often challenging or replacing
those articulated by non-religious agencies.

For example, many evangelical Christian groups express the geopolitical ambition of the Great Commission to 'make disciples of all nations'. The Great Commission is the instruction of the resurrected Jesus Christ to his disciples. They are a key justification for mission work and evangelism. In doing so, they practice what Bryant and Lamb (1999, 8) term the 'ideology of mission' whereby religious domination (expressed in terms of 'salvation') is the ultimate goal. Ideologically, they transcend the boundaries imposed by the state and enforced by indigenous religious groups by actively seeking to baptize people into a trans-ethnic, trans-territorial faith community that has historically been associated with Western imperialism (Nederveen Pieterse 1992; Wallace 2006). Constructing a higher level of authorization validates Christian claims to local religious markets, and challenges the (often state-imposed) regulatory controls that seek to contain their growth. Such assertions parallel those of Islamic social and political movements in Turkey, for example, which do not 'oppose the actions of any particular state or the structure of the global state system' but instead 'subordinate both to a functional role within a transcendental order defined by a religious faith' (West 2006, 280). Referred to as 'dissident geopolitics', the actions of globalist (and proselytizing) religions such as Christianity and Islam are driven by transcendental motives that, where necessary, show invariance towards the regulatory power of the state, and its territorial sovereignty. Such invariance is often a source of inter-group conflict, both religious and secular.

The nation, the state and religious identity

Tension often exists at the intersection of religious belief and identity, and national or territorial belonging. On the one hand, religious belief and identity can be seen to undermine national belonging. In Haiti, for example, McAlister (2005, 253) found the Christian identity to weaken territorial and national attachment, with Jerusalem 'displac[ing] the image of Haiti as nostalgic homeland'. In some instances, such 'displacement' is less symbolic in nature and has more obviously political undertones. For example, Christian children in northern Thailand worship God during Buddhist rites at school; a practice that is believed to be 'an act of defiance to the authority of the state', which in turn causes Christians to 'set themselves apart from the dominant religion of the society and also place themselves in an ambiguous, at best, relationship to a state that rules in the name of the Buddhist nation' (Keyes 1993, 262). While such 'defiance' is, in this instance, based on the actions of a minority religious group, in other instances, it can reveal the insecurities of a dominant religion. In Malaysia, Muslim agitators view Christianity as a proxy for foreign exploitation that is responsible for the prevalence of poverty and inequality among the indigenous Malay population (Jenkins 2007). The common thread that ties all of these examples together is that adopting a minority religious belief can set an individual apart from the dominant beliefs of society. Doing so can provoke dominant secular and religious agencies, and can provide a major barrier to religious assimilation.

In many cases, the minority religious groups against whom religious nationalists assert their authority are associated with diasporic communities (both emergent and entrenched). As Vertovec (2000, 5) argues, in many respects, the diaspora is inherently antagonistic, given its genesis as 'part of the postmodern project of resisting the nation-state, which is perceived as hegemonic, discriminatory, and culturally homogenizing. The alternative agenda – now associated with the notion of diaspora – advocates the recognition of hybridity, multiple identities, and affiliations with people, causes, and traditions outside the nation-state of residence'. Thus while religious nationalisms are boundary-enforcing and exclusory, the diaspora is often boundary transcending and inclusivist. The presence, actions and attitudes of diasporic communities poses a challenge to the exclusivity and authority claimed by religious nationalists, as they often 'reject the identity categories and social structures that nation states impose on them, opting instead to express identities based on a blurring of origin and destination and associated with loose, multiple connections to various groups, settings and practices' (Levitt 2001a, 4). More specifically, migrants are typically reliant upon 'symbols and ideas to imagine and locate themselves within a religious landscape that may be superimposed on, run parallel to, or obviate the need for one defined by national boundaries' (Levitt 2001a, 19). It is for these reasons that diasporic spaces are closely associated with the conquest or manipulation of host-country public space (e.g. Paerregaard 2001), and have become spaces of provocation and conflict vis-à-vis the nation-state.

On the other hand, religious belief and identity can complement national belonging and ideology. In many instances, religious and national belonging are aligned, but conflict with competing systems of belief and understanding. Vasquez (2008), for example, draws attention to the parallel worldviews of neo-Pentecostal groups and (hegemonic) US foreign policy. Both map the world in terms of a cosmic struggle between good and evil, between Jesus and the devil. In a similar vein, the prosperity gospel that is espoused by many neo-Pentecostal groups is also closely associated with the 'American Dream' and capitalist worldview. While creating domestic alignment, such worldviews can also be seen as hegemonic and overbearing, especially when applied to a non-American/ Christian setting. Accordingly, such worldviews support the 'neo-colonising' claims made against Christian missionaries, especially when operating in non-Christian, postcolonial contexts. Chapter 3 deals with the gap-filling activities of religious groups and expounds these ideas in more detail.

Religious buildings

Religious buildings – the church, temple, synagogue, *gurdwara*, *khovil* or mosque, for example – are the clearest identifiers of religious presence in space, and are religious spaces themselves. Often they are the focal point of analysis when 'religious space' is being considered, as is apparent from much of the foregoing discussion in this chapter. They are central gathering nodes for religious adherents, and provide venues not only for religious worship and instruction, but for social activities and community-building as well. In this capacity, they foster and enable group solidarity. On the other hand, they can also become divisive spaces that are used to sharpen religious identities and thought, and to create a distinction between self and other. They can alter the dynamics of, and create divisions within, communities (e.g. Connell 2005; Naylor and Ryan 2002), and are more often than not subjected to government proscriptions on their form and function (e.g. Kong 1993b). In extreme cases, religious buildings are eschewed in favour of outwardly secular spaces (e.g. the house) for religious worship, as religious buildings present a target that can be attacked. Such conflict is discussed in more detail in Box 3.20.

While buildings reflect presence, identity and (implied) acceptance, it is for these reasons that they can also be socially divisive. In many cases, planning guidelines (and decisions) for religious buildings often discriminate against particular religious groups. Greed (2011, 112), for example, shows how 'planning officers tend to treat applications by both Christian and Muslim faith groups with suspicion, as likely to be linked to "fundamentalism" and therefore to be dismissed as socially divisive'. Contrariwise, Greed argues that the spaces occupied by such faith groups tend to be socially and economically inclusive, and play an important contributory role to urban regeneration. More specifically, as Box 2.21 shows, religious buildings play not only an integral role in the (re) construction of diasporic immigrant communities, but also fuel intra-religious competition at the micro-scale over claims to space.

Box 2.21: The mosque and the (re)construction of the South Asian diaspora in the UK

The mosque is one of the most visible markers of South Asian (Indian, Pakistani and Bangladeshi) Muslim identity in the UK. In line with large-scale immigration from South Asia to the UK since the 1970s, the number of mosques needed to serve the Muslim community has mushroomed from 13 in 1963 to an estimated 1,000 in 2005 (Nielsen 1992). Of these, at least 44 can be found in Bradford, which is home to approximately 75,000 Muslims living within a small area close to the city centre. The construction of mosques reflects the belief and concern that 'if British-born and British-educated youngsters [of South Asian heritage] were going to be socialised in a context where the dominant culture was broadly secularising, and often hostile to minorities, Muslims would have to create spaces for the institutionalisation of Islam within the British nation' (McLoughlin 2005, 1046; see also McLoughlin 1998). In other words, the mosque was and is believed to be an important space wherein South Asian (religious) identities could be nurtured and strengthened. Mosques have also proven to play a central role in the social and political organization (both locally and transnationally) of the Muslim community.

Over the years, mosques have adopted numerous roles that go beyond being sites of religious instruction and praxis. These include the provision of sociocultural continuity for Muslims experiencing the dislocating effects of migration, racism or unemployment, advice centres, homework clubs, youth centres, elderly day-care centres and so on, and even Members of Parliament's surgeries (see Kalra 2000; McLoughlin 2005; Werbner 1996). Indeed, such spaces are of especial importance given the marginal position (religiously, but also socially, economically, culturally and often politically as well) of South Asian Muslims in the UK. The dense ethnic clustering in Bradford, for example, has contributed to the development of 'secure, institutionally complete and politically assertive [Muslim] communities' (McLoughlin 2005, 1046). Yet while there is a notable absence of mosques conflicting with the state, the development of mosque space has clear political undertones. As McLoughlin (2005, 1046, 1060) demonstrates, 'at the grassroots, the dominant mode of Pakistani-Muslim adaptation remains the deployment of culture and religion as bonding resources to maintain ethnic distinctiveness and so advance subaltern group interests'. More to the point is recognition of the fact that mosques are spaces wherein Muslims (especially new migrants from South India) can navigate the experiences of social exclusion that are an inherent part of diasporic life. The mosque is, in other words, believed to provide an exclusively Islamic space (or an Islamic 'haven') within the broadly secular environment of the UK.

Despite playing such an important unifying role for South Asian Muslim communities, mosques are also spaces of intra-religious competition. In Oxford in the early 1980s, for example, a dispute within the 1,000 strong Sunni Muslim community led to the splitting and reformation of the community along sectarian lines (Deobandi versus Barelwi), and the eventual founding of a second mosque (Shaw 1988). A similar example is provided by Lewis (1994), who documents how the opening of Bradford's first mosque in a terraced house in 1959 initially led to the Pakistani community to come together. Over time, however, ethno-religious rivalry and politics led to the splitting and expansion of the community (and mosques) along sectarian lines, showing how ethnic fusion eventually gave way to ethnic fission and the fragmentation of religious space. This underscores the fact that spaces of associational empowerment such as the mosque can also be sites of ideological, factional and sectarian struggle (see Werbner 1991).

The religious body and embodied religion

The most intimate scale of religious performance and analysis is the body itself. The body plays a vital role in the production of religious space, as it both occupies space and constitutes a space in itself. Bodies play an important role in religious praxis. They engender a sense of community and communality, and can bring meaning to the processes of religious worship. The religious body is, in other words, 'a site of signification in and of itself'; it plays a central role in the 'affective making of sacred space' (Holloway 2003, 1962), and provides an important focus for the study of everyday (or 'emplaced') religion (see Knott 2005b). More importantly, however, is the fact that because 'individuals are the vehicles of power' (Foucault 1980, 98) – and its points of application as well (Springer 2011) – the body plays an integral role in the competitive actions and violent outcomes of religious groups. Religious bodies are spaces to be constructed and controlled, just as much as religious buildings, countries and shrines are.

There are two ways of analysing and understanding the religious space of the body: the religious body and embodied religion. On the one hand, the *religious body* refers to the body of a religious person that is both an identifiable space in itself (e.g. through dress, custom or physical modification such as circumcision) and a body in space. On the other hand, *embodied religion* is both the internalization and externalization of religious practice (e.g. ritual, worship, penance) that gives meaning to religious experience. Each has a role to play in religious competition and conflict, and each is examined in more detail below.

On the one hand, the religious body (the body of a religious individual) is a space of religion. It is, accordingly, liable to regulation and control (and the politics therein) by religious agencies, given that religion often provides a 'totalising order capable of regulating every aspect of life' (Friedland 2002, 390). It is in the best interests of religious groups to (attempt to) control the bodies and reproductive capacities of its members if they are to retain (and grow) their authority and influence over time. For example, the religious segmentation of society has historically been reproduced by clerical (and, more indirectly, cultural) control over marriage and, by extension, injunctions against religious intermarriage. Over time, such control has contributed to the reproduction and growth (or demise) of religious communities, to the prevention of their dilution and, more pointedly, to the prevention of their dissolution by assimilation (Smith 1986; see also Brubaker 2012).

Religious bodies can also be conflictual and marginalized bodies. Young Asians living in the UK have, for example, been recognized as suffering from a 'culture clash' (Brah 1996) caused by the stresses and identity conflicts associated with the negotiation and management of a number of identities (e.g. Muslim, Asian, female) that may contradict, confront and compete with one another (see Knott and Khokher 1993; Anwar 1998). That such identities are often perceived to exist in binary opposition to each other (e.g. continuity versus change, alienation versus assimilation, tradition versus modernity, parental culture versus society-at-large) reveals how the otherness of some (minority) religious bodies presents a source of conflict that must constantly be negotiated. Moreover, immutable markers of identity such as race, ethnicity, gender and caste can reveal – or conflict with – religious affiliations as much as symbolic markers – such as the wearing of a crucifix, a *burqa* or *hijab*, a *bindi* or *tilaka* or prayer beads.

Religious dress can be a sign of authority, group identification and solidarity. Female conversion to Islam – and the associated proscriptions of dress and custom – can, for example, result in restricted mobility. This can be a source of significant tension, especially in Western contexts where 'at the end of the day, it might not be a "minor thing" to hand over to your husband the right to decide where you are and are not allowed to go' (Sultan 1999, 330–1; see also Wohlrab-Sahr 1999). In this case, the religious body is one that is restricted in its movement within and engagement with different (often public) spaces. How the religious body is managed and controlled within the public space of the school in Britain and France is explored in detail in Chapter 3 (Boxes 3.3 and 3.4). Such restrictions are also evident in some contexts that are hostile to minority religious groups. In Sri Lanka, for example, evangelical Christian pastors eschew traditional trappings of religious identity that distinguish them as religious leaders. Doing so enables them to avoid surveillance from anti-Christian factions, and to be more effective in engaging local communities (Woods 2012b).

On the other hand, embodied religion refers to the affective role of the body in creating religious experiences. This includes practices such as inspirited worship (e.g. speaking in tongues or 'glossolalia'), congregational dynamics (e.g. collective effervescence) or transcendental rituals (e.g. spiritual healing, exorcism). The embodiment of religious belief provides an important focus of analysis, as 'many features of religious life are implicit. It is hard to hold them constant or to determine their boundaries. They are deeply felt but often difficult to express' (Levitt 2001a, 4). While degrees of embodiment vary between and within religions – Scheifinger (2010, 196), for example, argues that Hinduism is 'fully embodied', whereas Doniger (1997, 183) makes the point that bodily detachment is 'the goal of most Hindu philosophical systems' – all religions provide some sort of internal resonance with their adherents.

Such resonance is not necessarily transcendental. The body can not only certainly give rise to implicit experiences or understandings of religion, but it can also be an object of religious discipline and even contempt. For centuries, Catholics have used flagellation as a form of penance, while regular periods of fasting among Christians and Muslims is a form of atonement designed to reconcile the adherent with their belief in God or Allah. On a more day-to-day basis, religious proscriptions on diet – for example, pork for Jews and Muslims, beef for Hindus, root vegetables for Jains – and alcohol is seen as a means of purifying the body while enacting belief. For some belief systems, the undesirability of the body provides a constant reminder of its impermanence, and the need to strive for more cognitive forms of enlightenment. In the Hindu sacred text the *Manusamhita*, it is, for example, stated that:

> [A man] should abandon this foul-smelling, tormented, impermanent dwelling place of living beings, filled with urine and excrement, pervaded by old age and sorrow, infested by illness, and polluted by passion, with bones for beams, sinews for cords, flesh and blood for plaster, and skin for the roof. (cited in Doniger 1997, 169)

Such a directive can be a source of inner torment for adherents, providing an ideal that necessitates an ongoing struggle with more profane bodily needs and desires. Taken to the extreme, the embodiment of religion can cause tension and antagonism within and between religious groups and secular agencies. Notable examples include public debates surrounding the circumcision of children and women, and religious opposition to contraceptives and abortion (Chapter 3; see Box 3.14).

The (ir)resolution of conflict over religious spaces

Having explored in some detail the causes and types of competition and conflict over religious space, this chapter ends by addressing the problem of conflict resolution. If we subscribe to Hassner's (2003, 4) view that sacred space is *inherently* problematic, the question of how conflicts over sacred space can be mediated and resolved appears to be insurmountable. Nonetheless, at the ideological level, two policy responses inform the management of space-related religious disputes. The first is the Hobbesian view that 'rejects the symbolic [i.e. religious] dimension of these disputes and treats them as standard territorial disputes'. The second is the Huntingtonian view that 'construes the intractability of these disputes as the products of religious forces beyond the influence of political actors'. A third is Hassner's own approach, which considers 'ways to problematize the social production and deconstruction of the sacred in pursuit of a solution for these disputes'. Doing so involves the co-option of religious leaders into the negotiation process, encouraging them to use their religious authority to help redefine the parameters and nature of religious spaces from a top-down perspective.

The Hobbesian approach rejects the symbolic dimension of conflicts over sacred space, treating them instead as standard territorial disputes. Such an approach is pragmatic insofar as it rejects the distinction between religious and political interests. Religious intentions are relegated to being nothing more than 'symbolic pretenses' that must be overlooked in order to 'expose underlying material interests' (Hassner 2003, 27). Given this approach, approaches to resolving conflicts over sacred space draw upon the same set of tools as other territorial disputes, namely, negotiation or arbitration which can result in the exchange or partition of territory, compensation or compromise. In other words, resolution has little to do with recognizing and reconciling the intrinsic spiritual qualities of (or attributed to) space, but the negotiation of its economic and political value instead.

On the other hand, the Huntingtonian approach accepts that conflicts over sacred space are essentially intractable as they are the outcome of religious forces that go beyond the control or influence of political actors. Reflecting the theory that religious identity is inextricably associated with conflict, the Huntingtonian approach accepts religion as an inherently disruptive force that manipulates and distorts the conduct of politics (Huntington 1996). Clearly the Hobbesian approach provides a more proactive and rational approach to conflict resolution, whereas the Huntingtonian approach is axiomatic insofar as it accepts that religion provides a dead-end when it comes to the negotiation and resolution of territorial and spatial disputes. In spite of this, the efficacy of the Hobbesian approach is far from guaranteed (see Box 2.22). Following that, Box 2.23 explores how state-religion competition (and conflict) over religious space has been mitigated against in Singapore.

Box 2.22: The failure of the Hobbesian approach in resolving the Temple Mount/Haram el-Sharif dispute in Jerusalem

The Camp David negotiations over Jerusalem in 2000 were symptomatic of the Hobbesian approach. While negotiators were able to find enough common ground to resolve a number of security issues, issues concerning Palestinian refugees, the Israeli withdrawal from Palestinian areas and even the division of the modern city of Jerusalem, the sovereignty of the sacred site at the heart of the old city proved to be an irresolvable stumbling block. President of the Palestinian Authority, Yasser Arafat, encouraged his negotiators to demonstrate flexibility when dealing with the Israelis, 'but do not budge on this one thing: the Haram [el-Sharif] is more precious to me than everything else' (cited in Hassner 2003, 27). In a similar fashion, Israeli Prime Minister Ehud Barak confessed to his delegates that the Temple Mount 'is the Archimedean point of our [Jewish] existence, the anchor point of the Zionist struggle . . . we are at the moment of truth' (cited in Hassner 2003, 27); while latterly explaining to US President George W. Bush that 'the Temple Mount is the cradle of Jewish history and there is no way I will sign a document that transfers sovereignty over the Temple Mount to the Palestinians. For Israel that would constitute a betrayal of its holy of holies' (cited in Hassner 2003, 29). Such quotes reflect the symbolic primacy of religious space, and its non-negotiable value to those who attribute it with sacredness.

Box 2.23: Mitigating against state-religion competition and conflict over religious space in Singapore

At first glance, Singapore, with its combination of a highly bureaucratized state (in both ideology and method) and a generally highly religious population, would appear to be a prime site for religion-state conflict over religious autonomy in religious spaces. State-religion competition in Singapore has primarily arisen as a result of regulations based on paternalistic considerations and a privileging of material-secular goals over spiritual ones. However, while competition over such autonomy has routinely taken place, it has rarely escalated into conflict. The pre-emption of conflict has been made possible by unique features in the relationship dynamic between state and religious groups.

As noted in the case study about religious relocation (Box 2.9), the Singapore state has often been able to co-opt religious leadership into acknowledging, endorsing and popularizing the primacy, or at least the need for, material progress. Second, ordinary people in Singapore have proved to be resourceful in devising alternative ways of maintaining a religious practice in particular (and maintaining religious meaning in general) in the face of restrictions on existing religious practices. This adaptability has been discussed with respect to religious relocation. Third, the containment of conflict has hinged on a universal acknowledgement that the government's regulations of religious practices (and hence, its curtailment of the autonomy of religious groups) has not systematically targeted a particular religious group to privilege another.

In addition to the state-religion competition over religious relocation, similar competition over autonomy has also arisen with respect to the government's ban on use of loudspeakers in mosques, and interference in religious education in *madrasah*s. The restrictions on loudspeakers in mosques, on having to face inward, rather than outward has been said to generate unhappiness among the Muslim community, which view the restriction as a proscription on Muslims' religious freedom (Kong 2006). However, the state has been effective in containing this resentment by citing the secular motivations (e.g. to curb noise pollution) of the restriction and demonstrating the non-discriminatory aspect of it: the state has argued that 'all communities were affected by the noise regulations, including Chinese operas, funeral processions, church bells, music during weddings, record shops, and places of entertainment. Even state-endorsed and state-encouraged nation-building activities were not spared, it declared, such as the recitation of pledges in schools' (Kong 2006, 911). Moreover, the aforementioned adaptability of religious groups in Singapore to circumnavigate restrictions and maintain proscribed religious practices has also been instrumental in managing discord. In this case, the Muslim community has migrated from issuing calls to prayer through loudspeakers to doing the same over Malay radio stations where non-believers are at liberty to avoid the station. In doing so, concerns about intruding into secular space have been avoided (Kong 2006).

State efforts to reform *madrasah* education has also been a source of tension between the state and the Muslim community. In 2002, in Singapore, there were six full-time *madrasah*s housed in premises distinct from mosques,

Religion and Space

and twenty-seven part-time mosques-based *madrasah*s. While the full-time *madrasah*s provide primary, secondary and pre-university education, the part-time *madrasah*s provide purely religious instruction to supplement the secular education program (Kong 2005a). In the late 1990s, the state embarked on a series of initiatives to reform the *madrasah* system in a way that secular education was not marginalized, even among full-time *madrasah* pupils, and to equip *madrasah* students with basic skills needed to participate in and profit from a knowledge-based economy. In addition to this paternalistic goal, the state's attempts to modernize *madrasah* education was also premised on the idea that attendance at national schools would foster a trans-religious national identity, which would accept and endorse modernization above all else. Given the sensitivity of proposed reforms and its implications about the autonomy of the Muslim community, the government was keen to adopt a consultative approach. Prior to legislation and implementation of reforms, the state engaged religious and community leaders in a series of dialogues to build a consensus over the need for reform in *madrasah* education (Kong 2005a). While this attempt at consensus building played a crucial role in pre-empting a fracture between the Muslim religious community and the state, the avoidance of conflict was also, in no small part, due to the Muslim community's ability to adapt in ways such that they would continue to maintain their autonomy. For example, prior to the reform initiatives, most *madrasah*s were dependent on endowments and state subsidies; after the prospect of reform was raised, many tended to modernize their facilities to avoid state scrutiny and embarked on private fund-raising campaigns to reduce their dependence on the state (Kong 2005a).

To understand competition and conflicts involving religious space, we need to consider whether such competition and conflict are to do with ownership of space or autonomy of activity (or both), whether they are inter- or intra-religious or between religious and secular forces, the scale at which they occur, whether they have escalated into violence or not, and whether and how they have been mitigated and resolved. In this chapter, we have sought to develop an understanding of the role of religious space in religious competition, conflict and violence by unpacking each of these dimensions. But, of course, competition and conflict does not just involve religious space, they erupt in secular spaces too. It is to such secular spaces that we now turn.

Religion in Secular Spaces

Introducing secular spaces

In contrast to religious spaces, secular spaces refer to areas where the primary purpose of social interaction is non-religious; the religious identity of an individual or group is not important in gaining access to such spaces; and the limits on personal and social conduct are established by secular/civic criminal laws and codes, rather than *divine* law. Secular law is justified by considerations of public order and the maintenance of essential social structures and institutions and not by a religious conception of morality. Such spaces have become a source of growing interest among scholars of religion in recent years. Building on the criticism that 'the secular' has been treated as a residual category of analysis and understanding (Wilford 2010), there has been a focus of attention on 'the spatialities of religion that lie beyond the church and the chapel' (Brace et al. 2006, 38; see also Kong 2010 on the 'unofficially sacred'), such as the home (Dwyer 2002; Kong 2002; Phillips 2009), the urban environment (Phillips et al. 2007), the labour market (Mohammad 2005) and the university campus (Hopkins 2011).

The secular environment plays an important role in shaping the spatial practices of religious groups and the religious identities of individuals. Strategies of competitive gain and religious growth increasingly reflect 'conscious decisions on the parts of local congregations to adapt to their secular environments' (Wilford 2010, 332) in order to make 'transcendent' (Taylor 2007, 423) systems of belief and understanding relevant and viable to contemporary audiences. The mapping of religious presence and meaning across secular space has led to situations that provide 'even greater opportunities for legitimising worship in what previous generations would consider distinctly *non-religious* places'

(Hopkins et al. 2011, 317, emphasis added). More specifically, Hopkins et al. (2011, 317) observe that:

> As processes of social differentiation and exclusion of religion from the public realm are being actively and covertly breached, scholars are increasingly accounting for the formation of new places that emerge out of the bringing together of sacred and profane.

As with religious spaces, there is a wide variation in the nature of secular spaces. For example, secular spaces may vary in terms of *ownership* (they can be privately or publicly owned), *purpose* (they can be concerned with providing education, entertainment or public services) and *control* (who is responsible for making and enforcing the rules of individual/social conduct in these spaces). Common examples of secular spaces include, private and government places of employment, state-run schools and public amenities (such as parks, markets, transportation networks, and hospitals). More specifically, in many Western contexts, the secular spaces of the skate park, pub, school and youth festival are as important (if not more so) than the church building when developing and enacting religious belief and identity, especially among younger generations of religious adherents (see Hopkins et al. 2011). Secular space has, in this sense, become an important (if not the most important) locus for the learning, exploration and transmission of religious ideas. Conversely, the encroachment of the religious into secular space has led to (and is a function of) many people enacting their faith in traditionally non-religious sites, such as the workplace, the classroom or the street (e.g. Leonard 2007, Olson et al. 2009). Such enactments are a source of tension in many societies, as they represent an assertion of religious agency where it may not necessarily be wanted.

Many secular spaces are often shared by secular and religious uses, that is, even religion can be an axis of social segmentation in an ostensibly secular environment. As Brubaker (2012, 4; after van den Berghe 1967) explains: 'Even when they are territorially intermixed, members of different religious, ethnic or national communities may participate in separate, parallel institutional worlds . . . [such as] school systems, universities, media, political parties, hospitals, nursing homes and institutionalised sporting, cultural and recreational activities.' What this means, ultimately, is that social segmentation along religious lines can still be generated and sustained in and through secular spaces. It is for this reason that such spaces are often liable to inter-religious and religious-secular contestation, regulation and control.

As is becoming apparent in our line of argument, with certain sorts of spaces it is not possible to classify them as either wholly secular or wholly religious. Wilford (2010, 329), for example, argues that 'the secularity of modern urban space' is, essentially, 'differentiated and fragmented space [that is] marked by specific limitations and affordances for religious activity'. Put differently, Wilford views secular spaces as those marked by a different – often more ambiguous – set of challenges and opportunities for religious praxis. Such spaces, which fall in the grey area between religious and secular spaces, are characterized as quasi-secular spaces in this book. Quasi-secular spaces are those that are affiliated to some religious group but perform primarily secular functions such as providing a secular education (e.g. mission schools), or providing medical services (e.g. hospitals and clinics owned by religious groups), or dispensing social support services (e.g. FBOs engaged in corrective social intervention or in the delivery of social services, including emergency aid). Generally, quasi-secular spaces are affiliated to religious groups and may or may not receive state funds to support their operations. Often, depending on whether quasi-secular groups receive financial/logistical support from the state, the jurisdiction over their activities is shared by the state and the religious group.

As noted with respect to religious spaces, religious competition in secular spaces can also be broadly broken down into competition between religious groups and competition between religious and secular (including the state) groups. Further, as with competition in religious spaces, both inter-religious and religious-secular competition in secular spaces can arise over competing ownership- or autonomy-related claims.

Ownership-related competition and conflict

This form of competition arises when religious groups demand new religious spaces (e.g. new places of worship). In doing so, religious groups enter into competition with the state, secular groups and, possibly other religious groups that might want the space for their own purposes. The demand for new places of worship is often made by religious groups which are new to a locality, to accommodate the religious needs of an increasing membership. In these cases, the resulting competition can be seen as another expression of the entrant-incumbent competition described in the previous chapter. In addition, the competition arising from the demand for new religious places can also be seen as a *variation* of the religion-secular competition over ownership of religious spaces, described in the previous chapter. There, competition and conflict resulted from the state's appropriation of *existing religious* spaces for secular purposes; the focus in this chapter is on the (converse) ownership claims of religious groups on existing secular spaces.

In many cases, religious groups wanting to own (previously) secular land for constructing a place of worship also face local opposition to the project. This local opposition could be based on concerns that building a place of worship will challenge the existing religious and cultural identity of the community; or the religious place – and the religious rituals performed there – will generate negative externalities such as noise pollution, traffic congestion and, in extreme cases, even disturb traditional family structures.

Two case studies illustrate how minority religions' attempts to acquire/own religious spaces have been contested by the state and/or society. This reluctance to allocate religious spaces can have potentially harmful social consequences, which include: giving rise to a society that might be permanently divided along communal lines; inhibiting the integration of new religious groups into society; and driving religious practices underground where they can no longer be monitored effectively.

Box 3.1: Resistance to new mosque developments in Australia and Western Europe

Dunn (2004) describes a classic instance of putative entrant-incumbent competition by throwing light on a spate of refusals by the local governments in Sydney, Australia, to applications for the development of Islamic religious institutions, including mosques, prayer centres and Islamic community halls in Sydney suburbs. These refusals have invariably been motivated by resident opposition to the idea of such (entrant) religious facilities in locations with a predominant (incumbent) Christian and Anglo-Celtic character. According to Dunn, 'resident objectors to mosques in Sydney have often claimed that "there are no local Muslims", that only outsiders will use the proposed mosque, or that the area is "Christian" and should not be allowed to become "Muslim"' (Dunn 2004, 333–4). While appellate courts have been prompt, in all such instances, to strike down the local government's refusal for mosque development, the fact remains that, at the grassroots, the entrant-incumbent competition generates significant acrimony. Accordingly, despite judicial victory, the right of the Muslims to own and develop religious space is open to violent challenges from Christian right wing and vigilante groups.

Voices against mosque building have also arisen in Italy, where, in 2008, a member party of the ruling coalition has been drafting a bill that would block the construction of new mosques in this heartland of Roman Catholicism. The bill proposes a ban on mosque building within half a mile of a church, oblige *imams* to speak Italian, link mosque size to the size of the congregation, forbid the call to prayer via loudspeakers and give the final decision of mosque development to residents via a referendum. The denial of ownership of religious space for entrant religions (Italy is home to over a million (minority immigrant) Muslims) is often based on the premises that mosque construction is 'an unfettered colonisation of Italian culture', and that, 'mosques discourage integration, and are places of cultural indoctrination linked to international terrorism' (*Daily Mail*, 16 September 2008).

The opposition of incumbent religious-political elites to entrant competition (or, entrant religion's religious spaces) resonates widely among the Catholic populace. However, conflict of this sort has the potential to alienate large sections of the significant resident Muslim population, who, deprived of a sense of belonging, can be vectors of self-perpetuating religious conflict that threatens to erupt into violence at the slightest provocation.

Similar opposition to new mosque building has also been witnessed in Switzerland, where the Swiss voted, in a referendum, to ban the construction of new minarets (US State Department 2010). In Germany too, a distinct rise in popular antipathy to new mosque building has been reported (US State Department 2010).

Box 3.2: Resistance to cults' ownership of religious spaces

For various reasons mentioned in the previous chapter, cults have found it harder to acquire and maintain religious spaces of their own. In addition to facing resistance from the state, cults have also experienced popular hostility from the local communities where they locate. The following examples show how mainstream (incumbent) religious groups can appropriate the general social misgiving against cults to make it harder for them to have continued or permanent access to their 'own' religious spaces. In Russia, for example, the Russian Orthodox Church (the dominant, incumbent religious group in Russia) has, through its patriarch Alexy II, argued for more stringent regulations in acquisition of religious places by 'deviant' religious groups – and, in general, for greater restrictions on religious freedoms – by arguing that they are needed for 'protecting the individual from destructive, pseudo religious, pseudo missionary activity that has brought obvious harm to the spiritual and physical health of people, and to the stability and civic peace in Russia' (Knox 2003, 87). In 1997, possibly on account of the pressure from the Orthodox Church,[1] some religious groups, including cults, were branded as non-traditional religious groups and were required to undergo annual registration, a highly cumbersome and restrictive process. This is made significantly harder for cults to acquire and maintain *permanent* religious spaces; in addition, responding to the spirit of the new law, landlords across Russia revoked rental/lease arrangements with groups such as Jehovah's Witnesses (Grim and Finke 2011).

Similarly, in Japan and Korea, countries noted for their high level of religious freedoms in the post-war period, cults have found it notoriously difficult to acquire and maintain religious spaces. Although there are no (or minimal) restrictions on the acquisition of property by any religious group, residents have generally opposed the location of cult-owned property (including places of worship/meeting) in their area. This opposition has largely been grounded on apprehensions, especially among older members in local families, that cults would weaken the family structure by inducting the younger members of the family (Kilbourne and Richardson 1982). As a result, religious spaces belonging to cults have become sites of persistent religious conflict and intermittent religious violence.

Autonomy-related competition and conflict

Generally speaking, autonomy-related competition in secular spaces takes place between the state and religious groups. As discussed in the previous chapter, most secular societies attempt to establish a division between religious and secular spaces; religious groups enjoy a high degree of autonomy in pursuing religious goals within religious spaces, in return for accepting state authority over secular spaces. In addition, secular societies also attempt to maintain the distinction between the religious and the secular by containing religious practices and the performance of religious rituals within religious spaces.

Despite this, religious beliefs and practices make frequent incursions into the secular sphere for a variety of reasons. First, because religion is a fundamental element of individual identity, individuals find it extremely difficult to create and maintain a religious-secular dichotomy of the self. Thus individuals carry signs and symbols of their private religious commitment into the *public* (e.g. through their clothing). The nature of religious commitment also works against the separation of the sacred and the secular. A system of religious beliefs is a complete worldview which does not distinguish between the private and the public or, mandate different types of conduct in secular public spaces and in private or religious spaces. Further, by carrying signs of their religious commitment in public, individuals perform an important sociological function. Outwardly visible, shared symbols of religious identity are devices that help to distinguish between 'friend and foe', and guide behaviour accordingly. Second, religions are social systems and thus, religious practices and rituals have a communal nature. Many sociologists in fact argue that it is the 'collectiveness' in religious performance that enhances it experiential value. Because many religious rituals require collective participation, it is that much more difficult to confine their performance to religious spaces. This is especially true when the religious spaces are too small to accommodate large religious congregations. Third, the nature of some religious rituals is such that they automatically bring religious practice into contact with secular spaces (e.g. pilgrimages and religious processions).

When religions encroach on public/secular spaces, states' responses to the encroachment lies on a continuum between the two poles of *accommodation* and *deterrence*. At the 'deterrent' end, state responses focus on building social and legal structures that reemphasize the distinction between the secular and the sacred by heavily restricting the expressions of religious identity in public. At the 'accommodation' end, the state is neutral towards (and, in many cases, endorses) public expressions of religious identity; the only limits placed on religious behaviour in public are those that are mandated by considerations of maintaining public order and protecting the interests of secular and other religious groups. While accommodationist strategies are based on acknowledging that the freedom of religious expression is an inviolable fundamental right (states adopting these strategies often have a history of cordial state-religion relations), deterrent approaches are underlined by the belief that a secular state must proscribe all religious activity in public spaces (states adopting these strategies, often, have had a history of religion-state conflict).

Regardless of the strategy that states adopt for managing the encroachment of religion into secular spaces, the potential for religious competition and conflict remains unabated. With deterrent strategies, the prime sources of religion-related conflict are tensions between disenfranchised religious groups and the state. The marginalization of religion in public life can also frustrate attempts by religious individuals and groups to maintain a coherent sense of their religious identity; these frustrations can be manifest in violent acts of subversion of state authority. On the other hand, accommodationist strategies run the risk of giving rise to intense inter-religious competition for scarce public resources, which might periodically become violent. In addition, when accommodationist states occasionally curb religious practices in public spaces in the larger interests of maintaining public order, they are met with vociferous opposition from religious groups, who view such curbs as unprecedented transgressions on religious freedom.

Autonomy-related competition and conflict tends to be symbolic in nature. Ideas surrounding identity and tradition are more often the cause of inter-religious and religious-secular competition and conflict than the practical advantages associated with religious presence in secular space. Such conflicts are particularly pervasive in the United States, where the dominant position of Christianity has persisted despite the constitutional separation of church and state. Throughout the country, Christian groups have assumed control of many public spaces – as shown by public displays of the Ten Commandments, the incorporation of the crucifix into official seals and the erection of nativity scenes and Christmas decorations in public spaces – which is increasingly a source of tension with minority, non-Christian groups (see Stump 2008; Barnett 2013). While Christian groups argue that nativity scenes, for example, are cultural traditions rather than displays of religious hegemony, non-Christian groups protest against the promotion of a single faith. In light of such protestations, courts have started to prohibit the display of overtly religious symbols (such as nativity scenes), while making allowances for less overt religious symbols that have strong cultural resonance (such as Christmas trees and lights). Indeed, nowhere is the symbolic display and tacit promotion of religion more contested than in the secular space of the school, which we cover in detail in a subsequent section, enabled by the organization of the remainder of this chapter in terms of sites in which religious competition over religious autonomy takes place, namely, civic and political spaces.

Formal spaces of education

Publicly funded educational institutions frequently witness some of the keenest competition over the autonomy of religious expression between the state and religious groups. This is due to the fact that the regulation of religion within schools directly impacts the ability of children to acquire and maintain a religious identity as well as their capacity for living amicably in a multi-religious society. Both sets of skills help children to acquire 'social capital', a key ingredient in maintaining social cohesion and religious harmony. However, Putnam (2002) distinguishes between two forms of social capital: *bonding* social capital refers to the building of solidarity among members of a group; *bridging* social capital, on the other hand, refers to the fostering of understanding and tolerance between members of different groups in a society.

In terms of regulating religion in secular educational institutions, competition arises because rules that lead to a high level of bonding social capital may result in low levels of bridging social capital. For example, allowing children/students to express their religious identity can help to build bonds among students of the same religious group based on shared religious customs. On the other hand, religion-based identification among students might result in religious 'cliques', which, in turn, might inhibit inter-religious understanding and tolerance, as well as the development of a trans-religious, civic identity. As will be discussed in a later section of this chapter, this problem of balancing bonding and bridging capital generates a lot of debate over whether faith-based schools should be supported by state funds. While religious individuals and groups demand more autonomy over religious practices (in order to build stronger intra-religious bonds), the secular state and other secular groups resist such demands (fearing the adverse impact of more autonomy on bridging social capital).

Against this background, we now turn attention to specific sources of religious-secular competition in public schools. Broadly speaking, such competition has centred on three main areas. The first is whether, and to what extent, students are allowed to wear religious garb in schools (e.g. the *hijab* or the turban). The second is whether, and to what extent, schools provide the infrastructure for students to maintain their religious practices (e.g. having canteens that provide halal or kosher food, making allowances for prayer time or religious holidays). The third is whether, and to what extent, schools provide religious education as a part of the curriculum.

As mentioned before, the outcome of religious-secular competition on all of the above issues is determined by whether the state adopts an accommodationist strategy or a deterrent strategy. The remainder of the section discusses each of the issues, with examples of how competition has been negotiated in two countries, UK and France, which, broadly speaking, employ an accommodationist and deterrent strategy, respectively.

In the historically Christian or secular countries of the West, there has been a lot of recent controversy over the right of Muslim school girls to wear the *hijab* in public schools (*Irish Times*, 4 June 2008; BBC Monitoring Caucasus, 24 December 2010). Where state laws have banned religious expressions (either generally or selectively) through restrictions on clothing in schools, the restrictions have given rise to pervasive and deep resentment among Muslim parents and religious groups, who see it as an intrusion on religious freedom. Such restrictions include not only the prohibition of the use of *hijab*, which has emerged as a prominent source of controversy, but also other clothing-related issues, such as school girls' attire for physical education classes. Objections to the use of *hijab* in schools (both by students and teachers) have been based on claims that wearing the *hijab* prevents the integration of Muslim minorities; legalizing the use of the *hijab* would irrevocably change the cultural ethos of the state; and even, that the use of the *hijab* is based on the premise of female inferiority (Fetzer and Soper 2005). Thus, restrictions on *hijab* use in public schools are justified by suggesting that their use erodes the development of bridging social capital. However, supporters of freedoms of religious expression also argue that allowing students to wear the *hijab* can produce bridging social capital, because it allows students to experience expressions of cultural difference on a first-hand basis, which makes them more tolerant of such difference in society at large.

When conflict over the use of *hijabs* in public schools remains unresolved, it can have negative social repercussions for affected minorities. There have been instances of Muslim parents withdrawing their children from public schools because of regulations banning the *hijab* (*Irish Times*, 15 September 2009; All Africa, 24 October 2009). In such cases, the affected Muslim girls have had to give up their education altogether or have had to rely on distance education, especially if there are no faith-based schools in the neighbourhood, or if private school education is too expensive. Muslim families which have accepted the restrictions (grudgingly or otherwise) have reported being ostracized by other members of the Muslim community. This shows how the ability to express religious identity through clothing in public schools (and, spaces in general) can give rise to bonding social capital, and the inability to do so, erode the same.

In several countries, school children, especially from minority religious communities, face other restrictions on their freedoms of religious expression in public schools. Fetzer and Soper (2005) note that in several Western European countries, Muslim religious groups have resented the lack of halal food in school canteens, the lack of designated spaces within schools for daily prayers, the lack of exemptions for Muslim students from classes to offer daily prayers or to participate in religious rituals on religious holidays.

These restrictions, along with those on wearing religious garb in schools, have the potential to breed suspicion against public schools among Muslim parents. Accordingly, as noted earlier, parents have sometimes responded by withdrawing their children from public schools to protect them from what they perceive as a destabilizing secular influence. In this context, many scholars have suggested that, at the heart of this competition over religious autonomy in public schools, is a debate about what 'multicultural' educational systems really mean. Chapman (1998), for example, suggests that educational policies in the West might be 'guilty' of equating 'secularism' with the 'absence of space to maintain religious differences'. This idea of secularism tends to treat religious values and practices as elements of an inherited culture, rather than of choice. On the other hand, religious groups push for greater support for religious practices in public schools, promoting 'multiculturalism' as the expression (rather than repression) of religious difference.

In many countries, historically, and oftentimes, constitutionally, certain religious groups have enjoyed a privileged relationship with the state (e.g. the Anglican Church in Britain). The hegemonic status of the religious group is reflected in the set of state-endorsed religious practices that are allowed within public schools as well as in the curriculum of (often, mandatory) religious education classes. In some instances, the influence of the dominant religious group may encroach into the subject matter of other classes as well. In some states in the United States, teachers are required by the curriculum to help students critically analyse evolutionary theory in science classes. Doing so provides an implicit framework for the validation of creationism, and reflects a more broad-based movement among conservative Christian groups that campaign for the explicit teaching of creationism in schools (*The New York Times*, 20 December 2005).

Outside of the classroom, school days might start with an assembly, incorporating some form of collective worship, which by law might predominantly take the form of worship practiced by the dominant religious group; or the religious education curriculum might focus more extensively on the hegemonic religious at the expense of the content on minority religions. In Britain, for example, the 1988 Education Act reaffirmed the constitutional hegemony of the Christian tradition, which specified that 'a majority of the acts of collective worship in state-run schools were to be "wholly or mainly of a broadly Christian character", and that in religious education the content "devoted to Christianity in the syllabus should predominate"' (Department of Education 1994, 16, quoted in Fetzer and Soper 2009, 39).[2]

In general, such provisions are highly likely to provoke autonomy-related competition by minority religious groups, who consider the laws as curbs on their ability to maintain their own religious identity even in supposedly 'non-religious' spaces such as public schools. For example, the Muslim community in Britain vociferously opposed the 1988 Education Act on the grounds that Muslim children would be coerced into participating in Christian worship rituals, or be ostracized within the school community at large (Shaikh 1992).

Box 3.3: Accommodation in Britain: A strategy for managing religion-state competition and conflict in public schools

Historically, the British political establishment has maintained cordial relations with the religious establishment, especially since the separation from the Vatican and the creation of the Anglican Church. In fact, both, the Anglican and Catholic churches have played a key role in lobbying for egalitarian treatment of minority religious groups and are considered by the government as important partners in the formulation of policies regulating educational/religious practices in public schools (Fetzer and Soper 2005; see also Rorive 2008).

Against this backdrop, public schools in Britain have been eager to accommodate minority religious practices, especially those of Muslims, within public schools through discretionary acts. School authorities have regularized the use of the *hijab* among Muslim school girls, only requiring that the *hijab* be in the same colour as the school uniform. In addition, in spite of the 1988 Education Act, schools have been careful to not impose Christian doctrine and practices on non-Christian students. Fetzer and Soper (2005) identify how collective worship practices at the morning assembly in several schools eschew a broadly Christian character, in favour of focusing on the moral content common to most religions. Similarly, the legal requirement of emphasizing the Christianity component of the religious education syllabus has been tempered by giving sufficient flexibility to local education authorities, and encouraging them to design religious education syllabi and worship practices with an eye towards the ethnic/religious composition of the student population (Fetzer and Soper 2005).

Broadly speaking, Fetzer and Soper (2005) report that public schools in Britain have been largely successful in accommodating Muslim claims for autonomy over religious expression in public schools. The wearing of the *hijab* is almost a non-issue and there is no strong opposition to religious education classes or collective worship practices. The relatively successful accommodation of religious difference may be attributed to a variety of reasons. These include a historically strong partnership between church and the state; church support for the protection of minority religious rights; a flexible regulatory environment that gave sufficient discretion to local authorities to interpret the 1988 Education Act in accordance with the demographic realities on the ground; and a concerted and sincere attempt to consult with, and co-opt minority community leaders in designing interventions to accommodate minority religious practices and in resolving school-religion conflict as and when it arises. That said, discretion can obviously lead to a lack of uniformity in the implementation of the law. For example, Fetzer and Soper (2005) point out that several schools take the Christian requirement of the 1988 legislation very seriously, provoking allegations of discriminatory and unfair religious practices in public schools from Muslims and other religious minorities.

Box 3.4: Deterrence in France: An alternative strategy for managing religion-state competition and conflict in public schools

Unlike in Britain, since the Reformation, the political leadership in France has had a largely hostile relationship with the religious establishment. The animosity between the religious and the political elite is crystallized in the concept of the *laïcité*,' the central principle guiding state-religion interaction in France. The strictest interpretation of the concept banishes religious belief and practice into the private domain and proscribes all public manifestations/expressions of the belief (Jezequel 1999, in Fetzer and Soper 2005). Softer interpretations of the term allow the state's encouragement of inter-religious understanding and promotion of public dialogue between religious groups, even in public schools (Jezequel 1999). Here again, the debate about whether an ideal secular state is repeated. Strict *laïcité* would define secularism as state neutrality in ensuring the absence of all religious expression from the public sphere; soft *laïcité* would define it as state neutrality in allowing (generally) all religious expression in the public sphere.

Against this backdrop, the use of the *hijab* has been a highly contentious issue in French public schools. The competition for autonomy was first dragged into the limelight in 1989 when three Muslim school girls were expelled by a public high school principal for refusing to remove the *hijab* on entering the school premises (Koulberg 1991, in Fetzer and Soper 2005). Through intense debates in the media involving state agencies, religious groups and parents, a general policy on the display of religious symbols in the classroom was formulated which, while not explicitly banning religious garb, proscribed 'ostentatious symbols that in themselves constitute agents of proselytism and discrimination' (Jezequel 1999, 90, quoted in Fetzer and Soper 2005, 71). This caveat – because of its ambiguity – has given rise to a wide variation at the local levels, in school authorities' responses to Muslim school girls wearing the *hijab* in school premises.

Liederman (2000) noted that, while there have been instances of school/college principals allowing girls to attend classes in the *hijab*, there are a significantly greater number of principals who have, and continue to, expel *hijab*-wearing girls, on the basis of the 'ostentation; and 'proselytism' clause. Often, principals are pressured into making the decision by the unionized teachers in the institutions, who are conspicuously in favour of a strict interpretation of *laïcité*. Whatever the motivation behind a ban on the *hijab* might be, Liederman (2000) documents a significant adverse impact on Muslim school girls affected by the ban. In addition to *hijab*-related withdrawals from schools in cases where Muslim parents have been financially unable to challenge the expulsion in court[3] (leading to either an abandonment of formal education altogether or a switch to education via correspondence), there are reports of prolonged psychological ill-effects of the official ostracism that *hijab* wearing or expelled Muslim school girls face in French schools on a daily basis.

While the *hijab* has been at the centre of autonomy-related competition between the state and Muslim religious groups, Muslim parents have also resented their lack of autonomy in avoiding secular practices in French public schools that they consider to go against their religious custom. For example, Fetzer and Soper (2005) report that parents continually attempt to seek exemptions for their children – under various pretexts – from going on overnight field trips (where boys and girls sleep in the same room), or from physical education classes (where Muslim girls are required to change into bathing suits and swim with boys).

As the preceding discussion demonstrates, the French state's approach to claims for religious autonomy has generally been to deter the expression of religious identity in public schools. As noted earlier, this has been partly the result of long-standing historical tension between religion and the state. However, if the British and French experiences are any guide, deterrent strategies might give rise to deep-seated rifts in society more so than accommodationist strategies, and pre-empt the fostering of a national identity. Accommodation of Muslim claims in Britain may facilitate the development of a 'British Muslim identity'. In France, however, efforts to build a trans-religious 'French' identity based on *laïcité* may fall short; with active deterrence, two polarized and mutually hostile identities, 'French' and 'Muslim' might instead be the outcome. Perhaps in recognition of this, educational authorities and school administrators have been gradually taking small steps towards the 'accommodationist' end; there have been directives to allow single-day absences to Muslim students for Id and recommendations to avoid conducting exams during Ramadan.

Box 3.5: Between accommodation and deterrence: The regulation of religion in public schools in Singapore

Singapore's strategy for the regulation of religion in public schools can usefully by characterized as falling in-between the accommodationist and deterrent paradigms. In its short history, Singapore has faced dilemmas concerning the use of the *hijab* in schools; special exemptions for Muslims to participate in Friday prayers and other significant religious rituals; special provisions for Muslims to ensure their participation in secular school activities (e.g. in terms of relaxing dressing requirements for physical education classes); and the design and delivery of religious instruction in national schools.

Given that Malays, who are almost invariably Muslims, are regarded as the indigenous population of Singapore (a status, which is constitutionally acknowledged, and hence comes with several religious privileges), Singapore's attempts at regulating religion have had less to do with integrating an immigrant minority, and more with building a national identity that supercedes an ethno-religious identity. As E. Tan (2008) explains, Singapore's banning of the *hijab* (or *tudung*) in national pre-university institutions is designed to expand the 'common' space shared between Singaporeans regardless of religious or ethnic affiliation. In spite of contestation by Muslim religious groups and parents, the state has held firm on the restriction, expressing concern that allowing religion-specific privileges will set a precedent for the accommodation of competing demands from other religious groups. At the same time, the state has balanced its unaccommodating stance on the *hijab* issue by accommodating Malay Muslim demands for religious autonomy on several other issues. For example, the use of *hijab* is not banned among adults (both those attending public universities and teachers in national pre-university educational institutions). Muslim religious holidays are accorded the status of public holidays and Muslim school children are granted special exemptions from classes to attend Friday prayers; and, female Muslim school children are allowed to eschew prescribed school attire, in favour of track pants, to attend physical education classes (E.Tan 2008).

While accommodation on other fronts has succeeded in containing resentment over the *hijab* issue in Singapore, the religion-state partnership (through the cooperation of religious elites) has also been critical in preventing the escalation of competition to conflict. As noted in an earlier discussion, it is accommodation of demands for religious autonomy, more than the enlargement of religious expression-free 'common space' that might contribute more towards 'Singaporeanising' the Malay-Muslim identity.

In terms of religious education, Singapore had a brief experiment with full-fledged religious education in national schools between 1984–9, which was largely state- initiated, developed and delivered. However, the provision (or lack) of religious education in national schools has not been a site of significant competition between religious groups and the state, partly because religious instruction in Singapore has historically been delivered through privatized, non-state organizations and mechanisms. As C. Tan (2008) points out, the provision of religious instruction in schools was primarily the outcome of a state assessment that it was an effective way to negate Western cultural influences that followed in the wake of rapid industrialization and modernization and posed a threat to desirable traditional social structures and institutions. Clammer (1991) further notes that the religious education curriculum was designed to distil common moral values between disparate religious doctrines/systems. A parallel can be drawn to the modifications made to collective worship practices in public schools in the UK (discussed earlier). Nonetheless, unlike in the UK, this has not drawn criticisms from religious groups that emphasizing commonalities between religions runs the risk of glossing over substantive differences between them and promoting not multiculturalism but an absence of cultural/religious difference.

Informal spaces of education

Informal spaces of education are those that are either privately owned and managed (and therefore exist outside of formal regulatory frameworks – e.g. tuition centres), or the informal spaces that can be found outside the classroom on formal education campuses (e.g. the playground, the university campus-at-large). Informality is often associated with ambiguity when it comes to religious regulation and praxis, with such ambiguity contributing to a politics of informality that must constantly be negotiated by students and staff of different religious affiliations. Ambiguity can also create opportunities for religious groups to generate competitive advantages by providing much needed educational services that enable them to disguise their religious motivations. Such opportunities and advantages are explored in a later section.

Box 3.6: The contested space(s) of the university campus: Muslim students in the UK

In a recent study of the experiences of Muslim (both British and overseas) students studying at a university in the UK, Hopkins (2011) explores the complex ways in which university campuses are constructed, contested and experienced by minority (and distinctly 'other') religious groups. He shows how the university campus is a contradictory space for minority religious groups, as it can be at once tolerant and diverse, and discriminatory and exclusionary.

On the one hand, the university campus is believed to be a tolerant and diverse space – a space of relative freedom. Spaces of the university campus are generally occupied by people who are more educated than the general public, making them relatively more tolerant of and liberal in their views towards religious diversity. As a result, Muslim students reported feeling comfortable, content and 'free' from racial and religious prejudice. On the other hand, the university campus was believed to be a discriminatory and exclusionary space – a space of surveillance and restricted access. The feeling of discrimination stemmed largely from guidelines produced by the British Department for Education and Skills designed to help universities identify potentially violent Islamic extremism in institutions of higher education. The ramifications of such guidelines – which aim to mitigate against moderate Muslims and non-Muslims being recruited into and groomed by extremist groups – are that they created spaces of institutional discrimination. Muslim students felt that as a result of such guidelines, 'their everyday movements [were being] monitored, surveyed and open to constant critique' (Hopkins 2011, 161). For example, a senior university administrator requested to be added to the mailing list of the Islamic Society (but not other religious societies) in order to monitor the group, an action that made the Muslim students feel less 'legitimate' than their peers.

The feeling of exclusion related more to the locations of facilities and the politics of access. The campus mosque, for example, was identified as being in a physically separate – and distant – location to the Chaplaincy Centre (which other faith groups used for worship). Not only was the location inconvenient, it was also described as being 'desolate' (Hopkins 2011, 164) and unsuitable for Muslim women to access by themselves. In addition, it was noted that halal food was difficult to obtain on campus and, more divisively, the dominance of a drinking culture and associated bars created spaces of restricted access for Muslim students. Moreover, the common practice of retiring to a college bar after a research group meeting or seminar caused many Muslim students to refrain from playing a more active role in the academic life of the university. Altogether, these examples reveal how 'some bodies have the right to belong in certain locations, while others are marked out as trespassers who are in accordance with how both spaces and bodies are imagined, politically, historically and conceptually circumscribed as being "out of place"' (Puwar 2004, 51). The informal spaces of the university campus can therefore help to reproduce subtle but undeniable feelings of institutional discrimination, exclusion and religious marginalization among the Muslim student body.

Spaces of employment

Broadly speaking, religion-secular and religion-state competition over religious autonomy in employment spaces share many characteristics with such competition in public schools. Thus, religious groups and individuals compete with state authorities to be free to express their religious identity by wearing religious garb at the workplace; to be allowed, without penalty, to maintain their religious identity through prayer and ritual-related practices at the workplace; and to be free to refuse to undertake jobs and/or comply with secular workplace rules when such jobs or rules infringe on some fundamental religious tenet or custom. In their pursuit to gain and maintain such freedoms, religious groups can come into direct competition with the state (when the employment contract is with the state); more frequently, however, religious groups compete with secular private sector employers, with the state and its agencies playing an adjudicating role in resolving the dispute.

As with managing autonomy-related claims in public schools, in general, state responses to demand for (greater) religious freedoms at the workplace have largely fallen in the continuum between accommodation and deterrence. Deterrent responses have been based on emphasizing the secular character of the workplace; uniformity in the treatment of employees regardless of their religion; asserting the employers' autonomy to establish and enforce workplace-related rules (as long as they do not violate labour laws); and, highlighting productivity-related losses that might result from allowing worship-related practices to take place at the workplace. On the other hand, accommodationist responses have been motivated by a desire to protect constitutionally enshrined guarantees of religious freedom and, in many cases, of freedom of conscience. It should be noted that there can be a wide gradation in the degree to which constitutional provisions protect religious freedom. Secular constitutions minimally guarantee protection against discrimination at the workplace based on employees' religious beliefs; more 'liberal' legal systems guarantee free exercise of religious rights at public workplaces; and finally, freedoms of conscience grant individuals exemptions from discharging otherwise binding obligations towards the employer in particular and the state in general. Freedoms of conscience, where they are provided, are generally interpreted broadly enough to extend exemptions to individuals 'who have no formal religious commitments but hold religious-like convictions' (Demerath 2007, 384).

In the previous section where we dealt with public (and formal) educational spaces, the pitfalls of adopting too deterrent a response to demands for greater religious autonomy were identified. Here, we focus on the problems associated with 'over' accommodation of claims for religious autonomy at workplaces. The central concern with accommodationist responses, especially salient with respect to granting freedoms of conscience, is that they set a precedent. The worry is that, once an individual is allowed to excuse himself or herself from duties on religious or conscientious grounds, it might open the floodgates for other such demands. Consequently, if conscientious objections to secular practices are consistently and universally granted, they will compromise the 'shared', 'common' foundations on which an effectively functioning society rests.

A clear example of this sort of a scenario is presented by the refusal of members of the Jehovah's Witnesses to bear arms or serve in the armed forces, on the grounds of religious doctrine. This refusal creates special problems for states where conscription is mandatory. While it might be possible for states to grant exemptions from military service to a small minority, it is practically infeasible to sustain military service as a national institution if a large majority were to seek, and be granted, such exemptions. Similar problems can also arise with accommodating demands for other religious free-exercise rights at the workplace (in terms of allowing employees to dress in accordance with religious requirements and engage in worship and other religious-related rituals at the workplace. The following case study represents the dilemmas that the United States, which adopts a highly accommodationist strategy towards demands for free religious expression at the workplace, has encountered at various points in its recent history.

Box 3.7: Competition for religious expression at the workplace in the United States

The United States has routinely faced a dilemma about balancing its constitutional commitment to religious freedom and the enforcement of secular aspects of labour law. The Supreme Court, in landmark decisions in 1965 and 1979, endorsed an extreme form of religious accommodation by extending the conscientious objector status to cover non-religious individuals. However, in many recent court rulings, a shift away from such extreme accommodation can be discerned. In 1990, the court allowed the state of Oregon to deny two Native American state employees the religious right to use peyote – an illegal psychotropic plant – in religious rituals, despite a long-standing custom (Demerath 2007). More recently, the court denied damages to a young woman who had been fired from her job as a check-out clerk with a large department store, for wearing a small gold ring in a pierced eyebrow. The affected woman had sued on the basis that the sacking violated her freedom of religion as a member of the Church of Body Modification (Demerath 2007).

More interestingly, upset by the 1990 Supreme Court ruling, the Congress had passed the Religious Freedom Restoration Act (RFRA) in 1993. The RFRA justified a wide variety of 'questionable' demands on the basis of personal religious practices; these included prison inmates petitioning for 'everything from drug use to conjugal visits as privately important religious rituals' (Demerath 2007, 384). The RFRA, unsurprisingly struck down in 1997, provides a classic instance of the slippery slope that accommodationist responses to religious free-exercise rights occupy.

Box 3.8: Singapore's 'contingent accommodationist' approach to religion and the workplace

In general, Singapore's response to managing claims for religious autonomy at workplaces can be classified as a 'contingent accommodationist' approach. Singapore classifies important religious holidays (but only those of the largest religious groups) as public holidays, encourages employers to be flexible in giving employees time off work to engage in worship and other forms of religious observance, and largely tolerates the use of religious garb among public sector employees (E.Tan 2008).

However, such accommodation of the demands for religious freedom are tempered by a clear acknowledgement that the importance of freedom of (profession and practicing a) religion is secondary to the goal of protecting and advancing the national/state/collective interest. Thus, members of the Jehovah's Witnesses have not been granted exemptions from National Service requirements nor have disruptive religious rituals been allowed at the workplace. Singapore courts have attempted to allow religious accommodation at the workplace, without sliding down a slippery slope by drawing a distinction between religious beliefs and actions that follow from religious beliefs. Courts routinely find the holding of religious beliefs, however objectionable they might be, to be legally unsanctionable; only actions that arise from such beliefs might be prosecuted (E.Tan 2008).

Public spaces

Certain religious practices (such as participation in religious processions and pilgrimages) by their very nature, involve the use of public spaces. Other more privatized forms of religious practices (worship rituals) are driven into public spaces due to the reduction of religious spaces – vis-à-vis secular spaces – in most countries. When religious practices 'threaten' to spill over into public spaces, competition between religious groups and the state takes place over whether, and how frequently, such practices are allowed. If they are allowed, further competition occurs over the extent to which religious groups retain autonomy in determining how such practices are conducted. Religious groups' demands for autonomy, in such circumstances, are based on the notion that the pilgrimage/procession route is a sacred place (according to Kong 2001b, 'unofficially sacred'); accordingly, religious jurisdiction ought to override the secular jurisdiction of the state. On the other hand, state resistance to such demands are premised on the notion that use of public spaces for religious purposes does not alter fundamentally the secular character of public spaces.

In general, collective performance of religious rituals enhances the value of the religious experience for the individual and generates bonding social capital. However, when such collective performance takes place in a public space, it can erode bridging social capital. For example, Fetzer and Soper (2005) report instances of anxiety among the secular/Christian sections of the German population at witnessing Muslims offering daily prayers in public spaces. German Muslims attribute such anxieties to a pervasive misconception that such worship rituals in public spaces constitute open attempts to proselytize. In extreme cases, public performance of religious rituals can (and have) generate(d) communal tension leading to inter-religious violence. In addition, religious processions and practices such as ancestor worship can generate significant negative externalities; they can cause traffic congestions, generate litter and produce noise and smoke pollution. Finally, public performances of religious ritual can, in many cases, have a negative impact on the well-being of the participants themselves. Large gatherings of people can potentially lead to stampedes (e.g. the annual 'chariot' festival in the Eastern state of Orissa has routinely witnessed stampedes involving significant number of fatalities (*The Times of India*, 3 July 2011); rituals involving the burning of paper and incense and fireworks can compromise fire safety (e.g. lunar new year celebrations in Bangkok, Thailand, result in scores of fires annually, leading to loss of life and property (Channel NewsAsia, 15 January 2009)); and, in rare cases, religious processions are easy targets for terrorist attacks (e.g. in Quetta and Baluchistan, in Pakistan, terrorist attacks on religious processions have claimed a significant number of lives in recent years [Pakistan Press International Information Services, 10 April 2004]).

Consequently, government attempts to ban or regulate religious processions are motivated primarily by public order considerations, social efficiency considerations and paternalistic considerations. In the wake of violence during an outdoor Jewish religious celebration in 2012, the local council of Outremont, a Montreal borough, decided to ban religious processions and parades on the basis of public order considerations (*Toronto Sun*, 6 April 2012). In Malaysia, there have been recent calls to ban religious processions altogether to minimize the resulting disruptions to secular social life (*New Straits Times*, 18 February 2010), a clear response to social efficiency considerations. In China, in 2011, local government authorities patrolled the roads to Hushan mountain in Qingdan, Shandong, to prevent people from performing ancestor worship and grave sweeping rituals at cemeteries on the mountain after fire from burning joss paper claimed several hectors of forests and killed two people (Xinhua News Agency, 5 April 2011). In Pakistan, bans on religious processions have been in place in Quetta, Baluchistan, to prevent participants of religious processions from being targeted by terrorists who have historically targeted dense populations moving through narrow, unmonitorable alleys (Pakistan Press International Information Services, 10 April 2004). This action may be said to stem from paternalistic considerations.

Whatever the motivations for banning or regulating religious practices in public places might be, religious individuals and groups have generally resented their resulting inability to engage in their religious practices in a traditional manner. In China, the curbs on ancestor worship rituals have provoked widespread insecurity among people who believe that non-performance of traditional customs will jeopardize the welfare of deceased ancestors in their afterlife, a direct cause of material misfortune for those who survive the dead (Xinhua News Agency, 5 April 2011). At the same time, the issue of regulating death rituals in public has drawn attention to the deep secular-religious rift in society, with several secular individuals and groups calling in the media for not just regulation, but outright bans on rituals they consider 'ugly', 'primitive' and 'environmentally damaging' (Xinhua News Agency, 5 April 2011).

Box 3.9: Proposed bans on religious processions in Penang, Malaysia

In Penang, Malaysia, in 2010, the state government came under tremendous criticism for initiatives to ban a religious procession (the Maulidur Rasul, the Prophet's birthday parade) (*New Straits Times*, 19 February 2010). In addition, the government – with the backing of a prominent progressive religious leader – called for a blanket ban on all religious processions as they created 'disturbances for the people' (*New Straits Times*, 18 February 2010). Supporters of the ban argued that roads are built for motorized conveyance and not processions; that no religious scripture requires religious processions to be held on public roads; and that such processions are discriminatory towards motorists who pay road tax.

This attempt to regulate a religious practice in public space tried to discredit the notion that the public performance of the said religious practice was necessary for the maintenance of religious identity. Relatedly, it was suggested that 'token' processions in the premises of religious groups (religious spaces) replace the public processions (as an example, it was suggested that the Hindu religious procession Thaipusam be moved to the temples in the Batu Caves [*New Straits Times*, 18 February 2010]).

Even more interestingly, just as proponents of the ban tried to dismiss the religious significance of public processions, opponents marshalled 'secular' arguments to keep the traditions alive and autonomous. Religious groups and their sympathizers noted that religious processions showcase Malaysia's cultural and religious diversity and are major sources of tourism-related foreign exchange. Ultimately, it was the risk of offending religious sentiment – and the potential electoral backlash – that led the government to stand down from pushing the proposal through.

This example is instructive because religious groups' opposition to the regulation of religious practices in public spaces invoked secular arguments and not merely claims based on constitutional guarantees of freedoms of religion. Religious groups' willingness to compete for autonomy on secular grounds is generally a positive development from the state's point of view, because it implicitly acknowledges that public performance of religious rituals might be to the detriment of society at large and that religious groups have an obligation to be mindful of the larger, collective good in pressing for the maintenance of and autonomy over extant religious traditions that are observed in public spaces.

Box 3.10: Truncated worship rituals in Singapore's public spaces

Rapid urbanization and the concomitant need for space for economic purposes has, over the decades, shrunk both religious spaces and residential spaces in Singapore. The result has been to push some private forms of rituals for Chinese religionists[4] (e.g. ancestor worship during the Seventh Month or Hungry Ghost Festival) into public spaces. In order to accommodate individual religious needs within spatial constraints, the state has provided infrastructure – such as common bins and receptacles in Housing Development Board (HDB) precincts (for the burning of paper money) – for shared use among residents. The early phase of adaptation to this notion of 'shared' rituals generated a fair amount of resentment among religious groups and individuals, who were concerned that sharing (public) ritual spaces compromises the requisite 'individualness' of the ritual and attenuates its efficacy (Tong and Kong 2000). Further regulations on Chinese worship rituals have involved limiting the size and numbers of incense sticks burnt and where they are burnt. Again, these regulations have been construed by many to be intrusions on religious autonomy that compromise the efficacy of religious ritual, especially given the belief that joss sticks are the medium of conveying worship to ancestors; hence, the bigger they are, the better the rituals (*Straits Times*, 9 October 1997).

In terms of religious processions, government regulations of the annual Thaipusam procession have been hotly contested. State regulations have encompassed performative elements of the ritual (by banning live or recorded music from accompanying those participating in the procession) as well as legislative elements (by setting a time bracket for the procession to take place and placing restrictions on the route of the procession, and have been justified on the grounds of public order (*Straits Times*, 15 January 2011). Affected members of the Hindu community have claimed that these curbs on religious autonomy have both symbolically and functionally affected the sanctity of the ritual (Kong 2005b), which nonetheless remains a prominent feature of Singapore's religious calendar. For example, Kong (2005b) reports that the lack of music on the processional route not only fails to generate appropriate religious ambience, but also negatively interferes with participants' ability to carry the *kavadi*.

That significantly truncated or modified worship rituals continue to persist has been a function of the following[5]: the powerlessness of religious individuals/groups to contest state regulations in any substantive manner; the co-optation of religious leaders in emphasizing that the aspects of religious practice made defunct via regulation were not integral to the sanctity of the ritual to begin with; the emphasis on the ideological hegemony of a secular state narrative of development; and the resourcefulness of the population at large to circumvent and, in innocuous ways, resist the regulation. For example, Taoists continue to use individual worship bins and place such bins in front of their homes to distinguish their offerings from those of others in violation of government regulations (Tong and Kong 2000) and Hindu youths accompanying Thaipusam processions make dustbins into drums when they are not being surveilled (Kong 2005b). It might be necessary for the state to tolerate these small token acts of resistance: they help to maintain a semblance of religious autonomy, without which the sense of religious disenfranchisement may put severe stains on belief systems and contribute to more subversive actions.

Media and arts spaces

In this section, we examine competition between religious and secular groups over the degree to which individuals and groups should be allowed to express anti-religious sentiment (either against religion in general or against a particular religious group), in traditional media[6] and arts spaces. These spaces include newspapers, magazines, books, brochures and works of art. The emphasis on the 'public' is crucial here. The fact that the opinion is expressed or protests are conducted in public makes such acts liable for government regulation and, accordingly, raise autonomy-related concerns.

Art (broadly conceived as a creative act, to include literature of any sort and physical and speech acts) has historically been a vehicle of protest. When works of art directly or indirectly trivialize, ridicule or criticize religious beliefs and practices, there is potential for (sometimes violent) conflict between religious groups or between religious and secular groups. In religious states (theocracies), the state religion is invariably protected from the public expression of insulting or critical opinion through punitive blasphemy laws (e.g. Saudi Arabia). At the other extreme, states protect the public expression of anti-religious sentiment through the strict enforcement of constitutionally enshrined laws guaranteeing freedom of speech/expression. The United States comes the closest to occupying this end of the policy continuum: it routinely accommodates acts such as the burning of religious texts (the Bible, Koran, etc.) and other religious paraphernalia (crucifixes and *burqas*, etc.) in public spaces (*The Dartmouth Review*, 29 February 2012; *The Washington Times*, 8 April 2011). Indeed, in the United States, religious freedom is often taken as a subset of freedom of speech (Demarath 2007).

In general, however, most multi-religious secular countries adopt an 'in between' approach: protecting the freedom of speech/expression while ensuring that the exercise of such freedoms does not compromise inter-religious and social harmony. Secular and religious groups try to influence this balancing act: religious groups argue for greater state protection from the public expression of anti-religious views by representing it as a human rights violation and an infringement of the religious freedoms of adherents. Secular proponents of free speech, on the other hand, demand greater freedoms to incorporate religious motifs and themes in creative arts (and, more generally, to be able to express anti-religious views) without the threat of state sanctions. The issue is not only debates within states but at a transnational level as well. In 2009, a resolution was put to the United Nations Human Rights Council by Pakistan on behalf of the Organisation of Islamic Countries; the resolution demanded state initiatives – including new legislation – to stop the 'defamation of religion'. Germany, on behalf of the European Union, opposed the resolution, arguing that 'human rights belong to individuals, not to institutions'.

Historically speaking, upholding constitutional commitments to freedom of expression while preventing the exercise of such rights from resulting in religious distress for, or causing offence to, believers has been challenging for many governments. Numerous episodes of intense competition between religions groups and between religious and secular groups will illustrate this. In 2006, a Danish newspaper printed – and refused to retract – cartoons depicting the Prophet Mohammed. Muslims around the world viewed the graphic representation as sacrilegious, and protested violently against this exercise in free speech (BBC News, 15 February 2008). In 2012, Salman Rushdie – the author of the Satanic Verses, banned in many countries due to its satirical portrayal of religious figures in the Quran – was denied entry by the Indian government to attend a literary festival in Jaipur, India, on the pretext that it would be unable to guarantee his safety. In addition, a scheduled address by Rushdie at the festival, via video conferencing, was cancelled, outraging proponents of free speech (*Legally India*, 30 January 2012). Media treatments of unpopular new religious groups can also act to foster negative public opinions against such groups and justify their persecution by secular groups and government agencies. State media in China and Iran have long campaigned to discredit and suppress the Falungong and the Bahai faith, respectively. Even in the United States, media coverage of the activities of Branch Davidians at Mount Carmel, Texas, was instrumental in building popular consensus for government action against the sect that led to the burning of the compound and the loss of lives of many women and children (Beckford and Richardson 2007).

Box 3.11: Blasphemy and Britain

The difference between religious (in this case, Islamic) and secular perspectives on the importance of freedom of religion came to the fore in the responses to Salman Rushdie's Satanic Verses, which Muslims believe to contain a deeply offensive portrayal of Prophet Muhammad. British Muslims led a petition to ban the publication of the book in the United Kingdom; engaged in marches to protest against the book's availability after it was published; and burnt copies of the book in public in a march in Bradford in 1989 (*Financial Times*, 24 June 1989). In addition, Muslims argued that Britain's existing blasphemy law should be extended to include Muslims (*The Guardian*, 14 February 1990).

What complicated matters was that, while the blasphemy law – a relic of the past – was largely unused, it had been called into action as recently as 1977 to successfully prosecute a magazine, 'Gay News', for its portrayal of Jesus (Fetzer and Soper 2005). Interestingly, while many secular voices in Britain have called for an abolition of the law (widely seen as archaic), British Muslims, in spite of the law's selective support for Christianity, have refused to join in this secular chorus. In fact, in 1998, Islamic groups in Britain supported efforts by a Christian organization to take a theatre company to court for having produced a play it deemed 'blasphemous' (Fetzer and Soper 2005).

Despite not actually benefitting from the law as it exists in its current form, Islamic groups' support for the law implies that they see it as a potential future tool for preventing defamations of Islam via the arts. Vigorous campaigns, resisted by the political establishment, to extend the law to cover Islam have been underway for some time now. More interestingly however, this case illustrates how otherwise divergent religions may rally around a shared cause – of acquiring and maintaining state protection against secular, creative affronts.

Political spaces

Demerath (2007) argues that in no country around the world is the separation between religion and state absolute; this includes the United States, where the Establishment clause in the Constitution is taken to set up an impermeable barrier between religion and politics. He suggests that 'because both religion and politics involve competing moral guidelines and ethical priorities, it is only natural that the two should inform – and occasionally inflame – each other' (Demerath 2007, 386).

To understand why, how and over what, religious groups engage in political competition (between themselves and with other secular groups), it is useful to start with a definition of political activity. We define political activity as any activity undertaken to influence the distribution of resources within a community and/or the development and enforcement of shared values among members of the community. Thus, political activity by religious leaders can be undertaken within congregations (religious spaces), where they rely on their teaching and leadership authority within the congregation to shape political attitudes and behaviour (Guth et. al. [1997] call this kind of political activity 'cue giving'). In addition, religious leaders can undertake political activity to achieve desirable resource allocation and social value systems outside congregations (i.e., in secular spaces); Guth et. al. (1997) call this kind of political activity 'direct action'. This section concentrates on competition that arises out of 'direct action'.

Based on what the relationship between religion in general (and, a religious group, in particular) and state/government is, Olson (2007) identifies four types of 'direct action' political activities that religious groups or their leaders might engage in: electoral activities, advocacy activities, partnership activists and gap-filling activities. These broad categories provide an analytical framework for understanding the nexus between religion and politics.

Olson (2007, 449) defines electoral activities as those that are undertaken to 'influence collective decision-making by shaping the selection of the individual who will make government decisions'. Thus, electoral activities include running for political office, campaigning, funding political campaigns, fundraising for political parties and so forth. Different constitutional regimes allow religious groups to engage in electoral activities to varying degrees: in religious states (Iran and Pakistan, for example) and religiously homogeneous states (Bangladesh, for example), having a religious affiliation is mandatory for holding political office; thus, competition arises within a particular religious group between moderates and extremes. However, there is very little religion-secular competition or conflict in the electoral arena.

At the other extreme, in 'anti-religious' countries such as China, participation of religious groups in electoral activities is completely banned. In addition, in order to hold political office at either national or provincial levels, individuals need to demonstrate their areligious credentials. In between these extremes, in most plural, secular countries, there is a wide variation in the degree to which religious groups are allowed to/actually participate in electoral activities. Generally, religious groups are not allowed by secular constitutions to run for political office. Exceptions to the rule are discussed later in the section. In spite of the restrictions on competing for political office, religious groups make their political presence felt for a variety of reasons: political parties or political individuals have religious leanings; the voting behaviour of people are frequently aligned with their religious preferences, which gives religious leaders the potential to be political king-makers (Norris and Inglehart 2004) and encourages political leaders to manipulate religious cleavages for electoral gain; and, even where religious involvement in electoral activities are constitutionally banned, weak states fail to stop religious groups from canvassing for votes for their political representative on religious grounds.

In general, the absence of religious involvement in electoral activities is positively correlated with more harmonious (and, at least, less violent) religious plural polities. Conversely, religious groups' involvement in electoral activities, either directly or indirectly, has a high risk of generating inter-religious conflict and communal tensions, especially in countries where a dominant (majority) religion coexists with significant minority religions. In countries such as Sri Lanka, Thailand and the Philippines, where the state has preferential relationships with the dominant religion, electoral competition between religious groups takes place on an uneven playing field. In Sri Lanka, for example, Buddhist monks have the right to run for public office and many occupy significant political positions

(Schober 2007). Accordingly, they have played a crucial role in legitimizing the state's repression of Tamil separatist claims; denying religious sanction to attempts at peaceful resolution of the conflict; and, supporting violent private anti-Tamil Tiger organizations such as the People's Liberation Front (JVP). As Schober (2007: 62) notes: 'Sinhalese monks defined for themselves a modern identity that openly claims monastic engagement with the political world'.

Finally, in Japan, the Soka Gakkai has actively campaigned for a greater political role for religious groups, including direct participation in elections (Shupe 1991). These claims have generated significant secular opposition to the idea not least because the Soka Gakkai is seen to be a 'radical' new religious movement.

In Thailand and the Philippines, the political influence wielded by religious leaders of the dominant religious groups (Buddhism and Catholicism, respectively) and their large say in determining who holds political office has contributed to violent Islamic separatist movements in Southern Thailand and Mindanao (Hefner 2007). In both cases, over-zealous programmes of defining the nation in terms of the dominant religious group – and the resulting over-enthusiasm over the assimilation of religious minorities into this exclusive national identity – has led to a religiously divided electorate. As noted before, when populations are inclined to vote along religion lines, it enhances the incentives that religious leaders have in participating in electoral activities.

Even in cases where the involvement of religious groups in electoral activities is constitutionally restricted, weak state structures and insincere enforcement have led to a violation of the laws and fomented communal tension. The following case study from India illustrates how a weak judiciary has allowed the country's constitutional commitment to secularism to be diluted by failing to contain religious groups' involvement in electoral activities.

Box 3.12: Confused courts and compromised secularism in India

The Indian constitution prevents religious involvement in electoral activity by stipulating that no organization can simultaneously be both a political and religious organization, soliciting electoral support in the name of religion or using religious symbols or promoting hatred for personal electoral gain are corrupt practices under the Representation of People (RP) Act; and every political organization sign a declaration, at the time of registration, affirming its commitment to secularism (Rao 2004). However, the Indian courts have delivered contra-secular verdicts in cases where political parties and candidates – especially from the Hindu right wing – have violated the RP Act.

In 1990, the Bombay High Court annulled the election of 12 Hindu right-wing members of the State Assembly, for having invoked *Hindutva* – the essence of being a Hindu – during their electoral campaigns and making statements and speeches that fuelled communal tensions. However, on appeal, the Indian Supreme Court reversed the lower courts' decision on the grounds that comments involving Hinduism or *Hindutva*, did not, per se, constitute invoking religion as both terms stood for a 'way of life or a state of mind' synonymous with Indian culture (Rao 2004, 396).

In similar circumstances in 1996, the Supreme Court overturned a lower courts' decision to annul elections of a prominent Hindu right-wing leader based on violations of the RP Act. Here, the Supreme Court ruling asserted that soliciting votes on religious grounds was not sufficient for the annulment of an election result; it needed to be shown that such soliciting had materially affected the outcome of the election. In another similar overrule of a lower court judgement, the Supreme Court stated that candidates belonging to a political party, which has a manifesto appealing for votes in the name of religion, cannot be charged with a corrupt practice as long as the candidate does not explicitly consent to such appeals (Rao 2004).

Together, these judgements have indicated the unwillingness of the judiciary to protect the spirit of secularism. Rao (2004) outlines several social-economic-demographic-political factors for why individual judges have been reticent in doing so. Whatever the reasons might be, the case study illustrates how the best intentions of keeping electoral activity free from religion can be neutralized by inadequate and half-hearted enforcement.

Box 3.13: Political innovation and minority religious groups in Singapore

Singapore has been able to effectively keep electoral activities (including running for political office, electoral campaigning and political fundraising) free from religious intervention by statutory design and strong enforcement. The Maintenance of Religious Harmony Act 1990 prevents religious groups from playing *any* part in electoral politics; however, as the above case study shows, constitutional provisions can be meaningless unless they are backed by uniform and consistent enforcement. The Singapore state, to its credit, has acted promptly against any infringement of the principle of separation between religion and politics. Preventing conflicts of interest – between religious loyalties and their secular commitments to the constitution – among state functionaries (political leaders, government officials, judges, etc.) has been the key to effective enforcement of state laws preventing religions' involvement in electoral politics. This, in turn, has been achieved by a technocratic governance, where the recruitment of state functionaries is (putatively, at least) based on secular, rather than ethnic/religious, merit.[7]

In addition, the state has managed to establish a secular agenda over which political competition takes place; this ensures that there is no scope for individuals bringing their religious preferences to bear on electoral issues or outcomes. Further, through its urban regeneration programme, the state has moved away from ethnically delineated residential areas (*kampungs*) by resettling the population in estates that are broadly representative of the national ethnic mix: this has played a key role preventing different electoral constituencies from having different ethnic (and relatedly, religious) majorities, thus negating the scope for religious-influenced behaviour (e.g. voting for a co-religionist) in elections.

However, this arrangement might be prejudicial to the chances of having representatives from minority religious groups in Parliament: such concerns have been addressed by a political innovation, the GRC (Group Representation Constituencies) system, to ensure that minority candidates are represented (*Straits Times*, 2 August 2008). Whatever other flaws the GRC system might have, they are better at representing minority interests – than having constituencies reserved for minority groups – while minimizing the role of religion in electoral activities.

Olson's (2007) second category of political activities – advocacy activities – calls for a definition of 'advocacy'. These are activities undertaken to affect government (or collective) decision-making by shaping public opinion. Thus, advocacy by religious groups leads to competition among religious groups and between religious and secular groups to establish hegemony over the 'ideological spaces' in a community. At its extreme, ideological competition is over whether secular or divine law should provide the foundations of civic/public morality (for example, in calls for the implementation of Syariah law). However, religious-secular ideological competition may just as well take place over attempts to win smaller battles: these include influencing the state to (de)criminalize homosexuality;

(de)legalize abortion and euthanasia; enact religious (or secular) sympathetic legislation related to cloning and genetic modification; and shape the curriculum for national schools to reflect a religious (or secular) bias.

In general, religious-secular competition over ideological hegemony can be classified into the following categories: secular demands for, and religious resistance to, the revision of existing laws; competition between religious and secular-religious groups over influencing the law on new forms of practice; and demands by religious groups for religious considerations to be restored in an ideological space that has been monopolized by secular considerations (e.g. the curricula in secular schools).

In all of the above forms of competition, we see that 'retaining control over the issues of their key myths, symbols and ideas is a major concern of religious organisations that are worried by the prospect of their sacred truths being stolen or misused by others' (Beckford and Richardson 2007, 399). In the remainder of this section, these categories of religious-secular competition for ideological hegemony are discussed with relevant country-based or issue-based examples.

Many modern legal regimes contain laws that are opposed by secular groups as archaic and because they encroach on individual liberties. However, the laws are, to a large extent, relics of a religious conception of morality; accordingly, religious groups resist secular demands for the repeal of such laws to maintain their historical role in shaping public morality and social conduct. For many religious groups, retaining such influence is essential to remaining *socially* relevant in an increasingly modernized world. Of course, religions can also strive for social relevance by doctrinal modification. Thus, religious canons can become more accommodating of pervasive social practices in order to maintain membership. The rapid proliferation of 'gay' churches in the United States is a case in point (*USA Today*, 19 October 2011). On the contrary, Iannaccore (1994) points out that by becoming less strict, churches become weaker. Further, there is a limit to how much modification a religious doctrine might be able to accommodate; constant adaptations of doctrine may make religion appear more like fashion.

Examples of competition between religious and secular groups include the vigorous early (and still lively) resistance of Catholic religious institutions to pro-abortion laws. In addition, the decriminalization of homosexuality has been violently opposed by religious groups in many countries. In India, for example, a Delhi High Court ruling to the effect in 2009 managed to manufacture a rare unity between its many religious groupings, who univocally protested against the deregulation *(Daily News & Analysis,* 3 July 2009). Even in countries where religious groups have been more accommodating of statutory changes – that better reflect changes in social realities – issues such as the state regulation of homosexuality remain bones of contention between religious and secular groups. As recently as March 2012, the Church of England vociferously opposed a proposed amendment that would recognize homosexual families on par with heterosexual ones, arguing that 'families' by definition, are heterosexual (*The Guardian*, 11 March 2012).

In addition to opposing the secularly motivated deregulation of the above practices, some religious groups have also been active in demanding greater regulation of, if not a complete ban on, new scientific activities. Developments in medicine, genetics and bioethics have potentially increased religions' role as a source to provide laws to regulate research and therapies (Beckford and Richardson 2007). While Palmer (2004) surveys the religious-secular competition for the right to regulate cloning-related issues, similar debates also exist over gene therapies and religion-based therapies (new-age healing, for example). With respect to religion-based therapies, secular groups have demanded stronger regulations based on secular consumer protection, patient protection and child protection principles (Beckford and Richardson 2007).

Finally, ideological competition between religious and secular groups have centred around the degree to which religious teachings may feature in the secular curriculum of secular educational institutions. An example of this is the intense religion/secular debate, in the early 2000s in the United States, over whether 'creationism' or 'Intelligent Design' should be included in the high school syllabus for Biology as one among many theories (including Darwinian Evolution) explaining the origin of mankind (*New York Times*, 20 December 2005). Similar debates have also punctuated curriculum design in subjects such as history and civics. When religious groups' demands for having religious 'facts' included in secular curricula have been rejected, they have given rise to a reluctance among religious parents to have their children attend secular schools. Fetzer and Soper (2005) report that many Muslim parents are hesitant to send their children to secular schools, citing inconsistencies between the secular curriculum and religious doctrine. On the other hand, when religious groups have succeeded in their agenda to have secular curricula contain religious 'facts', outraged secular groups have resisted their protest in routine and innovative ways. In 2005, outraged by the teaching of 'Intelligent Design' in Kansas Public Schools, Bobby Henderson, a physics graduate, wrote to the Kansas State Board of Education outlining an alternative religious cosmogony (Henderson 2005). Henderson supplied drawings of the supreme being of his religion, the Flying Spaghetti Monster. According to Cowan (2007, 360), Henderson's drawings of the 'supreme being' resembled a plate of 'pasta and meatballs with a pair of eyeballs mounted on breadstick stalks'. Henderson argued that if one religion's beliefs about the origins of intelligent life merited classroom time, then there was no room to deny the same treatment to another set of religious beliefs.

The following case study illustrates how advocacy by religious groups – in the interests of maintaining doctrinal integrity – can be to the detriment of secular and state interest, and promote intense competition to exert influence over public policy.

Box 3.14: The Roman Catholic Church and public health in the Philippines[8]

In the early 1990s, as HIV consciousness became pervasive among the population in the Philippines, prevention measures undertaken by the government included the promotion of the usage of condoms and the introduction of HIV-sensitive sexual education programmes in secondary schools. The Catholic clergy in the country mounted a strong objection to both the proposals on the grounds that safe sex solutions to the problem of HIV condone promiscuous and sexually permissive behaviour. In addition, the clergy argued that promoting early awareness of sexuality among adolescents, in conjunction with the encouragement of condom usage, would license irresponsible sexual behaviour and, by devaluing the concept of moral responsibility, produce only symptomatic cures.

As church and state went into an impasse over a proposed HIV-AIDS control bill, secular sections of the Philippine society, including the print and broadcast media, roundly criticized, what they considered, an over-jealous intrusion of religion on a critical matter of public policy, namely public health. In addition, among many government health workers, the dominant perception was that the clergy was trying its utmost to influence the government's HIV and reproductive health policies. In general, as a 2003 survey revealed, these public health officials do not see it as a part of their job description to promote pre-marital celibacy and abstinence and post-marital abstinence, even if most might adhere to these principles within private lives.

On the other hand, the clergy's opposition to pragmatic government interventions to contain HIV transmission has generated significant support among parents and school administrators who remain unwilling to endorse the introduction of a sex education module into the school curriculum.

The above instance of religion-state (and religion-secular) competition suggests how influential religious groups' advocacy-related activities can mobilize critical public support against government social intervention initiatives, leading to a policy standstill.

Box 3.15: Religious advocacy in Singapore – the case of AWARE

In Singapore, the religious-secular competition for control over ideological spaces has been largely non-existent. This has been largely due to the commonly acknowledged (by both religious and secular groups) hegemony of the state in framing collective goals and imposing its ideological narrative from the top. Nonetheless, skirmishes between religious groups and the state and religious and secular groups to exert ideological influence occur periodically. In 1987, 16 members of the Catholic community were arrested for aggressive social activism under the ISA (Internal Security Act). In connection with this episode, the Christian Conference of Asia was dissolved on the grounds that radical social action programmes are acts of political advocacy, which religious groups undertake to refrain from at the time of registration (Hill 2004). The controversy generated by the government crackdown on the involvement of religion in politics led to the Maintenance of Religious Harmony Act, which specifically bans political/social advocacy by religious groups (MRHA 1989).

Much more recently, the AWARE (Association of Women for Action and Research) saga showcased the potential for ideological competition between religious and secular groups to turn divisive. In March 2009, a group of conservative Chinese Christian women took over AWARE's executive council as they were unhappy with AWARE's alleged pro-gay education courses taught at some schools (*The Economist*, 7 May 2009). The old, liberal guard forced an extraordinary general meeting to table a no-confidence motion, which saw an unprecedented turnout and a spike in membership in the organization. At the meeting, the new council lost the no-confidence motion and resigned. Throughout the episode, the government did not actively interfere, but urged those involved to be tolerant, and to settle the issue democratically (Channel NewsAsia, 26 April 2009).

According to Olson (2007, 349), partnership activities constitute a third category of political activities and – as the name suggests – involve 'working with a government entity to address a specific problem or provide a specific service'. The potential for religion-government partnerships has continued to expand over time as governments have increasingly turned to faith-based initiatives (FBIs) and FBOs to share the economic burdens of social interventions and to improve the effectiveness with which such interventions are delivered (Farnsley 2007). FBIs enable organizations to deliver social services using public funds while retaining their religious character and identity.

That said, the provision of public funds for such FBOs mandate that they satisfy several criteria, including: not denying their services to members of other religions; not discriminating in recruitment against those who hold different religious beliefs; and, an abstinence from evangelization and proselytization-related activities in the course of administering publicly funded social support programmes (Farnsley 2007). Against this context, partnerships between the state and religious group can generate: inter-religious competition for access to public funds; inter-religious grievances over the abuse of public funds to boost religious market share; and religious-secular discord over how FBOs dilute the church-state division.

In numerous countries in Asia, including the Philippines, Papua New Guinea and Taiwan, FBIs have long been popular as they have legitimated culturally/ religiously dissonant social interventions initiated by the government (e.g. with respect to HIV interventions). Such partnerships between the state and religious groups have remained relatively uncontroversial, primarily because of religion's large influence on social life and a pervasive mistrust – especially among rural communities – of the policies of a remote, bureaucratized government.

In the United States, however, the 'charitable choice' law of 1996[9] – which weakened the restrictions on religious organizations competing for public funds to deliver social interventions – have prompted an escalation of debate among the pro- and anti-FBI camps about the viability and the constitutional legitimacy of these laws. While proponents of the laws have responded by publishing guidebooks informing congregations of their newly acquired entitlements to public funds (Esbeck et. al. 2004), secular individuals and groups have questioned, both, the efficacy and constitutionality of the new model (Kramnick and Moore 1997). Sider and Unruh (2001) pose a further dilemma by suggesting that many instances of social interventions – such as substance abuse rehabilitation or preventing criminal recidivism – are likely to be more effective when a spiritual dimension is present in the correctional strategy. When such spiritual exhortations can positively influence the impact of social aid, the legal restrictions against religious instruction as a part of aid administration can become contentious, even on secular grounds.

While secular concerns about the efficiency and legitimacy of FBIs have been routinely raised, the following case study illustrates how religious groups might find it difficult to use public funds to provide non-sectarian social services without compromising their religious identity or desiring religious outcomes. As Sider and Unruh (2001, 269) report, many FBOs view social services and evangelism as inextricably linked; many more may desire evangelistic outcomes without explicitly expressing this goal to clients – 'They hope to bring people to God through their actions, and not through their words.'

Box 3.16: Catholic adoption agencies and homosexuality in the UK

In 2007, in the UK, the Tony Blair government introduced the Equality Act, which would – once in effect – forbid schools, businesses and other agencies from refusing services to people on the grounds of their sexual orientation. In addition, Mr Blair categorically stated that FBOs will *not* be exempt from the provisions of the act (*Exeter Express & Echo*, 30 January 2007). The act will directly impact faith-based adoption agencies that have had a traditional partnership with the state in providing adoption services, by requiring them to not discriminate against homosexual couples wanting to adopt children.

Citing conscientious objections based on religious doctrine, the leader of Catholics in England and Wales, supported by the Church of England, has gone on record to warn that Catholic adoption agencies would close rather than place children with gay couples. Religious opposition to the indiscriminate imposition of the 'secular' Act has made way to the House of Commons, with Catholic MPs filing petitions that acknowledged the vital role that faith-based adoption agencies have played in placing children with caring families. They argued that these organizations would lose funding if the Act was applied to them and compromise the provision of a critical social service; and, called on the government to review its inflexible stand (*Exeter Express & Echo*, 30 January 2007).

Box 3.17: Faith-based Voluntary Welfare Organizations and the politics of partnership in Singapore

In Singapore, while political participation through electoral and advocacy activities by religious groups is expressly proscribed, state-religion participation has flourished in the provision of social services (E.Tan 2008). This relatively more accommodating attitude towards religious groups in the social sector is consistent with the state's idea of religions essentially as providers of personal spiritual bases to individuals and material support for the community.

Thus, faith-based voluntary welfare organizations (FBVWOs) have come to form an integral component in Singapore's 'many helping hands' social assistance programmes. The provision of social services by FBVWOs is generally 'faith blind and unconditional' (E. Tan 2008, 69). Indeed, FBVWOs cutting across religious faiths, report that their services are accessed by individuals of other faiths and denominations (Eng 2008; Mansor and Ibrahim 2008; Mathews 2008). While FBVWOs (especially those affiliated with proselytizing faiths) expressly deny that the scope for evangelical activity constitutes a key motivation in providing social services, most FBVWOs contain provisions for providing religious knowledge on a passive basis (i.e. to those who seek it).

The potential for faith-based social-service provision to contain evangelical messages or proselytization activities generates the risk of inter-religious tension. While Singapore has largely steered clear of conflicts of this sort – due to judicious self-regulation by FBVWOs themselves and the strict oversight maintained by regulatory watchdogs – continued emphasis on the need to keep the social sector free from evangelical zeal has been deemed essential. In this context, public service officers have sought to be informed by knowledge of the ways that an evangelical dimension may be present in a faith-based social service setting.

Sider and Unruh (2001) identify degrees of evangelism-social service nexus in the activities of FBVWOs. In ascending order, they are:

- *passive* (evangelistic materials and religious instruction/counselling are provided to those who seek it);
- *invitational* (clients are invited to religious activities where an evangelistic message is presented);
- *relational* (program staff/volunteers form relationships with clients and disseminate religious information/counselling to clients);
- *integrated, optional* (where service provision has a clearly religious character and volunteers explicitly invite clients to convert, while clients reserve the right to opt out of participating in/responding to religious practices/teaching); and,
- *integrated, mandatory* (where religious instruction in a core component of service delivery).

In outlining the degree to which religious content can be fused in social service provision, guidelines need to note that some forms of evangelical activity might be innocuous, while others can generate inter-religious hostility.

Mission schools in Singapore provide good examples in establishing the limits of acceptable evangelical and religious activity in the performance of a social function. These schools fall into the grey areas of FBOs, given their religious character and their secular function. Most such schools have at least a century-long tradition embracing a form of evangelism that would fall under what Sider and Unruh (2001) categorize as 'integrated but optional'. While religious practices (catechism classes, chapel services, etc.) are common at such schools – and often seen as indispensable to preserving their distinctive religious character – opt out provisions from religious practices for dissenting students have long been in place (Goh 2008). In addition, as Kong et. al. (1994) mention, Singapore's independent schools such as Convent of the Holy Infant Jesus (CHIJ) had put into place mechanisms to prevent the usage of public funds for proselytization and to schedule religious instruction for before and after school hours. As such, mission schools have largely been able to maintain their religious activities without generating any significant religious discord.

Nonetheless, sporadically, controversies about proselytization at such schools have arisen when opt-out rights are violated. For example, imparting religious instruction during secular class time gives no choice to students who do not want to receive such messages. More generally, due to the nature of the student–teacher relation, when teachers provide religious instruction within school hours, at times and places not designated for such instruction, the student's ability to opt out is tacitly compromised.

Finally, Olson (2007) identifies as a fourth type of religious activity in political spaces – 'gap-filling activities'. According to Olson (2007, 449), gap-filling activities involve working within the community to influence 'the distribution of resources or the enforcement of values directly – without government assistance'. Accordingly, gap-filling activities are equated with both charitable (i.e. material) or charismatic (i.e. spiritual) gifts, although such gifts are often distributed in tandem. Essentially, gap-filling activities by religious groups are more prominently and frequently observed in communities where safety nets for the socially and economically marginalized are not adequate. Conversely, it has been argued that economic growth (and the associated rise in economic security) obviates the need for religion to play a social (or gap-filling) function. In some cases, this has led to the retreat of religious groups from (or, at least, subservience within) the public domain and secular space (Norris and Inglehart 2004).

Gap-filling activities can provide a channel through which religious groups generate competitive advantages and grow. Indeed, the dramatic growth of Pentecostalism in many parts of Africa has been attributed to situations whereby 'neoliberal forces have eroded the capacity of liberal democratic states to provide education, health and welfare' (Comaroff and Comaroff 2003, 121). The ability of Pentecostal churches to provide such welfare and support has been a key reason for their growth. Moreover, in many postsecular Western cities the growing prominence of FBOs in urban environments is largely a reaction to the retreat of the state and secular agencies (and the associated safety nets they provide) in public life. The confluence of welfare provision and faith motivation is, however, an area that is replete with tension and ambiguity, as gap-filling activities can – in various ways – lead to allegations of the manipulation of under-privileged segments of society (e.g. the homeless – see Cloke et al. 2005, 2010).

In Washington, for example, Salvadoran migrant churches have been shown to keep in close contact with their sister churches in El Salvador in order to provide them with resources and funds, and to support community development projects (see Menjívar 1999). The motivations for such engagement and initiatives are, however, evangelism-driven rather than development-driven. As one interviewee commented, 'we only keep in touch with our own countries if it's going to help them accept Christ as their savior. And then the nationality doesn't matter any more. What's important is that we bring them the good news, the Word. This is a much better gift than any amount of money or clothes you can send' (cited in Menjívar 1999, 607). Thus even when transnational religious communities are given the option of arbitraging the development gap by supporting their home-country communities, they do so out of evangelical intent rather than needs-based necessity. In this instance, gap-filling activities provide little more than a pretext for evangelical engagement with society.

Because gap-filling activities are defined by the absence of state support – either financially or logistically – restrictions on combining social support provision with evangelical activity are generally absent. This, by implication, means that the potential for religion-state competition is greatly attenuated. However, gap-filling activities by religious groups can generate intense inter-religious competition, especially when the accompanying evangelical activity is aggressive and – by threatening to change the status quo of religious composition of a community – makes other religious groups insecure about losing adherents. The ethics of such activities are also a frequent topic of dispute, especially when the distribution of aid or other material resources is conflated (or perceived to be conflated) with religious instruction, evangelism and proselytism. When insecure groups constitute the majority religious faith of the community and wield considerable political power, they can impose political and social pressure on religious groups to cease their gap-filling activities.

Historically, gap-filling has been a bone of contention between Christianity/ Catholicism and the traditional religions of communities. Better-funded Christian missions often encouraged religious conversions – as a mode of expanding religious market share – among community members in order to enjoy economic and social benefits. Such benefits are viewed by some as a form of allurement that can impact the freedom of thought, and the freedom of religious choice (i.e. the freedom to think about religion in a critical and detached way) of the recipients. It has been argued that the recipients of charitable giving have become part of a culture of religious materialism, in which religion provides not just spiritual edification, but material benefits as well (see, e.g. Mahadev 2014). In light of this, it is clear that while in some instances 'charity can be reproduced as love and friendship, a gratuitious and creative giving', in many other it reflects 'a continuing pursuit of, control of, and power over the socially excluded other' (Cloke 2010, 233, 235).

Indeed, as discussed in more detail below, the acts of charity associated with gap-filling activities are often underwritten by 'an expectation and an implicit demand for acquiescence from the beneficiaries' (Hollenbach and Ruwanpura 2011, 1299), especially when such beneficiaries are from the most underprivileged segments of society. That being said, the vulnerability of recipients should not be implied. As Woods (2013a) highlights, the beneficiaries of charity are just as liable to exploit the providers as they are to be exploited. Many feign engagement with or interest in the religious undertones of the providers in order to be seen in a more favourable light; some even 'convert' in order to take advantage of the material benefits associated with religious affiliation, while maintaining their previous religious identities. Such dualistic religious behaviours highlight the agency of some recipients in being able to use religious groups to their own advantage. We explore in more detail below some of the issues surrounding the 'ethics' of the gift.

Box 3.18: Gap-filling activities and the ethics of the gift

Marcel Mauss's (1954) original theory of the gift articulated that even an apparently 'pure gift' – that is, one which is apparently given selflessly and without expectation of reciprocity – compels reciprocity in some way or another. Such compulsion is implicit to the act of gift-giving, as it is a deep-rooted part of human sociality. Such an insight complicates the gap-filling activities of many religious groups. Even if all measures are taken to ensure the 'purity' of the gift, it is difficult for the recipient not to feel indebted in some way or another to the giver. Such feelings are exacerbated when gifts are given by figures of religious authority. Moreover, in many postcolonial societies westerners can be treated with unduly high regard, further enforcing the feeling of indebtedness. Korf et al. (2010) take such logic one step further by arguing that in the context of post-tsunami Sri Lanka, the charitable acts of Christians – whether wittingly or not – generated a feeling of indebtedness and need for reciprocity among the receivers. In this instance, they argued that reciprocity would necessarily entail a return of religious patronage; a process that could result in religious conversion. Buddhist nationalists in Sri Lanka argue that when populations that are materially impoverished and/or socially disadvantaged are presented with gifts of charity, they are being forced into a position of duress: a process that is deemed to be 'unethical'.

In this sense, gift-giving can be viewed as a form of competitive action on behalf of religious groups; a strategy of evangelism or favour-winning that confuses material inputs with spiritual outputs. Although gifting and other gap-filling activities may, on the surface at least, help to address immediate material needs, the recipients can also be 'aided and ad(minister)ed and disciplined in additionally wounding ways' (de Alwis 2009, 122). Not only that, but gap-filling activities may evoke suspicion and distrust from other religious groups, given the potential for persuasion that such activities engender. In partial response to such actions (which are often embroiled within broader debates that intersect with ideas pertaining to religious nationalism and protectionism), some dominant religious groups have leveraged debates surrounding religious coercion and 'unethical' conversion in the pursuit of passing 'anti-conversion' legislation. While such legislation has proven to be problematic – and is rarely passed – it provides an extreme indication of how unfairly some religious groups view the charitable actions of others (see, e.g. Owens 2007).

The discussion in Box 2.4 with regard to India suggests that gap-filling activities continue to rouse suspicions of being pretexts for evangelical activities leading to mass conversions and – in states with weak security enforcement mechanisms – disrupt social harmony and endanger the security of individual and institutions involved in gap-filling activities.

Competition and conflict in quasi-secular spaces

Quasi-secular spaces are ostensibly secular spaces that are appropriated by religious groups in order to achieve a religious objective or outcome. As such, they are typically agentic, as they provide alternative channels that (often minority) religious groups can use to establish a spatial presence, to compete and to grow. They are also materially and symbolically ambiguous, and are often associated with the assertion or defence of religious identity. Accordingly, as religious asymmetry (i.e. the balance of power between competing religious groups) increases, minority religious groups often retreat behind secular spaces and practices in order to compete in less disruptive ways. In other words, rather than competing for presence in religious space, minority groups often occupy different (usually secular) spaces that enable new forms of competition to proliferate. Indeed, given Massey's (2005, 9) recognition of space as 'the sphere . . . of coexisting heterogeneity', it could be argued that all spaces – whether religious or secular – would have an element of the 'quasi' to them.

Given that such 'new' forms of competition typically blur the distinction between the religious and the secular, they are replete with politics and conflated ambition. In a more conceptual sense, quasi-secular spaces provide an important insight into the nature of sacredness and religious meaning. As Chidester and Linenthal (1995, 18) argue, the sacred is an 'empty signifier', yet 'by virtue of its emptiness could mean anything or nothing, its emptiness is filled with meaningful content as a result of specific strategies of symbolic engagement'. An examination of quasi-secular spaces therefore provides a revealing insight into how context 'determines the conditions for different communities to become established on the soil of a given society' (Hervieu-Leger 2002, 99) and the resulting assemblages of religion in space. In the highlands of Cambodia, for example, it has been argued that the quasi-secular spaces of the house church are in fact 'spaces where [Christian] highlanders can regain agency in the face of increasingly losing political and economic power' (Baird 2009, 459). Similarly, in post-conflict Croatia the Baptist Church leveraged 'secular advantages' (Henkel and Sakaja 2009, 51) in order to gain strength and build presence.

In what follows, we explore three variants of quasi-secular space: those that are sites of secrecy and subterfuge, those that enable informal patterns of worship, and those that are associated with sites of degradation. Each variant is embedded within ostensible secular space, but enables inter-religious and religious-secular forms of competition to proliferate. Following that, we expand the frame of consideration to include not just quasi-secular spaces – those that are primarily secular, but have a religious undertone – but quasi-*religious* spaces as well. Quasi-religious spaces are those that combine multiple religious meanings into a single space. In turn, this can cause confusion as to which group has legitimate claims to the space.

Quasi-secular spaces as sites of secrecy and subterfuge

As the regulation of religious groups increases, quasi-secular spaces become an increasingly important strategic tool used by minority religious groups to compete and grow. Specifically, the most competitive religious groups may appropriate secular spaces as strategies of secrecy (in order to be discreet) or subterfuge (in order to be misleading). The pervasive use of secular spaces by evangelical Christian groups operating within the 10/40 Window, for example, means that Christian activity is often more strongly associated with the secular spaces of social ministries than it is the church building.

Box 3.19: The strategic use of quasi-secular spaces by evangelical Christian groups in Sri Lanka

The actions of evangelical Christian groups operating in Sri Lanka are restricted by Buddhist surveillance and protectionism. However, rather than restricting the competitiveness and growth of evangelical groups, such restrictions usually encourage different strategies of growth instead (Woods 2012b, 2013a). Specifically, strong Buddhist surveillance encourages evangelical groups to evangelize through social ministries such as aid distribution, children's education and English tuition. Such acts have been termed 'clandestine proselytizing' (Gerhardt 2008, 920), and are typically reliant upon the occupation of secular spaces by evangelical groups. This invariably involves a conflation of the religious and the secular through different forms of engagement and space. It is such conflation that causes secular spaces to be imbued with a quasi-secular character, as the engagement is often driven by evangelical intent.

More specifically, Woods (2013a) shows that, rather than competing on religious terms, evangelical groups often meet a non-religious (i.e. secular) need of society, such as education, English tuition, medical care or food provision. The distribution of such services occurs within secular spaces that are not imbued with any overtly religious meaning or intent. Such services do, however, bring evangelical groups closer to local communities, and enable the process of religious influencing to begin. Accordingly, it is shown how 'acceptance into the social structure foreshadows acceptance into the religious structure, with evangelical intent permeating the behaviours and actions of frontier pastors' (Woods 2013a, 658). The focus on social ministries that are enacted through secular spaces enable evangelical groups to express religious agency in more subtle (and therefore less affrontive) ways, which can ultimately lead to he 'rupturing of the seemingly hegemonic spaces of the current [Buddhist] order, producing new lines of flight and new spaces of hope' (Cloke 2010, 234). It enables Christian groups to infiltrate the most hostile (and homogeneously Buddhist) villages, and to begin the process of religious influencing. Engaging society through quasi-secular spaces plays an important role in the re-framing of Christianity in the public domain. It has a generally positive effect, with the use of quasi-secular spaces being as much about changing community perceptions of Christianity as it is about religious competition, conversion and growth.

Quasi-secular spaces as sites of informal worship

In religious contexts where the presence and praxis of minority religious groups is restricted by a dominant religion, symbols of religious presence are often eschewed in order to avoid surveillance. Religious buildings, for example, are one of the clearest symbols of religious presence, and of the spatial encroachment of marginal or 'other' religious groups. As such, in these contexts, secular spaces are often used for religious gatherings and worship instead. For minority Christian groups operating in hostile religious environments, the house is typically used as a substitute for the church as it 'provide[s] an interface that camouflages the sacred other in the form of the secular' (Woods 2013b, 1062). Such spaces of informal worship constitute a second form of quasi-secular space; one that integrates both religious and secular practices and activities in one site.

Importantly, such quasi-secular spaces of informal worship also imbue minority groups with a degree of self-empowerment, autonomy and religious leverage. They are instrumental in enabling religious competition in contexts where it may otherwise be restricted. In China, for example, it has been widely accepted that the house church movement enabled the survival and promotion of Christianity during the Cultural Revolution (1966–76) and after (Kao 2009; Liu 2009; Wielander 2009). Since then, the use of secular spaces for religious introduction and instruction has expanded, with Yang (2005, 437) noting how McDonald's restaurants have become important gathering places for worship and Bible study in China, as 'it is an accessible and acceptable public place to meet a stranger without exposing one's home or office'. Quasi-secular spaces are implicitly more accessible than religious spaces, and more meaning-laden than secular spaces. In China, for instance, both McDonald's and Christianity are believed to be similar inasmuch as they share the same values of being 'progressive, liberating, modern and universal' (Yang 2005, 425).

Box 3.20: The strategic necessity of the house church in Sri Lanka

In Sri Lanka, regulation of evangelical Christian groups is high. It is therefore common for evangelical churches to 'operate in and through non-codified (often secular) spaces in order to downplay or camouflage their religious alterity' (Woods 2013a, 662). More practically speaking, many evangelical groups face difficulties in securing the official approvals (and funds) needed to legally register, build or expand a formal church building. Likewise, the formal renting of function rooms or other 'secular' venues for worship purposes is often frowned upon. Beyond such practical considerations, the use of houses to hold worship services serves a more strategic imperative as well. In a country where religious buildings are easily identified and respected, the house church downplays the competitiveness of evangelical groups. Their presence is harder to detect, because the physical appearance of the house is non-differentiated (or non-religious) in appearance. As a result, this enables churches to avoid the 'intense contestation' (Kong 2010, 757) that can arise from the outward appearance of religious otherness. More specifically, Woods (2013b) shows how house churches are constructed through the development of 'sacred networks' that emerge when a group of Christians assemble together for prayer, worship and bible study. Such networks are place-agnostic, meaning they are not dependent upon a particular (sanctified) location to yield effect. This renders the Sri Lankan house church an ephemeral, mobile and discreet movement that is almost impossible to regulate and contain. It also prevents surveillance, and reduces the risk of a building being taken away, razed or attacked by anti-Christian factions that may oppose the growth of Christianity.

Appropriating the secular space of the house for worship purposes also enables evangelical groups to infiltrate areas that are previously untouched by Christianity in a subtle and non-disruptive way. The Sri Lankan house church is typically devoid of any markings, objects or other ornamentation associated with Christianity. Such a non-descript appearance is intentional. Rendering the space 'religious' could be off-putting and inaccessible to non-Christians that may otherwise be willing to experience Christianity, as 'visiting a church building holds certain negative connotations that the presumed secularity associated with the house circumvents' (Woods 2013b, 1067). Such physical characteristics of the Sri Lankan house church are, however, markedly different from those in Singapore, for example. Kong's (2002, 1581) case study of a Singapore house church shows how the 'external facade of secularity' is in contrast to the 'internal presentation of religiosity' depicted by rows of chairs to replicate pews and stained glass windows. In Sri Lanka the veneer of the house is maintained in order to render it an accessible space; one that enables non-Christians to experience an alternative religion in an acceptable and non-threatening way.

While the Sri Lankan house church helps evangelical groups circumvent inter-religious conflict, it is imbued with a politics of its own. For many Sri Lankans, using the house as a place of worship is met with confusion as they tend to revere the permanence and symbolism of religious spaces, not quasi-secular ones. (Interestingly, this contrasts with the general acceptance of the house church in China, which is guided by a Marxist-informed interpretation of what constitutes 'religious space' – see Cheng 2003). In addition, services would often be disrupted by the everyday noises, smells and activities of the house and its occupants. The behaviours, attitudes and actions of the hosts would also be put under close scrutiny by attendees, as a lack of witness (or perceived religiosity) could invalidate the experience. As a result, many 'converts' to Christianity found it difficult to break with their past religions. This calls into question the effectiveness of the house church as a source of competitive advantage and growth, as it struggles to 'nurture clearly demarcated expressions of faith and encourages dualistic patterns of religiosity to evolve instead' (Woods 2013b, 1070).

Quasi-secular spaces of degradation

Crises – both natural and humanitarian – create numerous opportunities for religious groups to provide relief and engage communities through various gap-filling initiatives. Doing so often involves religious groups occupying secular spaces of degradation in order to pursue a religious directive. When this happens, such spaces become quasi-secular in character. The conflation of religious ambition (e.g. evangelism, proselytism) with secular action (e.g. reconciliation, development, relief) has triggered much criticism and debate from both religious and secular agencies. Such criticisms are exacerbated when spaces of degradation arise in less economically developed countries, and are appropriated by religious agencies from more economically developed countries, as the potential for economic exploitation and manipulation increases significantly.

Box 3.21: Christian charity in the aftermath of the 2004 Indian Ocean tsunami in Sri Lanka

The Indian Ocean tsunami that devastated various south- and south-east Asian coastal areas on Boxing Day 2004 provides a useful case study of how quickly, effectively and contentiously evangelical Christian groups react to crises. In Sri

Lanka, a variety of churches, religious NGOs and 'secular' NGOs with hidden religious motives, and FBOs entered the most adversely affected parts of the country in order to distribute aid and, in some instances, proselytize. Their reactions to the tsunami (in terms of both aid distribution and community reconstruction) were both rapid and generous, even though many of the organizations came from overseas. In particular, missionaries originating from America and South Korea arrived en masse to provide aid to those affected. Although the majority of missionaries arrived on tourist visas (meaning their intentions were either undeclared, or assumed to involve humanitarian work) allegations of aggressive proselytizing soon spread, especially the use of financial allurements (*aleppa*), incentives (*unanduwa*) and affection to encourage recipients to convert to Christianity.

Accordingly, the gap-filling activities of Christian-affiliated organizations in the aftermath of the tsunami were broadly criticized for exploiting a humanitarian emergency in order to proselytize. They were accused of 'distort[ing] the right to freedom of religion given the potential of conversion due to allurement' (Owens 2007, 329–30). Indeed, one group from Waco, Texas, went so far as to set up temporary 'tsunami ministries' in order to reach out to afflicted communities. Both Buddhists and mainline Christian churches condemned such 'culturally insensitive and hubristic activities' (Matthews 2007, 468), which received considerable attention in the international media. Such an example illustrates how secular spaces of degradation can easily adopt a quasi-secular character when they are appropriated and used by religious groups to achieve an overarching religious objective. Given that such objectives are often competitive in nature, the appropriation of such spaces is often associated with allegations of exploitation, and can be a precursor to conflict.

4

Globalization and Religious Competition and Conflict

Introducing globalization and religion

Even though there is no singular conception of what 'globalization' is, few would deny today that 'we live in a globalized world'. One useful understanding of globalization is as a process that incubates, fosters and makes indispensable, interactions between geographically remote individuals, communities, societies and nation(state)s. Thus, globalization has relied on, and has been driven by, 'globalizing' technologies, which increase the scope for, and the frequency and pace of, such interactions. Technological innovations – the hardware of globalization – include mass transportation systems; broadcasting systems; communication systems; and data storage and sharing systems. Such innovations have resulted in the emergence of cross-border networks that have, on the one hand, made life more connected and more fulfilling, but on the other hand, have made it more complex and confusing as well. As Taylor (2001, 202) explains:

> One of the most important factors creating unrest in today's world is the unprecedented noise generated by proliferating networks whose reach extends from the local to the global. As networks relentlessly expand, the mix of worlds, words, sounds, images, and ideas becomes much more dense and diverse. When this media-mix approaches the boiling point, multiple cognitive and cultural changes become inevitable.

Cross-border networks do not just enable the circulation of meanings, orientations and ideas, but they are often constitutive of them as well (see Emirbayer and Goodwin 1994). Networks are therefore integral to an understanding of the global movement and settlement of religion, as it is 'within and through networks [that] actors carve out spaces to dwell, itineraries, and everyday routines, drawing from religious symbols and tropes to reflect on and orient their own praxis and to "sacralize" nature and build environment' (Vasquez 2008, 169). As such, there has been a rethinking of the way that space is conceived. The production of space has evolved, from being an intrinsically bounded entity, to a 'constellation of connections' within 'wider cultural circuits' (Crang et al. 2003, 439; cf. Massey 1992). Such constellations contribute to the contestations that arise around transnational formations and imaginations, and have brought about dramatic changes in the way that religion is lived and enacted. Such changes are not welcomed by all, and can be both a cause and effect of religious competition and conflict.

Technological advancements change individuals' and communities' incentives for, and constraints against, greater interaction with the rest of the world. As Hannerz (1992, 218) correctly identifies, '[i]t must now be more difficult than ever, or at least more unreasonable, to see the world . . . as a cultural mosaic, of separate pieces with hard, well-defined edges. Cultural interconnections increasingly reach across the world'. Consequently, globalization has resulted in growing diasporas in various parts of the world. The proliferation of diasporic communities has caused the rapid pluralization of the demographic profiles in many countries; a highly interconnected, multipartite economic order; transnational communities linked by instant, costless communication; information sources (including media organizations) which are global in their reach and influence; not to mention new platforms for – governed by new protocols of – personal and public interaction. At the same time, new communities are formed that are often plagued by the emotional trauma associated with upheaval and physical dislocation from the home country, and exclusion and marginality within the host country (see Vertovec 1999; Vasquez 2008). As the modes of interaction have altered and multiplied, so too has the potential for social-political-economic-ideological competition.

Accordingly, globalizing pressures and processes have influenced the nature of religious competition by producing new sources of debate and new ways of (spatial) engagement; identifying new stakeholders; and, infusing a 'global', deterritorialized character into local, place-specific religious competition. Examples of how globalizing forces have mediated religious competition abound. For example, mass immigration of individuals from Asia and Africa to the west (North America, Europe and Australia) has given rise to diasporas – sustained through technology-enabled maintenance of ties to countries of origin – that demand freedoms for the practice of indigenous religious custom; this has resulted in debates over national identity and assimilation. In addition, the Internet has allowed for 'persecuted' new religious movements to circumvent state sanction and popular antipathy to remain alive and even flourish. The development of religious cyber spaces has also mediated religious competition in other ways. First, because of the ease in setting up and maintaining a religious website, the monopoly of religious specialists over religious ideology has been consistently challenged by lay co-religionists. Second, where such religious cyber spaces have been sophisticated enough to act as platforms for the performance of religious ritual (e.g. engaging in acts of worship, offering confession, issuing religious edicts, etc.), the 'authenticity' of the performance has been called into question. Nonetheless, where there are constraints on religious practices in physical spaces (e.g. on proselytizing in public or the observance of death rituals), their migration into a cyber religious space can/has also functioned as an adaptation helping to keep the ritual and the associated religious identity alive. Last but not least, the almost instant access to global events, combined with the ease of sharing information and communication through cyber social networks, have given rise to religious identities that are not geographically or politically contained. The coalescing of identities around religious affiliation – rather than, around place of residence or citizenship characteristics – is conducive to the development of an imagined community of coreligionists (an *umma* or a global Christendom, for example), which, as discussed in Chapter 2, can challenge and subvert state authority.

The preceding paragraph hints at ways in which the nature of religious competition can be affected by globalizing pressures. However, to systematically understand these effects and their implications for public policy, a conceptual taxonomy is needed. To that end, it is worthwhile noting that, essentially, globalizing processes are concerned with 'flows' or movements of people, goods, money, information and ideas across geographical and political borders. Appadurai (1996, 32) has proposed a highly influential template of understanding these global (especially, cultural) flows. In doing so, he re-conceptualizes culture as 'a complex, overlapping, disjunctive' interplay of flows that are built around five interrelated constructs: ethnoscapes, technoscapes, finanscapes, mediascapes and ideoscapes. While there is no distinct 'religioscape' or 'sacroscape' (as suggested by McAlister 1998 and Tweed 2006 respectively), Appadurai's five -*scapes* can easily be (and often are) appropriated by religious groups, imbued with religious meaning, and become an important part of religious praxis.

Ethnoscapes refer to 'landscapes of people who constitute the shifting world in which we live: tourists, immigrants, refugees, exiles, guestworkers and other

moving groups and persons'; *technoscapes* refer to 'the global configuration, also
ever so fluid, of technology, and of the fact that technology, both high and low, both
mechanical and informational, now moves at high speeds across various kinds
of previously impervious boundaries'; *finanscapes* refer to patterns of movement
and sites of accumulation of global capital; *mediascapes* refer to 'both the
distribution of the electronic capabilities to produce and disseminate information
(newspapers, magazines, television stations, film production studios, etc.), which
are now available to a growing number of private and public interests throughout
the world; and to the images of the world created by these media'; and, *ideoscapes*
refer to chains of images that are 'often directly political and frequently have to do
with the ideologies of states and the counter-ideologies of movements explicitly
oriented to capturing state power or a piece of it' (Appadurai 1996, 33–6).

Appadurai's (1996) emphasis on flows is a critical response to the treatment
of space as a clearly delineated, local entity that is bound together by a unified
cultural system (e.g. the congregation, the neighbourhood, the community). His
contention is that locality should not be automatically equated with stable and
self-contained places that are imbued with collective meaning, authenticity and
intimacy. Instead, locality is something that is produced by global (or, at least,
cross-border) flows that are 'constantly de-territorializing and re-territorializing'
in response to the 'circulation of people, commodities, knowledge and capital'
(Vasquez 2008, 167). Importantly, such flows are recognized as being place-making,
meaning they can lead to the creation of new (implicitly more flexible, dynamic and
often complex) spaces of understanding and meaning. Such spaces are inherently
political in as much as they are imbued with 'contested differentials of power, of
inclusion and exclusion, of cooperation and conflict, of boundary-crossing and
boundary-making' (Vasquez 2008, 169). Simply put, the spaces of flows that are
part and parcel of a globalized world exist at the intersections of dynamic fields of
domination and resistance. According to Tsing (2000, 327) such spaces are 'world-
making' and represent 'not just interconnections, but the recarving of channels
and the remapping of the possibilities of geography'. They can be a source of
emancipation as much as they can perpetuate structures of inequality, power and
control; they can be used as a source of competitive advantage by religious groups,
or they can provide a source of religious conflict. Whatever the outcome, they are
an increasingly integral constituent of religion in/and space.

Appadurai's five dimensions, with some modifications, can be easily and usefully
appropriated to categorize the influence of globalization on the nature of religious
competition. Accordingly, the remainder of the chapter is organized in five sections.
The first explores the new forms of religious organization and movement that have

arisen as a result of globalization. The second deals with (changes in) religious competition arising out of movements of people across national boundaries ('ethnoscapes'). The third examines how technological developments have impacted on traditional religious practices ('technoscapes'). The fourth pays attention to how the architecture of the modern financial system has remodelled existing forms of religious competition and conflict ('finanscapes'). The last section looks at how instant flows of images and narratives of events in the world have crystallized a transnational religious identity and effectively contributed to the globalization of local episodes of religious competition and conflict ('mediascapes' and 'ideoscapes').

Cross-border religious movement and organization in space

Processes of globalization have facilitated a change in the structure and operations of religious groups. This is particularly true for Christian groups which, in recent decades, have fragmented into smaller, more independent churches and denominations that are spiritually and organizationally different from their larger counterparts (e.g. Catholic, Anglican, Methodist and Baptist – see Jenkins 2007). Such fragmentation is, in part, driven by the desire to better leverage the processes of globalization that can lead to cross-border religious dissemination and growth. These organizations operate according to what Castells (2000) refers to as a 'network society' – one that is characterized by decentralized and flexible organization structures, and inter-connected webs of cross-border connections that enable the rapid and international spread of new religious movements. More specifically, it is the adaptive capacity of such movements that grants them a significant degree of competitive advantage as they are typically more responsive to – and better at meeting the needs of – religious consumers in the contemporary world (see Stoll and Levine 1997).

Flexible organizational structures

New religious movements are imbued with specific organizational characteristics that enable them to take maximum advantage of the processes of globalization, and to expand quickly and easily across borders. Globalization has fuelled the growth of transnational networks that bind together religious agencies around the world (see Haynes 2001). Such agencies feed off and strengthen each other's ideas, help each other with funds, contacts and introductions (both religious and secular), and form bodies that aim to improve the well-being of their (and other) community(ies). The cross-border networks that enable the flow of funds and ideas can be both uni-directional and multi-directional, simple and complex. They can both emancipate and empower, or control and subvert. The religious organizations that have been most successful in developing and propagating such networks have been described as 'liturgically lite and flexible' (Wilford 2010, 332), and have become voracious competitors in the marketplace(s) for religion. For example, Gerlach and Hine's (1968) analysis of the growth of the Pentecostal church in Latin America shows how the role of flexible (often decentralized) organization structures and embeddedness within international networks of funding and support can promote the international spread of religious groups, and their adaptation to various cultural contexts. Such networks often extend beyond both religion as well, helping to tie Pentecostal groups to non-religious (i.e. secular, often political) agencies, and to embed them within broader structures of power and authority.

The militant Islamic terrorist organization al-Qaeda provides a good example of a globally dispersed religious organization. Operating a multinational, stateless army of Islamic fighters, it relies heavily on globally dispersed networks of communication and command to expand its presence and to subvert enemy targets. Cooke and Lawrence (2005, 25) explain how al-Qaeda is 'structured around dispersed nodes that communicate with one another in non-linear space', meaning the 'network relies on neither hierarchical chain of command nor conventional rules of engagement. Rather it mobilizes nimble, dispersed and highly elusive units capable of penetrating and disrupting, or even destroying, massive structures'. Indeed, while Cooke and Lawrence refer to the military value of al-Qaeda's organizational structure, the same competitive logic applies to other globally dispersed and decentralized religious groups as well. For example, Pentecostal groups operating in Sri Lanka draw upon global networks of funding and support to further their evangelization efforts and, ultimately, to penetrate and disrupt the Buddhist religious structure. In both cases, it is clear that cross-border religious organizations rely on similar organizational structures in order to spread their influence, compete and grow.

Transnational religious practices and politics

For many globalized religious groups, gap-filling activities provide a core focus of their internationalization efforts. Saddleback Church in the United States, for example, runs training courses for laypersons and the staff of other

Christian churches. Such courses equip them with the skills needed to travel to underdeveloped parts of the world, and to partner with local churches, government, non-governmental and private sector organizations in order to help alleviate social problems such as poverty, disease and illiteracy (Wilford 2010). Transnational gap-filling projects such as these show how the movement of resources (in terms of funds, people, skills and ideas) is typically one way: from the developed to underdeveloped world, often from west to east (but increasingly intra-east as well). This can be problematic, not least for the neo-colonizing actions that it engenders, and the (often negative) reactions of local religious groups. The religio-cultural blending that is associated with transnationalism rarely – if ever – results in equal outcomes, but more often than not leads to the (re)production of dominant cultural representations, and associated structures of inequality (see Glick-Schiller 1997). In sum, transnational religious networks are catalysts for the cross-border growth of religious movements, and a key source of competitive strength and resilience.

Transnational religious groups are, however, often liable to undermine state sovereignty and can, in some instances, reflect an insensitivity to local customs and cultures. Developing this perspective further, it has been argued that such groups have 'weak and insignificant' ties to the spatial environment, and 'no local bonds' (Winter 1961, 103–4) as they tend to rely on a model of fellowship that is essentially placeless. Nuance is, however, needed, as transnational space is typically multidimensional, multiply inhabited and characterized by complex assemblages of networks, interactions and flows (see Crang et al. 2003). Transnational religious networks are a source of 'considerable worldly power' (Gerlach and Hine 1968, 28) that enable their constituent groups to be 'self-governing, self-supporting, and self-propagating' (Lechner and Boli 2003, 390). This can validate claims to local religious markets, and poses a problem to regulatory agencies (often associated with the state) that seek to curtail or control their growth.

Conversely, it has been shown how Islamist movements – alongside other types of politicized religious group – often accommodate themselves to state regulation, irrespective of transnational commitments, ties or aspirations. As Asad (2003, 200) argues: 'no movement that aspires to more than mere belief or inconsequential talk in public can remain indifferent to state power'. Thus, while the role of the modern nation-state has invariably been relativized by processes of globalization, it is not as redundant as some may argue. More specifically, it still plays a central role in the way that global (religious) networks are nucleated; it 'deploy[s] a whole host of legal, social scientific, ideological, bureaucratic, military, and geographic apparatuses to project itself globally and to extract surplus from transnational migrants' (Vasquez 2008, 173). Recognition of the power of the state is, in other words, believed to be a prerequisite to having a formal (i.e. publicly accepted) religious presence.

Moreover, such cross-border sharing of ideas, practices and resources often perpetuates structures of domination, control and inequality (see Levitt and Glick-Schiller 2004). The globalization of religion has been equated with the globalization of capital(ism); both are similar inasmuch as 'particularity [is] only a stepping strategy or stepping stone toward the production of globality' (Peterson et al. 2001, 40). Indeed, the 'production of globality' can be seen to reproduce global patterns of domination and exclusion. As Shamir (2005, 200) argues, contemporary globalization goes hand-in-hand with a 'mobility regime' that operates through a 'selective osmosis' that permits only certain types of movements through and across semi-permeable borders. Indeed, while the movement of people can be regulated and controlled, the movement of religious ideas and beliefs cannot. Such a mismatch often results in global processes not necessarily helping to diffuse global inequality through the blending of cultures and beliefs, but adding to it. This dynamic is explored in more detail in the next section on ethnoscapes.

Ethnoscapes

Historically, the movement of people across geographical locations has been the central instrument for the dispersal of religion around the globe. Conquerors (as in the case of Islam to the Indian subcontinent); colonizers (as in the case of Christianity to the Asian colonies); migrants (as in the case of Chinese religions to Singapore); merchants (as in the case of Hinduism to Bali and Cambodia); and, missionaries (as in the case of Buddhism to Sri Lanka and China) have all contributed to pluralizing religiously homogeneous societies, albeit through different methods (ranging from persuasion, to inducement, to force). However, the cultural and religious heterogenization produced by large-scale migration of peoples over short periods of time differs from the early attempts at disseminating religion, both in its scope for generating religious competition, and in the scale and intensity of such competition.

Sustained mass migration results in what may be termed as the import of whole religious traditions into an alien social-cultural habitat. In such circumstances, migrants' religion plays a vital adaptive function. Depending on the constraints imposed by the external social-political environment, the adaptation via religion can take two distinct forms. First, adaptation might involve reinforcing the religious distinction between migrants and natives and other migrants. Immigrants often use their religious identity to differentiate themselves from the alienating, 'foreign' environments that migration places them in: as Plüss (2009, 494) says, 'often, religious organisations are the first associations that immigrants set up in a new place of residence'. These organizations become sites for (and, later, symbols of) the evolution of a 'new' immigrant (and, distinct from the native) identity based on religious similarities that override cultural, economic and social differences between members. Such an 'alternative cartography of belonging' is often marked by the fact that 'religious icons and sacred shrines, rather than national flags, proclaim these religious spaces' (Levitt 2001a, 20). For migrant communities, it is often their religious identity – more so than their national identity – that helps them overcome the marginality associated with host-country life. Social networks that are spawned by the religious organization are sustained by high levels of bonding social capital and are important cogs in the wheels of migrant life; they provide avenues for socialization, economic opportunities, social safety nets, and provide channels via which migrants can articulate their grievances and social/political/cultural demands.

It is the proliferation and strengthening of such transnational social networks that gives rise to 'simultaneous embeddedness' – a metaphor that is believed to be integral to understandings of transnationalism and migrant's social life. Such a metaphor draws upon the fact that immigrants are often multiply located, and must therefore 'articulate multiple identities to negotiate the demands of different settings across the terrain delineated by the transnational social field' (Vasquez 2008, 158; see also Hannerz 1997; Nederveen Pieterse 2004). The net effect of being multiply located is the emergence of new – often innovative – cultural forms, alongside the desire to find stability in individual and collective identities. Both these transnational effects intersect with religious competition and conflict. In the first instance, the emergence of new cultural (and religious) forms can cause oppositional sentiment to arise among members of similar host-country religious communities. In the second instance, the desire to find stability in individual and collective identities can cause cultural and religious exclusivity, otherness and, ultimately, suspicion. In addition, the desire and, ultimately, failure to recreate a home-country religious environment can also result in feelings of disappointment and can cause feelings of alienation to perpetuate.

Box 4.1: Sacralizing the Brazilian diasporic home in Florida

Brazilian Pentecostals living in Pompano Beach, Florida, constitute a minority diasporic community. The diaspora is not large enough in size to warrant the establishment of formal immigrant organizations that can help them adapt. That, coupled with the fact that many of them live in an alienating environment marked by sprawling shopping malls, busy thoroughfares and gated (local) communities has caused many to carve out their own 'defensive spaces anchored in the domestic sphere' (Vasquez 2008, 170). Such strategies of defence are two-pronged. On the one hand, they re-assert their Brazilian identity through their homes by prominently displaying Brazilian flags and other symbols of their homeland. On the other hand, they sacralize their homes by constructing homemade altars to their patron saints – what Tweed (1999) calls 'transtemporal' and 'translocative' space. The Brazilian diasporic home is, in this sense, meant to symbolize both a slice of 'home' and a slice of 'heaven'; a defensive strategy that constructs the peace, safety and intimacy of the home in opposition to the danger, cruelty and impersonality of the street. Extending the metaphor further, Vasquez (2008, 170) suggests that the good-evil and purity-danger binary 'dovetails with a Manichean cosmos that opposes those who have been baptized in the Spirit (the church) to the temptation-filled outside world'. Central to such sacralization is the integration of interpersonal networks of relatives and friends in Brazil into the diasporic Brazilian home. Such networks are imbued with intimacy, trust, emotional attachment and meaning, causing the sacred domestic space to become like a 'home away from home'.

While the defensive space of the diasporic Brazilian home is one that clearly and overtly resists integration into the American way of life, it is also affected (and, indeed, compromised) by a more intrinsic politics of diasporic life. Many Brazilian migrants live in crowded and cramped apartments that lack the sense of community that is desired, because the inhabitants spend so much time working. Brazilian women in particular also stressed the day-to-day struggles they faced in trying to keep their families fed and healthy. Far from the domestic space being one of warmth and solidarity, therefore, it was more commonly one of alienation and mistrust. The constant struggle of reconciling the difference between the *real* home (in Florida) and the *imagined* home (in Brazil) is a problem faced by many migrant communities, and reveals both the role of religion in constructing a sense of religious similitude, and its limitations when faced with the secularizing limitations (e.g. housing, lifestyle, working practices) of the host-country.

Various reasons have been forwarded to explain why immigrants might choose religious differentiation as an adaptive strategy. Plüss (2009) argues that such a strategy is chosen when migrants experience difficulties in integrating into their new surroundings. Accordingly, a stronger distinctive religious identity provides a form of cultural continuity between their pre- and post-migration lives, which can alleviate the impact of 'uprootedness, alienation, racism and frustration' (Plüss 2009, 495). In addition, Vertovec (2000) suggests that migrants' emphases on religious differentiation is an expression of nostalgia for their homelands (i.e. religious involvement is a substitute for a pre-migration 'way of life'). In the UK, for example, McLoughlin (2005) shows how mosque space is used (and dominated) by *babas* (old, first-generation migrants from South Asia), whose primary orientation remains the Indian subcontinent. The mosque is a space wherein *babas* can escape their status as (socio-economically marginalized) 'nobodies' in the UK, and can regain the 'honour' they would experience in their homelands. The mosque is, in this sense, a space of transnational emancipation, and one of ethno-religious exclusivity as well.

Box 4.2: Jain diamond traders in Hong Kong

Plüss (2005) provides insights into the role of religious networks for Jain diamond traders in Hong Kong. Most Jains in Hong Kong are involved in transnational diamond trading firms that are based in India. Sharing essential or highly differentiated religious identities with co-religionists is key to succeeding in the diamond trade. Jain traders exclusively rely on religious networks to find guarantors to obtain credit from banks to finance the purchase of diamonds. In addition, a large proportion of social interaction between Jains takes place at the Jain temple: frequent and regular visits to the temple are signals to the community at large that one is not avoiding his guarantors and therefore, worthy of continued business trust.

Thus, economic expediency mandates and has sustained a largely unassimilated Jain immigrant community in Hong Kong, one whose members have resisted learning the Cantonese language or establishing any substantial social connections with the native Chinese population. The community continues to endorse and encourage the maintenance of this highly differentiated religious identity: for example, it continues to hire priests from India who are fluent in Hindi and Gujarati but do not speak English, let alone Cantonese.

Whatever migrants' motivations for maintaining an essentialized religious identity might be, it leads to a homogeneous religious culture (i.e. the religious tradition in the migrant's homelands and in their places of residence differ minimally). The implications of this for religious competition are several. First, attempts to extend cultural homogeneity over religious practices – what Lehman (2002, 299) calls 'fundamentalist religious globalization' – are based on arguments that religious beliefs and practices *need* to remain unchanged in a new culture. Thus, religious identities of migrants remain fundamentally opposed to – and continuously resist the hegemony of – the national identity of their adopted lands. The difficulties experienced by France in integrating its largely immigrant Muslim population – by emphasizing *laïcité as* the bedrock of national culture – is a clear example of how fundamentalist religious globalization can accentuate religious competition. Even in countries such as the UK, strategies to accommodate fundamentalist forms of religious globalization by searching 'for a national identity that will simultaneously acknowledges both diversity and sameness' have generated paradoxes of identity (Robertson 2009, 454). Robertson (2009, 457) continues: 'religion is greatly involved in the production and accentuation of this apparent contradiction. On the one hand, religion is frequently the major form of self-identification for migrants, while, on the other hand, intensification and politicization of this increases the tendency for actual or potential political elites to insist upon the formulation of ever sharper, civil-religious national identities for the host country'.

Lehman (2002) distinguishes between 'fundamentalist religious globalization' and 'cosmopolitan religious globalization'. Cosmopolitan religious globalization seeks to produce heterogeneous religious cultures, by incorporating elements of adopted country culture into home country religious tradition. This, to a degree, promotes integration and constitutes the other dimension of how religions might adapt in the face of migration. Plüss (2009) suggests that migrants may seek to attenuate their religious differences and hybridize their religious practices in order to gain greater access to social, political and economic resources. Thus, while cosmopolitan religious globalization might not reduce competition between religious groups and between religious groups and the state, they reduce the extent to which competition takes place on religious grounds.

Finally, the act of migrating can also release individuals from the religious constraints and expectations of their country of origin, and can provide the physical, social and cultural distance and dislocation needed to experiment with religious alternatives. In other words, new local contexts can both expose, and open migrants up to, new religious beliefs and needs. For example, the dislocation experienced by labour migrants from Latin America to Israel caused some to turn to religion in order to help them cope with their new circumstances, even if it was previously shunned (Kemp and Raijman 2003). In a similar vein, Vasquez and Marquardt (2003; see also Vasquez et al. 2001) explore the movement of Salvadoran youths to the United States in the 1980s. They show how young immigrants quickly became embroiled within American inner-city gang culture, and ended up being deported back to El Salvador after being convicted of committing a crime. In El Salvador they re-formed the gang affiliations that they had started in the United States, and were persecuted by a El Salvadoran state that was trying to impart law and order in the aftermath of civil war. Subsequently the deported gang members returned to the United States illegally, working as undocumented immigrants. The point to be made is that at different points throughout their migration pathways between El Savador and the United States, various Pentecostal churches made attempts to engage the youths and to introduce them to Christianity. The fact that such engagements are multiple and successful shows how these churches recognize the distress associated with having to navigate transnational social fields, and how they have become adept at meeting the emotional needs of migrants as a source of competitive advantage and growth.

Technoscapes

Innovations in media technology have historically affected the nature of religious practice and, consequently, the nature of religious competition. For example, printing has long been associated with the Protestant reformation; radio preachers and early televangelists were icons of American religious culture popularized by advances in broadcasting technology. Television continues to be a popular medium for the dissemination of religious discourse in the United States; pastors such as Billy Graham who combine religious passion with media nous are household celebrities (Hoover 2009). In India, as in the United States, the proliferation of television channels devoted exclusively to broadcasting content have given rise to two sociologically important phenomena. The first is a growing relationship between religion and commerce, with 'spiritual' television channels relying on charismatic individuals (and thereby promoting a cult of personality) to keep them commercially viable (much like the competition between secular talk shows). The second is a new possibility for television-mediated 24/7 religious experience while remaining rooted in secular spaces (e.g. houses) and engaged in the secular activities of everyday lives.

Since the 1990s, however, the development and popularization of the Internet have impacted religious practice in hitherto unprecedented ways (especially in societies with high Internet penetration and among individuals with easy and constant access to the World Wide Web). As Bunt (2009, 705) says, 'the Internet, within and between its different elements and forms, holds transformative potential for religions, in terms of representation, networking, by adherents, and application as a proselytising tool'. It has also opened up new (and encroached into old) spaces of religious practice, and has helped to both shape and alter the consumption and experience of religion in various contexts around the world. To understand this potential and how its actualization might (have) alter(ed) the dynamics of religious competition, two prior issues need to be addressed: the first concerns understanding why people/groups/institutions place/publish religious content on the web; second, given the vast amount of religious material on the web, some basic form of classifying the landscape of cyber-religious space is necessary.

According to Bunt (2009) religious material may be placed on the web for several purposes: to engender a sense of identity among existing believers (i.e. produce 'bonding social capital'); to explain religious beliefs or practices to outsiders (i.e. generate 'bridging social capital'); to encourage new adherents (i.e. to proselytize); and to represent offline religious processes and interactions[1] (i.e. to facilitate a vicarious religious experience). In addition to the above, Bafelli (2011) has noted that online presence has long become a prerequisite for most mainstream religious groups, if only to showcase their claims to being 'modern' and to avoid marginalizing the increasingly new media-savvy youth.

The politics of online presence

Online presence – and the techno-religious spaces associated with such presence – is implicated in various politics (see Kong 2001b). On the one hand, online content often originates from an international 'centre' and is consumed by audiences in both the 'centre' and 'periphery'. Such a distinction serves to re-enforce the international distinction between producers and consumers of religious knowledge, directive and influence. On the other hand, however, technology also provides the tools and resources needed for the 'periphery' to resist the ideological imperialism of the 'centre' through both discussion and debate, and the counter-posting of content. Vasquez and Marquardt (2000), for example, document how an apparition of the Virgin Mary that appeared on the windows of a bank building in a strip mall was soon published widely on the Internet, enabling Catholic devotees from around the world to experience the event. More to the point, however, is the fact that this example provided a template in cyberspace for the documentation and sharing of other sightings, meaning that other, often more 'peripheral' locations such as Bosnia-Herzegovina, Mexico City and Argentina could be viewed and accessed alongside the more traditional pilgrimage sites of Fatima and Lourdes. Altogether, they contributed to the co-creation of a 'global digital Marian devotional circuit', one that is 'anchored in particular localities which are beamed globally and stretched worldwide to allow those who cannot be present physically to experience the power of local hierophanies' (Vasquez 2008, 160). In this case, therefore, the Internet has helped transform the sacred landscape into one that is unbounded in cyberspace, and that enables apparitions to be viewed and compared with more established pilgrimage sites on the same terms.

Relatedly, techno-religious spaces generate new freedoms for their users. Such freedoms are numerous, and can be used to both positive or negative effect. They include: freedom from having to travel to and from, and interact within, Cartesian space; freedom from the inconveniences of time and scheduling; freedom of speech; and freedom from the social surveillance and controls determined by race, class and gender, or 'any other form of pretense' (Green 1997, 61; see also Dawson and Hennebry 1999). Indeed, it is the relative anonymity associated with techno-religious space that can enable such freedoms (especially freedom from social surveillance and control) to be exploited. To this end, techno-religious spaces can serve as emancipatory spaces. Brubaker (2012, 14; see also Anderson 2003), for example, shows how technology has helped connect marginalized second- and third-generation immigrant Muslims living in Europe to the *umma*. This has given rise to a form of 'transborder politicized Islam' that is 'nurtured primarily in cyberspace, articulated increasingly in English and promoted by a new class of Internet-based interpreters of Islam'.

Online presence is also affected by a politics of accessibility, which is often broken down according to age, language and class. Specifically, online content has traditionally been skewed – in terms of appeal and their ability to negotiate it – towards a younger, more economically advanced, and more educated usership. Moreover, it remains text-based and English-centric (see Kinney 1995). Additionally, in terms of engagement with, for example, online religious discussion forums, there exists an imbalance along the lines of gender. Men tend to dominate discussions and post more antagonistic comments, whereas women tend to contribute less, and in a more neutral manner (Herring 1996). While such broad-based observations may be more true in some contexts than they are in others, they are a useful way of illustrating the politics of accessibility.

Religion online versus online religion

As with motivations behind placing religious material on the web, religious websites also vary greatly in terms of their functionality (i.e. in terms of what they allow visitors to do on the sites). While some are static sources of religion-related information, others are highly dynamic, offering (to various degrees) the potential for religious interaction (through 'chat' pages, bulletin boards, RSS feeds, etc.), participation (through applications designed to mimic the actual offline performance of religious rituals) and experience (through sophisticated recreations of rare religious experiences such as pilgrimages). One way of classifying this wide range of religious 'material' on the web is to invoke Helland's (2000) basic distinction between *religion online* and *online religion*.

Religion online refers to the use of cyberspace by religious individuals, groups and institutions to provide information about religion (including about offline religious practices). Given that such information in available through alternative offline sources, 'religion online' is a simple, relatively uncomplicated way of extending a group's offline religious presence, online. On the other hand, *online religion* refers to the potential for Internet-mediated practice of religious faith; it refers to the ability of religious practitioners to engage in religious rituals on the Internet (either those which are representations of offline rituals or even entirely new religious practices). Brasher (2004, 4) provides a good example of what religion online might look like:

> Consider, for instance, a Web page titled Digital Avatar. Without leaving your desk chair, you can visit this virtual temple. The page opens to reveal not a temple building but rather a small, stunningly rendered image of a white-faced Shiva framed in black. Moving into the site, you discover a menu of worship experiences. Under a smiling Shiva mouth, hyperlinked text invites you to click on it to savour Shiva's cosmic delights. Other links offer 'take-away' religious experiences. You can download Shiva's image for later attempts to encounter his *Shakti*. If it's meditative bliss you seek, you can download the *aum*, the mystical utterance of Vedic praise that expresses and affirms the totality of creation. For those who need or want visual stimulation as well, a QuickTime movie file with accompanying sound allows you to meditate to an eerie, mystical, rapid alternation of Shiva images.

With regard to the Internet-mediated practice of religious faith that is part and parcel of online religion – and the associated observation that 'when entering cyberspace some form of disembodiment occurs' (Scheifinger 2010, 209) – a number of preconditions are needed for the experience to be deemed authentic.

Integral to such rituals is the need for users to feel like they are part of both a felt and shared experience simultaneously (Kinney 1995); something that is becoming increasingly possible with advancements in digital technology. That said, however, practices such as confession among Catholics remain relatively resistant to technological uptake (using the phone, e.g. or Internet-mediated confessions). Zaleski (1997) suggests that this is because of the limited exchange of energy (or *prana*) through electronic media, which makes practices such as confession seem vacuous when not conducted in a physical face-to-face setting. On the contrary, Scheifinger (2010, 205) argues that the experience of conducting *pujas* and other forms of Hindu ritual practice online 'is a good thing because it results in some sort of felt or actual detachment from the body' – an ideal state for Hindus. It is the sense of disembodiment associated with online religion that can either dampen or enhance the experience of religion. Whichever way it is conceived, it is clear that online religion changes the conditions for and expectations of religious experience for those involved. Altogether this suggests that online religion is more of a complementary resource for religious adherents than it is a substitute for offline experience.

Associated with the practise of religious faith online is the potential for online religious community-building. While it is unlikely that online religious communities will ever be able to command the same sort of commitment and loyalty as, for example, a congregation that visits a church premise every Sunday for in-person worship and communion, they do provide new avenues for religious communities to grow and expand, especially across borders (see Rheingold 1993). Such growth and expansion can cause existing community boundaries to be redrawn, negotiated and dismantled in ways that can both strengthen and weaken religious affiliations, and cause animosity within and between religious groups. Oosterbaan (2010), for example, shows how the Google-powered Brazilian version of Facebook, *Orkut* (with a reported 16 million users), is used by Christian pastors as a tool to evangelize the Brazilian diasporic communities in Amsterdam and Barcelona. In this sense, *Orkut* is viewed as an integral resource to the 're-territorialization' of Christianity in Europe (see also Hervieu-Leger 2002).

Technoscapes and religious competition and conflict

Against this backdrop, it is possible to appreciate how the 'technoscapes' of the globalized world can give rise to new forms of religious competition and inflect traditional sources of conflict. (New) competition associated with cyber-religious spaces has arisen over the access to online religious material and interaction; the authority of religious leaders/scholars to determine the content of religious postings and the scope of religious practice on the Internet; and the authenticity of Internet-mediated religious rituals and experience.

Access-related problems arise when religious groups/institutions try to determine who has access to their cyber-religious space, both in terms of accessing religious content and in terms of participating in communication platforms such as chat rooms on the website. On the one hand, the problems of granting indiscriminate access runs the risk of a desecration of the cyber-religious space through web vandalism, posting of anti-religious material that undermines the plausibility of the group's religious doctrine and exposure to counter-proselytization movements. On the other hand, restricting access to members of the religious group inhibits the use of the web as a resource for evangelical activity. Further, since much of informal Internet-mediated interaction takes place under the cloak of anonymity, a foolproof method of restricting access to 'insiders' can be prohibitively costly. Challenges are most acute for New Religious Movements, for a variety of reasons. These movements are most likely to use the web as a medium for information dissemination and proselytization; however, as Cowan (2007) points out, the Internet favours counter movement activities. Cowan (2007) suggests four reasons for this: the architecture of the web encourages unrestricted replication of (damaging) material across multiple websites; there is no process by which material posted to the web is vetted for accuracy; endless replication continuously degrades the counter movement allegations to over-simplified straw men; and, religious groups have limited resources to counter sustained web-based anti-group propaganda. Further, as Barker (2005) notes, most new religious movements possess an esotericism in doctrine, the plausibility of which, for insiders, might be undermined by repeated contact with outsiders.

Authenticity-related competition arises over whether religious experiences mediated through the Internet have genuine religious merit. These experiences include worship rituals, joining online congregations, and other forms of sacramental participation. Arguments in favour of computer-mediated ritual highlight the fact that it lowers the costs of religious participation and hence is an indispensable innovation for maintaining high levels of participation on otherwise time-intensive religious rituals. On the other hand, religious traditionalists denounce the notion of computer-mediated ritual, citing its lack of experiential verisimilitude and immediacy. The sights and smells of actual worship are missing, the communality of worship is not palpable and there is no sense of action and engagement (Bafelli et al. 2011). Religious leaders have generally sided with the traditionalists: it is worthwhile noting that a growth in computer-mediated religious ritual runs the risk of bypassing the clergy as mediators between the worshipper and the worshipped.

Authority-related competition arises over who has the authority to provide spiritual guidance and religious counsel, disseminate religious knowledge, issue religious edicts and arbitrate on religious disputes (both doctrinal and praxis related) on the Internet. The popularity of the Internet and its capacity to deliver both religious and secular 'knowledge' instantaneously has given rise to a new generation of 'instant experts'. The resulting 'democratisation' of religious knowledge and interpretation – in spite of their alleged lack of credibility – have, in turn, democratized religious discourse on the Internet and in the process bypassed the traditional authority of religious leaders trained and qualified to interpret and comment on religious doctrine. This has given rise to intense competition between religious scholars and lay 'experts' over the monopoly to interpret religious scriptures and issue religious edicts. At its extreme, such competition runs the risk of fragmenting unitary and coherent systems into mutually inconsistent interpretations. Larsson (2005) sums up the debate on the positive and negative impacts of the democratization of religious 'knowledge; as follows: 'on the one hand, the Internet can be seen as an opportunity to liberate the individual from his or her social context or cultural bonds. On the other hand, it can be seen as a threat to theological order and religious authority. From this point of view, the Internet is merely fostering relativism and sectarianism, thus leaving the individual in an existential world'.

Box 4.3: The politics of 'religion online' in Singapore

Given high rates of Internet penetration in Singapore (in excess of 80%) and the high religiosity of Singapore's population, one would expect it to be a site for intense competition between religious leadership and the religious commoner over authority, authenticity and access. However, a survey of Internet and religion in Singapore suggests that Singaporean religious leaders generally endorse the use of the Internet for religious purposes (Kluver and Cheong 2007). However, most religious leaders surveyed subscribe to the concept of online religion rather than religion online. In other words, while they consider the Internet to be a valuable tool for disseminating religion-related information and evangelization, they do not think the medium to be suited for the practice of religious ritual (such as engaging in pilgrimages or virtual worship practices). In rejecting religion online, religious leaders in Singapore share the concerns of their compatriots elsewhere about the inauthenticity of Internet-mediated religious practices (and favour the Durkheimian notion of flesh and blood participation in religious ritual).

The survey draws attention to some authority-related concerns. For example, Buddhist monks express reservations about the publication of *tantric* knowledge and method on the Internet (Kluver and Cheong 2007) because 'exposing' *tantric* practices on the Internet would create a potential for them to be experienced without the guidance and oversight of a spiritual leader.

Generally, however, the broad-based acceptance of the Internet as a medium of acquiring religious information implies that religious leaders' concerns about a diminution of their religious authority are minimal. This is further vindicated by the survey where religious leaders cite engagement with the young – who are the most likely to challenge traditional structures of hierarchy – as a prime motivation for their support for the adaptation of the Internet for religious purposes (Kluver and Cheong 2007). This can be attributed, in part, to a Singaporean (and in general, an East Asian) culture of respect for age, expertise and scholarship. Thus, even if religious commoners were to use the Internet as a medium of acquiring religious knowledge, they are more likely to want to have such knowledge validated by religious leaders.

Kluver and Cheong (2007) report that the most significant concern about 'religion online' for leaders of mainstream religious groups is the threat of counter-movement material on the Internet. Cutting across religious lines, religious leaders express anxiety that 'cultic groups', including the Falungong, might impersonate themselves as 'religious groups' and 'create websites of harm' (Kluver and Cheong 2007, 12). This apprehension about 'cults' can be attributed to an entrenched linguistic tradition in Singapore, which ascribes a pejorative connotation to the word (Hill 2004).

Box 4.4: The Vatican and the Internet

In 2002, the Pontifical Council of Social Communications, in a document titled 'The Church and Internet' first addressed the role of the web in the way that Roman Catholics live and practise their religion. In this document, the Church asserted its responsibility to 'safeguard the boundaries of acceptable belief and practice that could be challenged by unregulated computer mediation' (Cowan 2007, 358). The document also unequivocally emphasized that 'virtual reality is no substitute for shared worship in a flesh-and-blood community' and that 'there are no sacraments on the Internet, and even the religious experiences possible there by the grace of God are insufficient apart from real world interactions with persons of faith' ('The Church and Internet', cited in Cowan 2007, 358).

In spite of this proscription, there is evidence to suggest that at least some Catholics consider some form of worship through the computer as valuable parts of their religious lives. For example, Catholics, unable to travel to a Chapel where the Blessed Sacrament has been kept for devotional purposes, report resorting to websites that upload digital images. In addition, several such online worshippers have reported miracles and apparitions associated with their online worship (Cowan 2007).

This discussion reveals how the competition for the authenticity of computer-mediated worship can take place, between those who find it expedient and experientially satisfactory to do so, and those who deny the religious virtue of such practices, a priori.

Box 4.5: Islam and the Internet

Islam's first forays into the Internet took place through initiatives of 'religiously lay' students of technology at Western universities. Since then, Islamic websites have grown in popularity despite low levels of Internet penetration in the predominantly Muslim parts of the world. Various factors are attributed to the popularity of Islamic websites: their inclusivity in creating an online 'public' that transcends age, nationality and gender (and even sexuality); their ability to foster debate on controversial issues such as organ transplantation and in-vitro fertilization (issues sidestepped by clerics); their use of vernacular languages; and, their promise of providing easy access to religious guidance through online *fatwas* (or, religious edicts) (Bunt 2003 and el-Nawawy and Khamis 2009).

Traditionally, the capacity to issue such edicts was dependent on being able to draw practical inferences from Islamic primary sources (*itjihad*); this capacity had to be honed through years of religious education that culminated in membership of the religious elite (*ulama*). However, the ease with which online interpretations of the Quran can be accessed has given rise to a form of (instant) expertise, labelled by Bunt (2003) as 'e-*itjihad*'. As a result, the circle of individuals who 'can' interpret the Quran and issue fatwas based on such interpretations has proliferated vastly. In the unregulated domain of Islamic cyberspace, interpretations of Quran provided by instant experts multiply and generate a folk Islam that continuously challenges and contests the religious authority of the *ulama*. Consequently, the Islamic cyberspace is faced with what some view to be a crisis of religious authority.

While the technoscapes of globalization have generated new forms of religious competition – involving new issues and new participants – they have also facilitated the adaptation of endangered forms of religious doctrine/ritual in ways that have minimized the potential for conflict. Unpopular (and, sometimes state-shunned) new religious movements have been able to circumvent public hostility-, deregistration-, publication-related bans and so forth by temporarily migrating to cyberspace. Consequently, an 'offline' community has been replaced by an online one and 'offline' proselytization has been replaced by an online soliciting for adherents. Bafelli et al. (2011) cite the example of the new Japanese religious group Hikari no Wa, an offshoot of the vastly unpopular Aum Shinrikyo. Hikari has faced public protects wherever they have tried to establish teaching/worship centres and the stigma associated with public engagement with the group has been a major obstacle against new recruitment. Faced with these constraints, Hikari has migrated all of its operations – including intra-group interaction and proselytization – to the relative safety of the Internet, away from public scrutiny.

In addition, technological development has played a vital role in allowing religious individuals and groups to maintain religious practices in some alternative form. For example, Kong (2011) described the relatively new practice of online mourning and memorialization that has developed in China; there, users are able to offer flowers, tea, candles, incense and prayers as part of their mourning rituals via a memorial website.

Box 4.6: Disseminating the Alpha course among transnational elites in Singapore

Originating in London, UK, the Alpha course is designed for non-churchgoers to explore Christianity in a relaxed environment. When Nicky Gumbel took over the running of the course in 1990, it evolved from a tool used to educate newly baptized Christians to a means of attracting non-Christians into the church. The course itself is free, lasts fifteen weeks, and is globally convergent. This means that every course around the world is run according to the same agenda (i.e. specific topics – such as 'Who is Jesus?', 'Why and how do I pray?' – are covered in the same order); even each 'Alpha evening' follows a recommended programme. Every evening will usually start with an informal meal, followed by Nicky Gumbel's talk for the week (usually delivered via video CD or other technology-mediated means), and then small-group discussions. In the nearly thirty years since it started, it has reached a global audience. In 2010 the Alpha course was being taught in at least 163 countries, and reached out to over 16 million people (Kong 2013).

The global reach of the course has been greatly facilitated by technology. Its website – www.alpha.org – is well-designed, easy to use and highly personal. Starting and running a course is designed to be as simple (and as structured) as possible, thus minimizing any potential barriers or obstacles to global dissemination and replication. Importantly, it also downplays its religious messaging, making it accessible and non-threatening to the non-Christians it targets. In addition, the website acts as a central repository for course materials. The website includes both a 'TV' tab that enables users to login and watch Nicky Gumbel's past talks, as well as a link to the Alpha Shop that enables course organizers to purchase starter packs, video and audio tapes, video CDs and printed literature (and other Alpha paraphernalia, such as stickers and posters). Both the technologies of the Alpha website and shopping portal represent a type of religious globalization that enables the global reproduction of religious practices, from London to the world.

Kong's (2013) case study of the Alpha course in Singapore does, however, show how the appeal of the course is somewhat limited in scope. The types and content of the materials used, the method of instruction and the logic of religious persuasion are shown to appeal more to a transnational elite audience than the masses. Kong (2013) shows how there are three facets of Gumbel's talks that appeal to such an audience: first, his use of cultural references (e.g. Leo Tolstoy, Robert Louis Stevenson) and humour that appeals to (and is understood by) a well-educated audience with an international outlook and understanding; his arguments appeal to the intellect, using evidence-based approaches that are driven more by rational and logical thought than superstition or 'faith'; and his evocation of global and cosmopolitan landscapes and lifestyles that resonate with transnational elites.

Such characteristics appeal not just to skilled migrants living and working in Singapore, but to the well-educated and well-travelled (and, implicitly, higher income) echelons of Singapore society as well. By way of contrast, when the course was run in a lower-middle-class neighbourhood, the organizers experienced high drop-out rates, largely because attendees found the course (especially Gumbel's humour) difficult to understand. Given that Singapore's Christian community tends to be better educated and higher income, it is clear that the Alpha course serves to reproduce and reinforce the socio-economic profile of Christianity in Singapore, while producing and reproducing a transnational (elite) religious community.

Finanscapes

One of the key elements of globalization has been the evolution of an interconnected global financial system. Such a system – brought into being as much by technology as by a relentless pursuit of financial profit – is characterized by the potential for almost instantaneous movements of capital (and at short notice); the fluid nature of the ownership of capital; and sophisticated, often incomprehensible, instruments (investment products) to enable mass participation in the race to make quick monetary gains over short periods of time.

Consequently, successful participation in the new global financial system requires a set of skills and attributes that are at odds with the sort of qualities that usually underpin religious virtue: the former increasingly valorizes the short run, while religious rewards such as salvation and 'other-worldly' pleasures are 'compensations' (the term is due to Stark and Bainbridge [1996, 305]) for patience; the former encourages speculation, while religious doctrines normally advocate prudence; and, more generally, the former promotes an extravagant, consumption-oriented lifestyle that is self-centred, while religions preach an abstemious, spiritually aligned and other-regarding life. Thus, modern finanscapes promote increased competition between religious and material values, which might contribute to a 'fractured' self that is highly alienated. In short, the modern financial system with its temptations and tantrums contributes to the production of anomie, more than any other aspect of globalization.

Religious groups have responded to this philosophical/conceptual dissonance in essentially one out of three different ways. One response has centred around advocating for a reorienting of social and political resources away from promoting material towards spiritual ends. A clear example of this strategy emerged in the aftermath of the 2011 riots in the UK, where religious leaders lay the blame, either explicitly or by implication, squarely on the secularization/materialization of society (Kent News, 20 August 2011). Many sought to see the riots as driven by a 'sense of entitlement' among the youth, a sense engendered by a global economic system that putatively breaks the traditional, protestantist, connection between 'work' and 'economic reward' (*The Guardian*, 28 March 2012). As a result, there was active lobbying for religion to play a greater role in chaperoning society towards 'morally desirable' ends.

A second, more reconciliatory approach has been for religions to legitimize the pursuit of material ends as a religiously worthy goal and therefore to portray material success as a form of divine blessing. Many strands of evangelical Christianity, including but not limited to Pentecostal brands, seek to do this.

Historically, Pentecostalism has been most prevalent among economically and socially marginalized communities. As a result, early versions of Pentecostalism tended to emphasize the importance of 'other worldly' rewards. However, because of the upward socio-economic mobility of adherents, newer interpretations have sought to legitimize individual material pursuits and profit-seeking. This alteration in stance has been made possible due to Pentecostals' decentralized organizational structure (Hefner 2009). For example, New Pentecostals are known to preach a 'prosperity gospel' which declares that 'health and wealth are divine gifts delivered to all who are suitably faithful' (Hefner 2009, 156). It is noteworthy that adopting such diametrically opposed stances to wealth acquisition can itself generate inter-religious competition over religious doctrine and interpretation. Hefner (2009, 156) goes on to note, for instance, that 'the expensive cars and clothing flaunted by some prosperity pastors disturb Catholics, mainline Protestants, and even many traditional Pentecostals'. More than that, some scholars (e.g. Glick-Schiller 2005; see also Vasquez 2008) have also drawn comparisons between prosperity theology, the globalist ambitions of Christianity (enshrined by the Great Commission, for example) and the close ideological affinity with neo-liberal capitalism typically advocated by elites in the United States. As previously mentioned, given such a web of close associations, it has been argued that the prosperity gospel used by Christian groups to gain traction in frontier territories around the world could be a carrier of neo-imperialist thought and action.

A third response by religious groups to financial activity has been more selective. In such cases, religious groups have objected, on doctrinal grounds, against particular financial instruments and practices, and not universally against the whole system. A case in point is Islam's rejection of derivatives and other interest-based financial instruments as anti-religious. This opposition has led to the creation of an alternative financial regime constituted by Islamic banks that provide opportunities for 'religiously pure' investments (Plüss 2009). Indeed, Islam's injunction against some conventional financial products and the emergence of competing Islamic banks have led to a large number of 'secular' banks offering Islamic investment portfolios.

In addition to posing conceptual conundrums for religious groups, modern finanscapes have influenced the trajectory of religious globalization, in terms of whether it moves in the direction of fundamentalism or cosmopolitanism. The high mobility of money across national boundaries has corresponded to the ease with which diasporic religious organizations have been able to rely on home country organizations for financial support (and avoid dependence on state/ social resources in the adopted country). As Plüss (2009) mentions, migrant religious organizations' financial dependence on state/society in the adopted country acts as incentives for integration, hybridization of religious practices and a cosmopolitan religious globalization. By implication then, financial independence of religious organizations – sustained by readily mobile capital – can give rise to deterritorialized, religious identities and a fundamentalist religious globalization that is more prone to challenging state authority (at best, tacitly and at worst, through active acts of subversion).

Finally, even when diasporas are not involved, religious organizations which receive international financing might also develop a deterritorialized identity based on shared religious affiliation with the donor. As such, conflicts of interest, loyalties and authority might arise. In extreme cases, local religious institutions may espouse a pan-religious sentiment that challenges the goals and policies of the nation-state in question.

Box 4.7: Proscriptions on the overseas financing of religious groups in Singapore

In Singapore, the importance of financial independence of organizations in preventing conflicts of interest has generally been acknowledged in policymaking. For example, measures preventing political parties from receiving financial assistance from religious groups or international sources have long been in place to ensure that state policies remain immune to religions or foreign political influence. In addition, religious groups in Singapore are required to be registered under the Societies Act (chapter 311), and under this act, groups which are 'formed under the instruction of a foreign organisation or is affiliated to a foreign organisation or whose major source of funding is from outside Singapore' are not allowed to be registered. This measure prevents foreign influences from having a direct and sustained impact on local religious groups.

The attitude of the Singapore state is that preventing religious organizations from assuming a deterritorialized identity is key to retaining control over religious organizations. Such control has been an important element in Singapore's ability to generally co-opt religious groups into furthering (secular) state goals and endorsing state policies. In this context, even though financial flows from outside to religious organizations in Singapore can reduce the fiscal burden of the state, given their destabilizing potential, there is a continued need to monitor and regulate such flows. Such regulations can play a vital role in ensuring that religious organizations in Singapore are, primarily, national organizations and operate in accordance with the national – rather than, a trans-national – agenda.

Mediascapes and ideoscapes

The defining features of the modern mediascape are the rate at which ideas are transformed into images and the rate at which such images are transmitted across national boundaries.[2] The central consequence of this, combined with an explosion in media penetration around the world, has been a spatial compression of the world; to use a metaphor, the world is now available in real time in the living rooms across the world. The blurring of spatial and temporal distances on such a large scale has an unprecedented potential for generating empathy. For example, it is much easier to be moved by people dying (in, say, religious violence) right in front of one's eyes, in high definition at that, than to be moved by a textual description of the same in a newspaper (or, still less, a history book). Thus, media, through its image-centricity and disregard for geographical distances, makes its 'audience' 'participate' in the events of the world.

The influence of such a mediascape on religious competition is significant, both in its scope and its scale. The resultant expression of religious essentialism by diasporic groups is ambiguous. On the one hand, intimate connections with the homeland through media narratives could facilitate stronger connections with the religious tradition of the homeland; this, in turn, might inhibit the hybridization (heterogenization) of religious culture, resist integration and sustain deterritorialized religious identities. The global spread of the ultranationalist Hindu ideology of *Hindutva* has, for example, been attributed to the activities of professional Indians (entrepreneurs, doctors, software engineers, journalists and scholars) located in various diasporic communities around the world. Such communities have the resources and technological savviness to spread and sustain the message of *Hindutva* around the world via the Internet. Indeed, not only are they able to promote the message, they have also been successful at reconciling the seemingly antithetical messages of racial and religious primordialism that *Hindutva* engenders with 'hypermodernist, deterritorialized, and de-centered cyber-spaces' (Vasquez 2008, 174). Such reconciliation highlights the power of mediascapes in driving religio-political awareness and support; the effect of which is most noticeable in the election of Narendra Modi – a Hindu nationalist and proponent of *Hindutva* – to the role of prime minister of India in May 2014.

On the other hand, immediate media(ted) experience of events from the homeland could weaken nostalgic feelings for the homeland; and, if Vertovec (2000) is right about religion being a substitute for the homeland, then constant exposure to events in the homeland could weaken incentives for developing an essentialized religious identity. The evidence is inconclusive as to which of the two effects dominates.

There are yet other ways via which mediascapes could lead to a globalization of local religious competition. The first of these appeals to the nature of participation that image-intensive media representations of local events invites. Chris McGillion makes an effective criticism of media's role in promoting an individual's unreflective engagement with (events in) the world, by suggesting:

> Interiority, the capacity to step back from places and events and contemplate their meaning is an essential ingredient of the religious imagination. But it is also one of the casualties of an image-driven culture . . . Internet-generated images . . . invite reaction not reflection, and invite it at the speed of instinctive, rather than considered responses. What we gain in information we lose in sight and, over time, perhaps, in the capacity even to think insightfully. (*Sydney Morning Herald*, 23 December 2000)

Thus, television and the Internet encourage reflexive (and, not reflective) response and provoke emotional attachment (rather than critical evaluation) of media content. When the media presents stories of localized religious persecution, violence or resistance in simplistic, graphic forms, it is easier to establish empathetic bonds. The simplicity in presentation also implies that key local details are often kept out of the reportage in a way that maximizes its universal appeal. The resulting empathetic bonds are crucial first steps to building transnational religious identities.

Second, the possibilities of transnational interaction with co-religionists over new media give rise to the possibility of communities that are deterritorialized. Such communities are held together by more primordial forms of identification, like religion, and come to resemble a cyber-*umma*.[3] Transnational religious communities online due to their deterritorialized status necessarily have a predisposition towards viewing local religious ethnographies as a part of a grander global narrative. As a consequence, they tend to distil all local nuances (social/economic and political) from an episode of local religious conflict in such a way that all that remains is an example of religious conflict. By creating a single discourse of religious conflict, which is widely disseminated through conventional and new media, these communities are then able to elevate small, localized conflicts into global planes. Local ideological entrepreneurs might then take over and escalate the scale of conflict by infusing local participants (in the conflict) with the consciousness that they are part of a 'battle' more grand than fighting for a better quality of life, or against corruption, or against inequality and so forth. As Juergensmeyer (2009) has noted, the elevation in status of the conflict (from local to global, from material to spiritual) contributes significantly to the intensity of subsequent violence.

Box 4.8: Indonesia and the rise of Islamism

Woodward (2007) offers insightful analysis of the rise of Islamism in Indonesia and the underpinning factors. Since the early 2000s, such a phenomenon has been characterized as an example of the globalization of religious conflict. Four factors are cited to support such a view: the communication revolution focused international attention on the conflict; economic and ethnic conflicts were reinterpreted as religious ones; Christian and Muslim participants in the conflict saw it as an element in a larger global struggle for ideological hegemony; and Christian and Muslim representations of the conflict, which were initially part of a propaganda war carried out almost exclusively on the Internet, gradually spilled over into mosques and churches around the world.

Projections by either group – of the violence committed by another – are in overtly simplistic terms, as is necessary to capture a global imagination. In addition, simple messages serve as more powerful symbols. An Islamist website in the UK, Islamicawakening.com, for example, describes Muslim victims of Christian 'atrocities' in East Indonesia in the following terms (Woodward 2007, 97):

'IMAGINE now a land where Muslims have been brutally murdered by the thousands. Not only murdered and beheaded etc. but afterwards mutilated, hearts cut out and eaten or pounded to make a gunpowder mix for ammunition.
IMAGINE a land where Muslims are burnt alive while performing *Salaat ut-Taraweh* last Ramadan.
IMAGINE women being raped in mosques by savages including priests who afterwards pass comments like the flesh of the Muslimahs were delicious in front of their families who await their turn for death.
IMAGINE an imam being killed and buried only to be exhumed later, crucified, his genitals chopped off and stuffed in his mouth with pieces of raw pork. The earth shook and only that act of Almighty Allah stopped them from going further.
IMAGINE the sick and wounded treated on the floors of mosques and make do areas with compound fractures held together with external fixtures made of bicycle spokes . . . wounds covered with honey and cloth. (By Allah's will, the wounds healed and the union of the bones occurred.)
IMAGINE Christian doctors who for the past few years have made it their mission to snuff out newborn Muslim babies or doing caesarean hysterectomies in an attempt to curb the growth of the Muslim community.'

On the other hand, Christian accounts of Muslim 'atrocities' are equally polemical. Descriptions posted on a New Zealand Evangelical website, the Christian Broadcasting Network and the Christian Solidarity Worldwide, include the following descriptions:

'Cries come out from the mosque whipping the Muslims into frenzy and calling upon the military and the police to join them in a fight to defend the religion of

Allah and to wipe out the Christians . . . once they have sufficient people through they then attack the Christian positions, killing, maiming, burning and looting.

The Christians do not attack, they just defend their positions, and while under attack sing some of the most beautiful worship hymns of history to praise and glorify Jesus Christ even as they are under siege'; and,

'An elderly couple was burned to death in their house. Bullet holes still riddle what's left of the buildings.'

The above examples illustrates how transnational religious communities can result in globalizing local conflict through a process of religious essentialization (reimagining an ethnic-economic conflict as a religious one); and, a process propaganda involving graphic images and overly simplistic text. Such globalization contributes to even more violent conflict, as participants come to associate violence – through the exhortation of local ideological entrepreneurs – with grander concepts of martyrdom and salvation.

Finally, to look at these dynamics from another perspective, mediascapes can also be used to localize hitherto globally oriented religious networks and flows. Doing so is often a strategy used to garner international support for a locally relevant cause. A good example of this is the massive demonstrations against the punitive immigration reforms proposed by the US House of Representatives in 2006. Unexpectedly, more than half a million demonstrators materialized in Los Angeles to protest against the reforms; similar marches also took place in Chicago, Omaha, Phoenix, Dallas, Atlanta, Salt Lake City and New York. Orchestrating the marches were diffuse networks of immigrant advocacy groups, which included the Catholic and evangelical Protestant churches. Such groups worked closely with Spanish-language radio hosts and TV news anchors to encourage migrant communities to attend the demonstrations, carrying the flags of the United States and their country of origin to symbolize their dual sense of belonging. Interestingly, traditional media were used over online media as the immigrant communities being mobilized had limited access to the Internet, showing how 'we need to be sensitive to the differential access and use of media' (Vasquez 2008, 175). Such mobilization of immigrant communities using religious networks and media agencies (many local radio stations are actually owned by evangelical churches) surprised the mainstream media and English-speaking public, as it reflected not only the political activism of immigrant religious communities, but also the power that immigrant religious groups have to mobilize their communities against the state apparatus.

5

Social Resilience and Religion

Introducing social resilience

Social resilience may be defined as 'the ability of groups or communities to cope with external stresses and disturbances [that arise] as a result of social, political and environmental [and economic] change' (Adger 2000, 347). Such changes are necessarily adverse in character, and at such a scale that they affect large groups of people, often at the same time. In other words, social resilience is the ability of a group to either absorb, adapt to or to mitigate the influence of negative changes in the external environment. Both the triggers of social resilience (i.e. the changes that cause external stresses) and their effects (i.e. the communities implicated by such changes) are space-bound, and implicate individuals, communities and groups at various (and often multiple) scales of analysis (Robinson and Carson 2015).

Any discussion of social resilience necessarily involves an understanding of vulnerability, even though the idea of 'resilience' has started to supplant that of 'vulnerability' in academic discourses. While some view resilience as the opposite of vulnerability (e.g. Adger et al. 2005), others – especially geographers – argue that the relationship between the two concepts is one of multiple inter-dependencies rather than one of detached independence. Vulnerability is the exposure of society to various stresses (i.e. circumstances that disrupt livelihoods and require some sort of adaptation), and the associated loss of security. Vulnerable groups are those that are persistently and pervasively subject to such stresses and losses, which are often linked to underlying social, economic, cultural, political and environmental drivers (see Chambers 1989). As shown in the preceding chapters, such groups are often targeted by religious groups for the purposes of upliftment and, in some instances, proselytization. In this sense, vulnerable groups are often a focus of religious activity, and a driver of inter-religious and religious-state competition and potentially conflict.

Social resilience is a collective process that is dependent on the strength and solidarity of the group rather than the individual (de Tocqueville 2000; see also Lin et al. 2001; Sampson et al. 2005). Religious groups often play a central role in developing social resilience during times of upheaval and change. Indeed, it has been recognized that the 'group' is often more effective than the state in making decisions and taking immediate action to address the problems or issues that individuals may face. According to de Tocqueville (2000), the 'group' is often more agentic than the state in developing social resilience, as it is typically more flexible, adaptive, responsive and sensitive to the needs of its constituent members. In contrast, the efficacy of the state is often compromised by its atomized structure, bureaucracy and separation from society. Key factors that contribute to the development of socially resilient groups include legitimacy, either inclusivity or exclusivity (depending on context) and trust (see Harriss and de Renzio 1997; O'Riordan et al. 1998). That said, the capacity for resilience is never distributed homogeneously or equitably within and through religious groups (or any other social groups for that matter) (Weichselgartner and Kelman 2015). As highlighted in previous chapters, groups – especially religious groups – are political agents in as much as they are guided by their own interests, resources, preferences and capabilities. Invariably, therefore, there is a politics of resilience than intersects in various ways with different religious groups (and the spaces they occupy) and state power. Such a politics of resilience is a sub-field that requires closer attention, not least because of the intricate webs of power, marginality, governance and social (and religious) capital that it can expose (Wisner et al. 2012; Robinson and Carson 2015; Weichselgartner and Kelman 2015).

Our concern in this book is with the ways in which religious groups are able to build social resilience and strengthen themselves in the face of upheaval and change. In the sections that follow, we first examine how religious groups develop social resilience, followed by the proactive and reactive capacities of religious groups. Following that, we focus on disaster response as a form of social resilience, and social resilience as a means of regulating religious groups.

Religious groups and the development of social resilience

The social resilience of religious groups is believed to be stronger than that of other (often secular) social assemblages such as the household, the school or the peer group. This is largely because of the greater capacity of religious groups to build and maintain a sense of identity and belonging among their members (Ellison 1993), to provide support systems for families (Mahoney et al. 2003), to connect members to a higher authority (Blaine and Crocker 1995) and to more generally provide for the physical, mental, emotional and spiritual needs of members and their families (Taylor et al. 1997; e.g. Carlson et al. 2002; Wiley et al. 2002; Ball et al. 2003). Importantly, in many contexts, religious buildings – mosques, churches, temples and so forth – serve not only as places of religious instruction, but as community gathering places as well. They are instrumental in developing a sense of identity and relationships which contribute to social resilience, and often function as distribution channels through which aid and other resources can flow. As McGregor (2010) highlights in the context of post-tsunami Aceh, Indonesia, the destruction of mosques was acutely felt, with local communities deeming the reconstruction of mosques to be more important than the reconstruction of houses. This put Christian NGOs in a difficult position of trying to meet local community demand and to further the development objectives of their overseas donors, while trying not to compromise their own religious standpoint. Their success in being able to meet these various demands was reflected in the ability to blur conceptual boundaries, notably by building secular 'community centres' instead of Islamic mosques.

As is evident above, religious groups can play integral roles in the development and strengthening of social resilience. More often than not, they have the 'potential to influence individual and community well-being through a diversity of strategic pathways and in a diversity of ecological contexts' (Pargament and Maton 2000, 502). The 'diversity of strategic pathways' and the 'diversity of ecological contexts' can be re-conceptualized as the difference between the proactive capacity and reactive capabilities of religious groups (after Walker et al. 2006). It should be noted that there have been growing calls within the academy for research to shift away from resilience as a descriptive concept that explores and explains what has been done (i.e. the reactive capabilities of groups), towards a more normative agenda that identifies what should be done (i.e. the proactive capacity to influence change) (see Weichselgartner and Kelman 2015). This shift requires that the discourse be expanded to incorporate hitherto understudied aspects of resilience, such as entitlement, access, choice and equity. Such aspects come into sharp focus when religious groups are the enablers of resilience, and we highlight these issues in the examples and analyses that follow.

The proactive capacity of religious groups

The 'strategic pathways' that religious groups use to build social resilience take the form of strong intra- and inter-religious relationships developed during 'peace time', that is, when threats – whether economic, political, social, cultural or environmental – are not imminent. They are premised on strong ties of trust within religious groups, and from a broader state-societal perspective, on trust between religious groups as well as between religious and secular groups. These relationships of trust then become valuable when adversity strikes. Government leaders seeking to resolve crises would benefit from being able to harness these relationships of trust and the resources and capabilities that arise from such robust relations. A society in which the strategic pathways are well-harnessed – or the proactive capacities usefully exploited – is one which helps people anticipate adversity, and create options that will help to prevent, minimize or avoid altogether vulnerable circumstances. It is proactive in the sense that it aims to identify and address needs before they evolve into significant social problems. The ability to help pre-empt adversity (at least, human-made ones) and effect positive social change is one of the marks of a robust and resilient society.

The proactive capacities of religious groups are built up over time. Apart from the shared commitment to a belief system, the strength of ties is often also enabled by the provisions that religious groups offer: the fellowship that leads to a sense of a group and purpose that is larger than oneself, as well as the provision of goods and services for members and non-members. Thus religious groups help to strengthen their communities through the provision of various forms of capital: social, cultural, symbolic, economic, political and so on (after Bourdieu 1986). And yet as Davoudi (2012, 306) recognizes, 'in the social world, resilience has as much to do with shaping the challenges we face as responding to them'. Thus religion not only provides a sense of solidarity in the face of adversity, but also a shared framework within which negative changes in the external environment can be interpreted and understood. Taken to the extreme, such frameworks can insulate religious groups and communities from the world around them, and enable cultic behaviours to flourish (see Box 2.6). Having said that, in most instances, developing a sense of resilience is integral to the development of religious (and, more broadly social or 'human') communities (Robinson and Carson 2015).

Accordingly, the strategic pathways of religious groups are often planned, managed and long term in approach. For example, the work of FBVWOs, plays a big part in building a sense of commitment among adherents and non-adherents, with provisions in areas such as healthcare, education, drug rehabilitation, eldercare, childcare and so on. In the United States, for example, it was estimated in the early 1990s that 37 per cent of all volunteer activity was church-related (*Washington Post*, 26 March 1994), and that church congregations donated more money to community causes than private corporations ($6.6 billion versus $6.1

billion respectively) (*Washington Post*, 10 June 1993). As discussed in Chapter 3, the fact that such engagement involves religious groups playing a secular role in society (often an important one) is not without contention, given the easy conflation of religious and secular goals, and the shifting of power from secular to religious agencies. Nevertheless, the active engagement in such welfare activities can and does help to build commitment, trust and capacity that can be called upon in times of adversity. From the perspective of policymakers seeking partners in building social resilience, it is therefore necessary to understand how religious identification and belief is in itself a source of strength and comfort for many adherents, and how religious groups organize themselves to provide goods and services for members and non-members.

The ability of religious groups to provide their members with the support and resources needed to build a sense of resilience is often attributed to modernity, and the associated dismantling (or, at least, weakening) of traditional support structures for society (e.g. the family, the neighbourhood). As Giddens (1990, 114) observed: 'many individuals may be searching for new ways of establishing the kinds of trusting relationships which are essential for their sense of security but which are no longer necessarily provided by families and neighbourhoods'. Attachment to a religious group and belief in a religiously mandated worldview can therefore engender a form of social resilience that may become stronger or weaker over space and time, and according to the individual needs and circumstances of its members. Such worldviews can also, however, separate individuals from the community and communities from society-at-large. This dynamic becomes especially pronounced – and contentious – when imparted by non-domestic religious groups (notably, Christian charities working in non-Christian religious contexts – see McGregor 2010; also Robinson and Carson 2015).

Social resilience may also be interpreted as a society in which inter-religious relations are well-managed and where competition does not escalate into conflict, much less violence. In this regard, evidence suggests how fractiousness can be proactively minimized and resilience enhanced via sound management by state authorities. For example, in situations of entrant-incumbent competition and conflicts (as discussed in Chapter 2), sound management on the part of the state may include enshrining in the constitution protection for the evangelical activities of minority religions, which, when combined with effective law enforcement, avoids fractious entrant-incumbent religious competition. Singapore's policies with respect to sustaining the freedom of minority religions to compete for religious market share against incumbent religions is one example of how, generally speaking, religiously plural polities might develop harmoniously.

While allowing free entry to 'new' or 'foreign' religions, Singapore also clearly delineates the rules of competition and scrupulously enforces the rules and penalizes breaches, whether by entrants or incumbents. In such a situation, resilience against conflict is enhanced.

Other actions not reliant on state policy and management are also evident. The rapid and peaceable spread of Christianity in post-war South Korea can be attributed, in part, to the fact that key members of early post-war governments openly adopted Christian beliefs, which protected evangelical missions from reprisals by the dominant religions of the day (Confucianism and Buddhism). Of course, other factors also played a part. As Adams (1995) suggests, a key reason for the lack of any antagonism to Christianity in South Korea was the fact that the incumbent religions did not see Christianity as a 'foreign' or 'colonising' religion, since Japan was the colonial power that ruled Korea between 1905 and 1945 and Korean Christians contributed to the nationalist movements against Japanese occupation as well as, resisting the imposition of Shinto as a civil religion. Joint participation in a trans-religious cause by incumbent and entrant groups builds a sense of solidarity and softens entrant-incumbent competition.

What the above examples suggest is that a society may be able to avoid religious conflict and violence through the successful use of law, policy and enforcement, and is in that sense, resilient, but it may also be resilient to such adversity for other reasons that are grounded in the confluence of specific historical, political, social, cultural, economic and even personality factors.

The reactive capabilities of religious groups

The 'diversity of ecological contexts' that Pargament and Maton (2000) refer to as the contexts within which religious groups have the potential to influence individual and community well-being are precisely the contexts within which religious groups may be called upon to shore up resilience. They include the range of socio-economic and environmental spaces within which religious groups operate, helping individuals and communities cope with and limit the damage from adversity, and to recover from and adjust to positions of vulnerability. The reactive capabilities of religious groups are called upon to assist with damage limitation, rehabilitation and the future mitigation of the effects of adversity. Such capabilities are reactive in the sense that they are only leveraged once an adverse situation has developed, and a state of vulnerability established.

Religion's reactive capability may be called upon at both the level of the individual and the community. In the case of the former, religious groups often help individuals cope with, or recover from, personal setbacks. This is usually in relation to offering psychological and emotional support, and the population that benefits from religion's reactive capacity often comprises the socio-economically vulnerable individuals (e.g. youth, the elderly, women, disabled and so on). In the case of the latter, religious groups may help entire communities afflicted by various types of disaster (either environmental, political, social or economic). The focus is on providing aid and relief, and the target population is often spatially (and/or temporally) vulnerable. For example, the Jewish Family Service in southern Florida maintains an 'Emergency Care Contact List' of senior citizens that are vulnerable to hurricanes, the aim being to better deliver services and assistance during times of need (Leeds 2006). As with the examples of gap-filling activities discussed in Chapter 3, these forms of 'help' can be leveraged as a source of competitive advantage that enables religious groups to attract and retain adherents, and in some instances, to promote divisive forms of religious exclusivity (Marshall 2005).

How religious groups respond to disasters provide some of the clearest examples of their reactive capabilities. Indeed, disaster response is a very specific form of social resilience that is enacted through clearly defined spaces. As we discussed in Chapter 3 on quasi-secular space, religious groups are often closely associated with disaster relief efforts. The ways and means of conceptualizing and delivering relief do, however, differ markedly between groups, contexts and spaces. As Patterson et al. (2010, 138) rightly acknowledge, 'not every [religious group] is equal and not all [religious groups] are beneficial'. Religiously-guided (or even driven) forms of social resilience can have both positive and negative effects.

On the one hand, well-organized and well-functioning groups that are trusted by their members and society-at-large can leverage their moral authority to encourage co-operation and teamwork when it is needed. Many governments do not possess such authority. Given that they are often more locally entrenched than the apparatus of the state, religious groups are also recognized as having stronger abilities to assess need, to distribute relief in a more efficient and equitable manner, and to (re)build a sense of social cohesion within and between communities that may have been disrupted by disasters. For these reasons, many (religious) groups are integral to disaster response efforts, and often provide an important link between government agencies and local communities. Such efforts are often associated with an integrated approach to social resilience that is based on the idea of pooling resources and capabilities with a view to scaling-up their potential impact. In other words, the more religious groups (irrespective of affiliation or denomination) and secular agencies work together, the better the potential outcome. In the aftermath of Hurricane Katrina in the American state of Louisiana, for example, a large, informal and loosely structured group of interdenominational faith leaders co-ordinated a series of meetings that led to the organization and distribution of relief and information, and the development of longer term disaster contingency and recovery plans (among other things – see Patterson et al. 2010, 138). In this instance, working together had positive effect for both society and inter-religious relations.

Box 5.1: The role of religious ritual in the aftermath of Hurricane Katrina

The Hurricane Katrina case shows how the emotional trauma caused by physical displacement can be mitigated by ritualistic religious practices. In 2005, Hurricane Katrina swept through the eastern seaboard of the United States. It caused devastation throughout the state of Louisiana and, in particular, the city of New Orleans. The hurricane caused large-scale evacuation from the city, with significant numbers of people remaining displaced from their homes for years afterwards. Despite such displacement, communities were rapidly and effectively re-built, often along religious lines. Indeed, since the founding of New Orleans in 1718 and the arrival of Catholic missionaries shortly thereafter, religion has played an important role in the public and private spaces of the city. Ursuline nuns built a shrine for Our Lady of Prompt Succor, which has been described as a 'new form of Marian devotion [i.e. devotion to the Virgin Mary]' (Carter 2007, 10) that is now closely associated with miraculous activity, and permeates the daily lives of adherents. Many have built altars or shrines in their homes, with the saint considered by many to be 'a cherished regional cultural symbol of quick help in times of need' (ibid. 11).

In the aftermath of Hurricane Katrina, Carter (2007) shows how ritual and religious practice played an important role in building social resilience. In particular, she shows how the practice of Marian devotion enabled individuals and communities to develop a sense of local connection (despite displacement) and well-being through the development and strengthening of social and spiritual relationships. Many re-built Marian shrines in front of their devastated homes, a reflection of how 'the continuing power of religious belief and commitment provides a basis for enduring solidarities' (Levine 1992, 15–16). The sharing of stories of miraculous intervention in the aftermath of Katrina served to both strengthen belief and grow the community of adherents. Not only that, but such sharing and strengthening often occurred at the shrine of Our Lady of Prompt Succor and other places of worship – both public and private – which in turn became places of socio-spiritual unification. This shows the important role of 'social networks and webs of relations between people, divine forces, materials, and places' (Carter 2007, 11) in building social resilience. Indeed, such networks and webs served to increase feelings of safety and security by making people feel like they are part of a community. In turn, they provide the capabilities needed to prepare for, withstand and adapt to the effects of environmental disaster.

On the other hand, the efficacy and intentions of religious groups can also be called into question. Partnerships with the government can reduce the independence and autonomy of religious groups (in terms of deciding how funds or relief are to be used). In turn, this has been shown to affect the moral authority of groups and, in some instances, the loyalty of their members. For these reasons, some groups eschew government funding in order to retain their autonomy (see Cain and Barthelemy 2008; also Pipa et al. 2006). Presumably, unbeknown to them, groups may also encourage action that is detrimental to their members, or to society-at-large. Indeed, as Weichselgartner and Kelman (2015, 253) recognize, 'while resilience may be important to support and maintain systems in a desirable state, it may also maintain a system in an undesirable state, making recovery or transformation difficult'. To this end, groups may, for example, instil a false sense of security (or a desire to maintain community solidarity) that could cause their members to remain in a vulnerable location. Likewise, they may encourage practices that exacerbate, rather than mitigate against, vulnerability. Some groups may act in an exclusionary manner, one that unfairly privileges members over non-members, and can lead to a monopolization of resources, information and access. When such exclusionary practices are attributed to religious groups, the politics of social resilience come to the fore.

Exclusionary practices are often associated with a more autonomous approach to disaster relief, one that privileges isolated efforts to provide disaster relief to afflicted areas and communities. Working autonomously may enable faster response times (as there is less bureaucracy involved in the decision-making process), but in the same measure, it can also reduce the accountability of religious groups. As Lemyre et al. (2005; see also Smit and Wandel 2006) argue, not only does the group act as a resource that facilitates processes of adaptation and resilience in the aftermath of disasters, but it is also one of the most important actors and stakeholders in such processes. Specifically, group resilience 'serve[s] to mitigate the impacts of adversity and strengthen community capacity to deal with existing and future events' (Lemyre et al. 2005, 319). Such strengthening can be a source of opportunity for religious groups, most notably in terms of changing community perceptions of a minority religious group, or more contentiously, for the recruitment or conversion of new members.

Finally, it should be noted that while religious groups can contribute to the development of social resilience, they can be regulated by it as well. Social resilience can, in other words, be a form of religious regulation, especially in contexts where majority religious groups seek to mobilize communities against the encroachment of minority players. Such a dynamic is clearly at play in Sri Lanka, where adherents of the majority Buddhist seek to informally regulate the competitive actions and outcomes of minority Christian groups. More specifically, the US State Department's International Religious Freedom reports (2003–10) suggest that within Sri Lanka, civil society is actually more assertive in regulating minority religious groups than the state: Government Regulation of Religion scores 6/10, whereas Social Regulation of Religion scores 9.4/10 (where 10 is the highest rate of regulation – see Woods 2012b). Indeed, the Sri Lankan case shows how civil society can take the lead (albeit in often quite punitive and reactionary ways) in regulating religious groups when the regulatory apparatus of the state is seen as weak or ineffectual. Such a dynamic is most pronounced in rural village settings where social resilience to Christian growth is strongest. At the local level in Sri Lanka, it is often therefore civil society and not government agencies that dictates the limits of religious freedom. In this way, the resilience of religious groups may be a limiting rather than enabling factor.

6

Conclusions: (Re)Conceptualizing Religion and Space in a Globalized World

This book has weaved together different understandings of religion and space in the modern world. We have focused particularly on how various forms of religious competition, conflict and violence are enacted in and through different spaces, and how space itself can serve an agentic role. While the book examined religious and secular spaces as two distinct categories of analysis and understanding, it is clear from our discussion of quasi-secular spaces that such categories are rarely mutually distinct. Instead, space – whether categorized as 'religious' or 'secular' – is invariably constructed, used and managed by people and groups in order to achieve an objective or to further an agenda. As has repeatedly been shown in this volume, space is not only a locus of religious activity, but is also a tool used by religious groups to engage society, to exert authority and to reinforce or subvert a dominant order, regime or discourse. It is for these reasons that space is such an important analytical lens that can help reveal and illuminate the inherently complex inter-relationship(s) between religious groups, the state and society.

Through the five preceding chapters, we have explained and elaborated on how religious competition and conflict intersect with space. We have shown that space can be both a cause and effect of religious competition and conflict, as it reveals and enables expressions of religious power and control. The evolution of spatial theory – from the 'insider' standpoint of Mircea Eliade, to the 'outsider' standpoint of Henri Lefebvre and other social constructionists – provides a framework within which to understand religious competition and conflict. They enable an understanding of how religious and secular claims to space are, and have been, negotiated in the post-war period of modernity. To further offer a conceptual frame for examining the nature of claims to space, we introduced the notions of ownership- and authority-related claims to space. We thus examined in Chapter 2 competition over religious spaces (using the lens of ownership and autonomy), why competition can escalate into conflict (with a focus on the issues of centrality and exclusivity), and why such conflicts are often so difficult to resolve (with a focus on the issue of indivisibility). Further, we highlighted the importance of scale as an analytical overlay, and examined various scales of analysis– from the religious mapping of the world, through to the religious body and embodied religion.

The counterpart to Chapter 2 on religious spaces is Chapter 3, which focuses on secular spaces, where we similarly examined ownership- and autonomy-related competition, this time, over secular spaces, from both inter-religious and religious-secular standpoints. Numerous types of secular spaces were examined – educational spaces, both formal and informal, employment spaces, media spaces and political spaces.

Our division of space into religious and secular, while reflected in their treatment over two separate chapters, is in part empirical, in part heuristic. Thus, in the latter section of Chapter 3, we introduced the notion of quasi-secular spaces, referring to those spaces that are appropriated by religious groups in order to achieve a religious outcome. In many ways, these are the 'unofficially sacred' spaces Kong (2001) urged scholars to pay attention to, and which has led to numerous studies (see, e.g. Holloway 2003; Valins 2003; Campbell 2005; Brace et al. 2006; Ismail 2006; Pollard and Samers 2007).

In Chapter 4, we turned attention to how globalization has given rise to new spaces of religious competition and conflict, examining how globalization has caused understandings of space to evolve in line with the growing focus on transnational networks and flows, and the globalization of religious movements. We drew on Arjun Appadurai's five constructs – of ethnoscape, technoscape, finanscape, mediascape and ideoscape – to examine the effect of different facets of globalization on religious competition and conflict. We examined how the movement of people around the world and the resulting ethnoscapes contribute to a strengthening, weakening or inter-mixing of religious traditions and identities, and shape occasions for religious competition and conflict. We also discussed globalization-enabling technologies (such as TV and the Internet), and show how such technologies have changed the nature of and potential for religious experience, instruction and competition (through a dual focus on online religion and religion online). We then focused on finanscapes and explored how participation in a global financial system (and the associated pursuit of material values) can both conflict with religious values and influence the globalization trajectories of religious groups (i.e. towards fundamentalism or cosmopolitanism). Finally, through our examination of mediascapes and ideoscapes, we explored the transformation and transmittance of religious images, the emotional (rather than critical) interpretation of such images, and the ways in which such interpretations can be exploited to further a religious objective.

Whereas all the previous chapters examined the conditions that lead to and exacerbate religious competition and conflict, in Chapter 5, we focused on how religious groups can become agents of social resilience and change that are often more powerful than the state (and other secular institutions). We examined how religious groups strengthen themselves – and thus become more competitive – by engaging socially vulnerable groups, and within broader contexts of environment vulnerability. Both the proactive capacities and reactive capabilities of religious groups were considered.

As demonstrated in various ways throughout the book, religious spaces are intimately entwined with global processes. More often than not, religious spaces are 'avatars' of globalization. It is clear that in a globalized world, religion is not a bounded phenomenon that can be fixed within buildings, localities, or even the nation-state. Instead, religion 'circulate[s] globally, becoming localized in paradoxical ways that alternatively foster a cosmopolitan hybridity or erect new exclusionary boundaries in the name of purity' (Vasquez 2008, 153). Contrary to the proscriptions of the modernization and secularization theories outlined in Chapter 1, religion today is mobile, diffuse and compelling. It can serve as an anchor, 'orient[ing] itinerant individuals and groups in time and space' (Tweed 2006, 262), but it can also be anchored itself by buildings and bodies. Whichever way it is conceived, it is clear that religion always serves a bridging function; it connects ideas of – and claims to – universal truth with the salvation or redemption of the self. Religion is never static. It is always on the move, finding expression in spaces that may or may not be imbued with competing claims, meanings and identities. Religion, like space, is always in the process of becoming. It is never static.

In addition to processes of globalization raising questions about the changing forms of religion, they have also contributed to new understandings of the way that space is produced, imagined and analysed. Such understandings can be conceived in terms of the compression and distanciation of space and time in a globalized world. On the one hand, advances in communications technology (driven for the main part by innovations in the capitalist regime of global production and consumption) have accelerated the pace of life. This has caused distances to shrink (or compress), thus 'annihilating space through time' (Harvey 1989, 293). The net effect of such 'annihilation' is that space becomes less clearly defined, and more enmeshed within global networks of production and understanding. On the other hand, the same advances have served to disembed social relations from local contexts of interaction, instead 'restructur[ing them] across indefinite spans of time-space' (Giddens 1990, 21). The net effect of such 'restructuring' is that space opens up new possibilities for engagement and interaction.

The global imperative is not, however, one of unbounded expansion and freedom of expression. On the contrary, as Shamir (2005, 214) rightly contends, globalization is too often 'overtheorized in terms of social openness and undertheorized in terms of social closure'. Closure does, in many respects, paint a more accurate image of the power asymmetries and intransigence that the processes of globalization exacerbate. As this book has illustrated in various ways, when religion is added to the mix, the potential for ongoing forms of exclusion, exploitation and subjugation is heightened. As Vasquez (2008, 151) argues, the study of religion in/and space should 'assume that complexity, connectivity, and fluidity are preponderant features of our present age, without ignoring the strong countervailing global logics of segregation, surveillance and control'. Religious spaces are features of the connections within which they are enmeshed; they are not static, nor are they prescribed. Instead, they exist and are imbued with meaning and resonance at various scales of geographical analysis – from the global to the embodied. They are completely relational and often, therefore, the focus of the competing ambitions of different religious groups, or of religious and secular agencies. That such claims to space often degenerate into inter-religious and religious-secular competition and conflict reflects a dynamic that is difficult to resolve, and often becomes more pronounced with time. To understand religious competition, conflict and violence, therefore, requires that attention be paid to the spaces that are both medium and outcome of such relations. This then is the crux of the book's contributions.

Notes

Chapter 1

1   We are grateful to Sovan Patra for suggesting this conceptualization.

Chapter 2

1   It is worth being careful about the usage of the terms 'cults' or 'sects'. After all, some
    of today's mainstream religions, including Buddhism, Christianity and Islam, were
    yesterday's 'cults'. A more recent example is the steady growth of the Methodist
    church from 'cult' to 'mainstream religion'. In this sense, when cults compete for
    religious market share, they are in fact attempting to shed the tag of being a 'cult' to
    join the religious mainstream.
2   This has close parallels to the recent phenomenon of 'reconversion' programmes
    undertaken by Hindu right-wing organizations in India to bring converts to
    Christianity back into the 'Hindu fold' (Josh 2009).
3   In Singapore, the government is empowered to acquire land, through compulsory
    purchases by the Land Acquisition Act of 1966. Once the Act is invoked, land
    owners have no legal recourse, in terms of challenging the purchase; they can only
    appeal about the quantum of compensation. See Kong (1993a).
4   The influence of both these factors in managing dissatisfaction over religious
    relocation is most clearly seen in the events following the government's decision
    to acquire the land in Queen Street on which the Sikh Central temple was located
    (Kong 1993a).

Chapter 3

1   After 1990, when the Supreme Soviet passed a legislation guaranteeing religious
    freedom for all communities, there was a rapid spurt in the presence of religious
    groups in Russia, including Evangelical and Pentecostal groups and cults such
    as Jehovah's Witnesses. However, as the new groups rapidly increased their own
    membership at the expense of the market share of the Orthodox Church, there was a

steady decline in the support for religious freedom at the highest levels of religious and political leadership. For greater historical detail, see Froese (2008) and Wanner (2004).

2   That said, the act also provided parents with the right to withdraw their children from the religious education classes or collective worship practices.

3   Since 1997, after a ruling that the *hijab* was not in itself 'ostentatious', French courts have sided with students challenging their expulsion from schools (Fetzer and Soper 2005).

4   'Chinese religionists' is a term that encapsulates Taoism, ancestor worship and various other Chinese folk religions that are practiced throughout China and among Chinese diasporic communities.

5   As noted in the previous chapter, this is the same set of variables that have helped the state to comprehensively and effectively regulate religious practices in religious spaces.

6   New media will be discussed in Chapter 4 where technology and religious competition are discussed.

7   One exception to the rule is the well-publicized unwillingness on the part of the state to put Malay-Muslims in frontline positions in the Armed Forces (e.g. as pilots). Interestingly, this deviation from the technocratic principle (itself, a bulwark against conflict of interests) has also been justified by an appeal to the need to prevent a conflict of interest (see Hill [2004] for a discussion of the issue). In 1987, open admission of the government's position on this issue provoked strong anti-government sentiments among sections of the Singaporean Malay community.

8   The material for this case study is drawn from Apilado (2009).

9   While in the early models of religion-state partnerships for social service provision required faith-based agencies to maintain an essentially non-sectarian character, the new laws have allowed organizations to retain their sectarian identity as long as they did not use direct government funds for sectarian purposes. If the funding was indirect – for example, through vouchers bought by clients who had a free choice of service providers, even this minimal restriction did not apply (Sider and Unruh 2001).

Chapter 4

1   Although a key religious innovation mediated by the Internet has been the development of 'online religion' that has no offline equivalent or presence, given the relatively early stage of such fully online religions, they are excluded from the analysis here.

2   This is true for both conventional and new media; the only aspect that distinguishes the two forms is the potential for interactivity: conventional media draws a clear

line between image production and image consumption; new media, however, makes it possible to be at once a producer and consumer.

3   The use of the Islamic *umma* is only for expositional purposes. One can easily think of a cyber-Christendom, for example.

References

Adams, D. J. (1995) 'Church Growth in Korea: A Paradigm Shift from Ecclesiology to Nationalism', in M. K. Mullins and R. F. Young (eds), *Perspectives on Christianity in Korea and Japan: The Gospel and Culture in East Asia.* Lewiston: E. Mellen Press, 13–28.

Adger, W. N. (2000) 'Social and Ecological Resilience: Are They Related?' *Progress in Human Geography*, 24 (3): 347–64.

Adger, W. N., T. P. Hughes, C. Folke, S. R. Carpenter and J. Rockström (2005) 'Social-Ecological Resilience to Coastal Disasters', *Science*, 309 (5737): 1036–9.

Agnew, J. (2006) 'Religion and Geopolitics', *Geopolitics*, 11 (2): 183–91.

Albin, C. (1991) 'Negotiating Indivisible Goods: The Case of Jerusalem', *Jerusalem Journal of International Relations*, 13 (1): 45–76.

Allievo, S. and F. Dassetto (1999) 'Introduction', *Social Compass*, 46: 243–9.

Anderson, A., M. Bergunder, A. Droogers and C. van der Laan (2010) 'Introduction', in A. Anderson, M. Bergunder, A. Droogers and C. van der Laan (eds), *Studying Global Pentecostalism: Theories and Methods.* Los Angeles: University of California Press, 1–9.

Anderson, B. (1983) *Imagined Communities: Reflections on the Origin and Spread of Nationalism.* London: Verso.

Anderson, J. W. (2003) 'The Internet and Islam's New Interpreters', in J. W. Anderson and D. F. Eickelman (eds), *New Media in the Muslim World: The Emerging Public Sphere.* Bloomington: Indiana University Press, 45–60.

Anwar, M. (1998) *Between Cultures: Continuity and Change in the Lives of Young Asians.* London: Routledge.

Apilado, D. B. (2009) 'The Issue of HIV/AIDS in the Philippines', in J. Bautista and F. G. L. Khek (eds), *Christianity and the State in Asia: Complicity and Conflict.* Oxon: Routledge, 131–54.

Appadurai, A. (1996) *Modernity at Large, Cultural Dimensions of Globalisation.* Minneapolis: University of Minnesota Press.

Asad, T. (2003) *Formations of the Secular: Christianity, Islam, Modernity.* Stanford, CA: Stanford University Press.

Azaryahu, M. and A. Golan (2001) '(Re)Naming the Landscape: The Formation of the Hebrew Map of Israel 1949–1960', *Journal of Historical Geography*, 27: 178–95.

Bafelli, E. (2011) 'Charismatic Blogger? Authority and New Religions on the Web 2.0', in E. Bafelli, I. Reader and B. Staemmler (eds), *Japanese Religions on the Internet: Innovation, Representation and Authority.* Oxon, UK: Routledge, 118–35.

Bafelli, E., I. Reader and B. Staemmler (2011) 'Media and Religion in Japan: Innovation, Representation and Authority', in E. Baffelli, I. Reader and B. Staemmler (eds), *Japanese Religions on the Internet: Innovation, Representation and Authority.* Oxon, UK: Routledge, 20–38.

Baird, I. (2009) 'Identities and Space: The Geographies of Religious Change amongst the Brao in Northeastern Cambodia', *Anthropos*, 104: 457–68.

Baker, C. and J. Beaumont (eds) (2011a) *Postsecular Cities: Space, Theory and Practice*. London: Continuum.

Baker, C. and J. Beaumont. (2011b) 'Introduction: Rise of the Post Secular City', in C. Baker and J. Beaumont (eds), *Postsecular Cities: Space, Theory and Practice*. London: Continuum, 1–11.

Ball, J., L. Armistead and B. Austin (2003) 'The Relationship between Religiosity and Adjustment Among African-American, Female, Urban Adolescents', *Journal of Adolescence*, 26: 431–46.

Barker, E. (2005) 'Crossing the Boundary: New Challenges to Religious Authority and Control as a Consequence of Access to the Internet', in M. T. Højsgaard and M. Warburg (eds), *Religion and Cyberspace*. Oxon, UK: Routledge, 67–87.

Barnett, L. (2013) 'Freedom of Religion and Religious Symbols in the Public Sphere'. Background Paper of the Legal and Legislative Affairs Division, Library of Parliament, <http://www.parl.gc.ca/content/lop/researchpublications/2011-60-e.pdf> (accessed 20 March 2015).

Basch, L., N. Glick-Schiller and C. Szanton Blanc (1994) *Nations Unbound: Transnational Projects, Postcolonial Predicaments, Deterritorialized Nation-States*. Amsterdam: Gordan and Breach.

Beaumont, J. (2010) 'Transcending the Particular in Postsecular Cities', in A. L. Molendijk, J. Beaumont and C. Jedan (eds), *Exploring the Postsecular: The Religious, the Political and the Urban*. Leiden: Brill, 3–17.

Beckford, J. A. (1978) 'Accounting for Conversion', *British Journal of Sociology*, 29 (2): 235–45.

Beckford, J. A. and J. T. Richardson (2007) 'Religion and Regulation', in J. A. Beckford and N. J. Demerath III (eds), *The SAGE Handbook of the Sociology of Religion*. London: Sage, 396–418.

Berger, P. (1967) *The Sacred Canopy: Elements of a Sociological Theory of Religion*. New York: Anchor Books.

Blaine, B. and J. Crocker (1995) 'Religiousness, Race and Psychological Well-Being: Exploring Social Psychological Mediators', *Personality and Social Psychology Bulletin*, 21 (10): 1031–41.

Bouma, G. (2007) 'Religious Resurgence, Conflict and the Transformation of Boundaries', in P. Beyer and L. Beaman (eds), *Religion, Globalization, and Culture*. Leiden and Boston: Brill, 187–202.

Bourdieu, P. (1986) 'The Forms of Capital', in J. G. Richardson (ed.), *Handbook for Theory and Research for the Sociology of Education*. New York: Greenwood, 241–58.

Bourdieu, P. (1989) 'Social Space and Symbolic Power', *Sociological Theory*, 7: 14–25.

Brace, C., A. Bailey and D. Harvey (2006) 'Religion, Place and Space: A Framework for Investigating Historical Geographies of Religious Identities and Communities', *Progress in Human Geography*, 30: 28–43.

Brah, A. (1996) *Cartographies of Diaspora*. London: Routledge.

Brasher, B. E. (2004) *Give Me That Online Religion*. New Brunswick, NJ: Rutgers University Press.

Brereton, J. P. (1987) 'Sacred Space', in M. Eliade (ed.), *The Encyclopedia of Religion*. New York: MacMillan, 525–35.

Brubaker, R. (2012) 'Religion and Nationalism: Four Approaches', *Nations and Nationalism*, 18 (1): 2–20.

Bruce, S. (2002) *God Is Dead: Secularisation in the West*. Oxford: Blackwell.

Bryant, M. D. and C. Lamb (1999) 'Introduction: Conversion in a Plural World', in C. Lamb and M. D. Bryant (eds), *Religious Conversion: Contemporary Practices and Controversies*. London: Cassell, 1–19.

Buchanan, J. (1981) 'The Return of the Ikhwan – 1979', in D. Holden and R. Johns (eds), *The House of Saud*. London: Sidgwick and Jackson, 511–26.

Bunt, G. R. (2003) *Islam in the Digital Age: E-Jihad, Online Fatwas and Cyber Islamic Environments*. London: Pluto Press.

Bunt, G. R. (2009) 'Religion and the Internet', in P. B. Clarke (ed.), *The Oxford Handbook of The Sociology of Religion*. Oxford: Oxford University Press, 705–22.

Cain, D. S. and J. Barthelemy (2008) 'Tangible and Spiritual Relief after the Storm: The Religious Communities Responds to Katrina', *Journal of Social Service Research*, 34 (3): 29–42.

Campbell, M. (2005) 'Sacred Groves for Forest Conservation in Ghana's Coastal Savanna's: Assessing Ecological and Social Dimensions', *Singapore Journal of Tropical Geography*, 26: 151–69.

Carlson, T. D., D. Kirkpatrick, L. Hecker and M. Killmer (2002) 'Religion, Spirituality, and Marriage and Family Therapy: A Study of Family Therapists' Beliefs about the Appropriateness of Addressing Religious and Spiritual Issues in Therapy', *The American Journal of Family Therapy*, 30: 157–71.

Carter, R. L. (2007) *Understanding Resilience through Ritual and Religious Practice: An Expanded Theoretical and Ethnographic Framework*. 2007 Summer Academy on Social Vulnerability, United Nations University.

Casanova, J. (1994) *Public Religions in the Modern World*. Chicago: University of Chicago Press.

Castells, M. (2000) *The Rise of the Network Society: The Information Age: Economy, Society and Culture*. Oxford: Wiley-Blackwell.

Chambers, R. (1989) 'Vulnerability, Coping and Policy', *IDS Bulletin*, 20: 1–7.

Chapman, C. (1998) *Islam and the West: Conflict, Coexistence or Conversion?*. Exeter, UK: Paternoster Press.

Chen, C. (2002) 'The Religious Varieties of Ethnic Presence: A Comparison between a Taiwanese Immigrant Buddhist Temple and an Evangelical Christian Church', *Sociology of Religion*, 63 (2): 215–38.

Cheng, M. (2003) 'House Church Movements and Religious Freedom in China', *China: An International Journal*, 1: 16–45.

Chesnut, A. (2003) *Competitive Spirits: Latin America's New Religious Economy*. Oxford: Oxford University Press.

Chidester, D. and E. T. Linenthal (1995) 'Introduction', in D. Chidester and E. T. Linenthal (eds), *American Sacred Space*. Bloomington: Indiana University Press, 1–42.

Chivallon, C. (2001) 'Religion as Space for the Expression of Caribbean Identity in the United Kingdom', *Environment and Planning D: Society and Space*, 19: 461–83.

Clammer, J. (1991) *The Sociology of Singapore Religion: Studies in Christianity and Chinese Culture*. Singapore: Chopmen.

Cloke, P. (2010) 'Theo-Ethics and Radical Faith-Based Praxis in the Postsecular City', in A. Molendijk, J. Beaumont and C. Jedan (eds), *Exploring the Postsecular: The Religious, the Political and the Urban*. Leiden: Brill, 223–41.

Cloke, P. and J. Beaumont (2013) 'Geographies of Postsecular Rapprochement in the City', *Progress in Human Geography*, 37 (1): 27–51.

Cloke, P., S. Johnsen and J. May (2005) 'Exploring Ethos? Discourses of Charity in the Provision of Emergency Services for Homeless People', *Environment and Planning A*, 37 (3): 385–402.

Cloke, P., S. Johnsen and J. May (2010) *Swept-up Lives: Re-Envisioning the Homeless City*. Oxford: Wiley-Blackwell.

Comaroff, J. and J. Comaroff (2003) 'Second Comings: Neo-Protestant Ethics and Millennial Capitalism in Africa, and Elsewhere', in P. Gifford, D. Archard, T. A. Hart and N. Rapport (eds), *2000 Years and Beyond: Faith, Identity and the 'Common Era'*. London: Routledge, 106–26.

Connell, J. (2005) 'Hillsong: A Megachurch in the Sydney Suburbs', *Australian Geographer*, 36: 315–32.

Cooke, M. and B. Lawrence (eds) (2005) *Muslim Networks: From Hajj to Hip Hop*. Chapel Hill: University of North Carolina Press.

Cowan, D. E. (2007) 'Religion on the Internet', in J. A. Beckford and N. J. Demerath III (eds), *The SAGE Handbook of the Sociology of Religion*. London: Sage, 357–76.

Cox, H. (1965) *The Secular City: Secularization and Urbanization in Theological Perspective*. New York: Collier Books.

Crang, P., C. Dwyer and P. Jackson (2003) 'Transnationalism and the Spaces of Commodity Culture', *Progress in Human Geography*, 27 (4): 438–56.

Davoudi, S. (2012) 'Resilience: A Bridging Concept or a Dead End?' *Planning Theory and Practice*, 13 (2): 299–307.

Dawson, L. L. and J. Hennebry (1999) 'New Religions and the Internet: Recruiting in a New Public Space', *Journal of Contemporary Religion*, 14 (1): 17–39.

de Alwis, M. (2009) 'A Double Wounding: Aid and Activism in Post-tsunami Sri Lanka', in M. De Alwis and E. Hedman (eds), *Tsunami in a Time of War: Aid, Activism and Reconstruction*. Colombo: International Centre for Ethnic Studies, 121–38.

de Tocqueville, A. (2000) *Democracy in America*. Edited and translated by H. Mansfield and D. Winthrop. Chicago: University of Chicago Press.

Dehghani, M., K. Sagae, S. Sachdeva and J. Gratch (2014) 'Analyzing Political Rhetoric in Conservative and Liberal Weblogs Related to the Construction of the "Ground Zero Mosque"', *Journal of Information Technology & Politics*, 11 (1): 1–14.

Demerath, N. J. III (2007) 'Religion and the State; Violence and Human Rights', in J. A. Beckford and N. J. Demerath III (eds), *The SAGE Handbook of the Sociology of Religion*. London: Sage, 381–95.

D'Epinay, C. (1969) *Haven of the Masses: A Study of the Pentecostal Movement in Chile*. London: Lutterworth.

Deutsch, K. W. (1953) *Nationalism and Social Communication: An Inquiry into the Foundations of Nationality*. Cambridge, MA: MIT Press.

Dobbelaere, K. (1981) 'Secularization: A Multi-Dimensional Concept', *Current Sociology*, 29: 3–153.

Doniger, W. (1997) 'Medical and Mythical Constructions of the Body in Hindu Texts', in S. Coakley (ed.), *Religion and the Body*. Cambridge: Cambridge University Press, 167–84.

Dunn, K. (2004) 'Islam in Sydney: Contesting the Discourse of Absence', *Australian Geographer*, 35 (3): 333–53.

Durkheim, E. (1965) *The Elementary Forms of the Religious Life*. New York: Free Press.

Durkheim, E. (1984 [1894]) *The Division of Labour in Society*. New York: Free Press.

Dwyer, C. (2002) '"Where Are You from?": Young British Muslim Women and the Making of Home', in A. B. Blunt and C. M. McEwan (eds), *Postcolonial Geographies*. London: Continuum, 184–99.

Eade, J. (1996) 'Nationalism, Community, and the Islamization of Space in London', in B. D. Metcalf (ed.), *Making Muslim Space in North America and Europe*. Los Angeles and London: University of California Press, 217–33.

El-Nawawy, M. and S. Khamis (2009) *Islam Dot Com: Contemporary Islamic Discourses in Cyberspace*. New York: Palgrave Macmillan.

Eliade, M. (1958) *Patterns in Comparative Religion*. New York: Sheed & Ward.

Eliade, M. (1959) *The Sacred and the Profane: The Nature of Religion*. Translated from French by W. R. Trask. San Diego: Harcourt Brace Jovanovich.

Eliade, M. (1991) *Images and Symbols*. Translated by Philip Mairet. Princeton, NJ: Princeton University Press.

Ellison, C. G. (1993) 'Religious Involvement and Self-Perception Among Black Americans', *Social Forces*, 71 (4): 1027–55.

Emirbayer, M. and J. Goodwin (1994) 'Network Analysis, Culture, and the Problems of Agency', *American Journal of Sociology*, 99 (6): 1411–54.

Eng, K.-P. K. (2008) 'Delivering Welfare Services in Singapore: A Strategic Partnership between Buddhism and the State', in A. E. Lai (ed.), *Religious Diversity in Singapore*. Singapore: Institute of Southeast Asian Studies, 505–23.

Esbeck, C., S. Carlson-Theis and R. Sider (2004) *The Freedom of Faith-Based Organizations to Staff on a Religious Basis*. Washington, DC: Center for Public Justice.

Farnsley, A. E. II (2007) 'Faith-Based Initiatives', in J. A. Beckford and N. J. Demerath III (eds), *The SAGE Handbook of the Sociology of Religion*. London: Sage, 345–56.

Fetzer, J. S. and C. Soper (2005) *Muslims and the State in Britain, France and Germany*. Cambridge: Cambridge University Press.

Foucault, M. (1980) *Power/Knowledge: Selected Interviews and Other Writings 1972–1977/Michel Foucault*. Edited by C. Gordon. New York: Pantheon.

Foucault, M. (1984) 'Of Other Spaces: Utopias and Heterotopias', *Architecture / Mouvement /Continuite*, 5: 46–9.

Fox, J. (2009) 'Integrating Religion into International Relations Theory', in J. Haynes (ed.), *Routledge Handbook of Religion and Politics*. New York and London: Routledge, 273–92.

Friedland, R. (2002) 'Money, Sex and God: The Erotic Logic of Religious Nationalisms', *Sociological Theory*, 20 (3): 381–425.

Froese, P. (2008) *The Plot to Kill God: Findings from the Soviet Experiment in Secularization*. Berkeley and Los Angeles: University of California Press.

Ganguly, S. (2001) *Conflict Unending: India-Pakistan Tensions Since 1947*. New York: Columbia University Press.

Ganguly, S. (2007) 'The Roots of Religious Violence in India, Pakistan and Bangladesh', in L. E. Cady and S. W. Simon (eds), *Religion and Conflict in South and Southeast Asia: Disrupting Violence*. London and New York: Routledge, 70–84.

Gardner, K. (1995) *Global Migrants, Local Lives*. Oxford: Clarendon Press.

Gellner, E. (1983) *Nations and Nationalism*. New York: Cornell University Press.

Gerhardt, H. (2008) 'Geopolitics, Ethics, and the Evangelicals' Commitment to Sudan', *Environment and Planning D: Society and Space*, 26 (5): 911–28.

Gerlach, L. P. and V. H. Hine (1968) 'Five Factors Crucial to the Growth and Spread of a Modern Religious Movement', *Journal for the Scientific Study of Religion*, 7 (1): 23–40.

Giddens, A. (1990) *The Consequences of Modernity*. Stanford, CA: Stanford University Press.

Glick-Schiller, N. (1997) 'The Situation of Transnational Studies', *Identities*, 4: 155–66.

Glick-Schiller, N. (2005) 'Transnational Social Fields and Imperialism: Bringing a Theory of Power to Transnational Studies', *Anthropological Theory*, 5 (4): 439–61.

Goh, R. B. H. (2008) 'Mission Schools in Singapore: Religious Harmony, Social Identities, and the Negotiation of Evangelical Churches', in A. E. Lai (ed.), *Religious Diversity in Singapore*. Singapore: Institute of Southeast Asian Studies, 362–80.

Gorlizki, Y. (2000) 'Class and Nation in the Jewish Settlement of Palestine: The Case of Merhavia, 1910–30', *Journal of Historical Geography*, 26: 572–88.

Greed, C. (2011) 'A Feminist Critique of the Postsecular City: God and Gender', in J. Beaumont and C. Baker (eds), *Postsecular Cities: Space, Theory and Practice*. Leiden: Brill, 104–19.

Green, N. (1997) 'Beyond Being Digital: Representation and Virtual Corporeality', in D. Holmes (ed.), *Virtual Politics: Identity and Community in Cyberspace*. London: Sage, 59–78.

Grim, B. J. and R. Finke (2011) *The Price of Freedom Denied: Religious Persecution and Violence*. Cambridge: Cambridge University Press.

Guth, J. L., J. C. Green, C. E Smidt, L. A. Kellstedt and M. M. Poloma (1997) *The Bully Pulpit: The Politics of Protestant Clergy*. Lawrence: University of Kansas Press.

Habermas, J. (2006) 'Religion in the Public Sphere', *European Journal of Philosophy*, 14 (1): 1–25.

Hall, J. (2003) 'Religion and Violence: Social Processes in Comparative Perspective', in M. Dillon (ed.), *Handbook for the Sociology of Religion*. Cambridge, NY: Cambridge University Press, 359–81.

Hannerz, U. (1992) 'The Global Ecumene as a Network of Networks', in A. Kuper (ed.), *Conceptualizing Society*. London: Routledge, 140–60.

Hannerz, U. (1997) *Transnational Connections: Culture, People, Places*. New York: Routledge.

Harriss, J. and P. de Renzio (1997) 'Missing Link or Analytically Missing? The Concept of Social Capital. A Bibliographic Essay', *Journal of International Development*, 9: 919–37.

Harvey, D. (1989) *The Condition of Postmodernity*. Oxford: Blackwell.

Hassner, R. (2003) '"To Have and to Hold": Conflicts over Sacred Space and the Problem of Indivisibility', *Security Studies*, 12 (4): 1–33.

Haynes, J. (2001) 'Transnational Religious Actors and International Politics', *Third World Quarterly*, 22 (2): 143–58.

Hecht, R. (1994) 'The Construction and Management of Sacred Time and Space: Sabta Nur in the Church of the Holy Sepulchre', in R. Friedland and D. Boden (eds), *Now Here: Space, Time and Modernity*. Berkeley: University of California Press, 181–235.

Heelas, P. and L. Woodhead (2005) *The Spiritual Revolution*. Oxford: Blackwell.

Hefner, R. W. (1993) 'World Building and the Rationality of Conversion', in R. W. Hefner (ed.), *Conversion to Christianity: Historical and Anthropological Perspectives on a Great Transformation*. Berkeley: University of California Press, 3–45.

Hefner, R. W. (2007) 'The Sword against the Crescent: Religion and Violence in Muslim Southeast Asia', in L. E. Cady and S. W. Simon (eds), *Religion and Conflict in South and Southeast Asia: Disrupting Violence*. London and New York: Routledge, 33–50.

Hefner, R. W. (2009) 'Religion and Modernity Worldwide', in P. B. Clarke (ed.), *The Oxford Handbook of The Sociology of Religion*. Oxford: Oxford University Press, 152–71.

Helland, C. (2000) 'Online-Religion/Religion-Online and Virtual Communitas', in J. K. Hadden and D. E. Cowan (eds), *Religion on the Internet: Research Prospects and Promises*. London and Amsterdam: JAI Press/Elseiver Science, 22–36.

Henderson, B. (2005) 'Open Letter to Kansas School Board', <http://www.venganza.org/about/open-letter/> (accessed 20 April 2012).

Henkel, R. and L. Sakaja (2009) 'A Sanctuary in Post-Conflict Space: The Baptist Church as a "Middle Option" in Banovina, Croatia', *Geografiska Annaler*, 91: 39–56.

Herring, S. (1996) 'Bringing Familiar Baggage to the New Frontier: Gender Differences in Computer-Mediated Communication', in V. I. Vitanza (ed.), *CyberReader*. Needham Heights, MA: Allan & Bacon, 144–54.

Hervieu-Leger, D. (2002) 'Space and Religion: New Approaches to Religious Spatiality in Modernity', *International Journal of Urban and Regional Research*, 26 (1): 99–105.

Hill, M. (2004) 'The Rehabilitation and Regulation of Religion in Singapore', in J. T. Richardson (ed.), *Regulating Religion: Case Studies from Around the World*. New York: Kluwer Academic/Plenum, 343–58.

Hollenbach, P. and K. Ruwanpura, K. (2011) 'Symbolic Gestures: The Development Terrain of Post-Tsunami Villages in (Southern) Sri Lanka', *Journal of Development Studies*, 47: 1299–1314.

Holloway, J. (2003) 'Make-Believe: Spiritual Practice, Embodiment and Sacred Space', *Environment and Planning A*, 35: 1961–74.

Hoover, S. M. (2009) 'Religion and the Media', in P. B. Clarke (ed.), *The Oxford Handbook of The Sociology of Religion*. Oxford: Oxford University Press, 688–704.

Hopkins, P. (2011) 'Towards Critical Geographies of the University Campus: Understanding the Contested Experiences of Muslim Students', *Transactions of the Institute of British Geographers*, 36: 157–69.

Hopkins, P., E. Olson, R. Pain and G. Vincett (2011) 'Mapping Intergenerationalities: The Formation of Youthful Religiosities', *Transactions of the Institute of British Geographers*, 36: 314–27.

Huntington, S. (1996) *The Clash of Civilizations and the Remaking of World Order*. New York: Simon & Schuster.

Iannaccore, L. R. (1994) 'Why Strict Churches are Strong', *American Journal of Sociology* 99 (5): 1180–1211.

Introvigne, M. (2002) '"There Is No Place for Us but to Go Up": New Religious Movements and Violence', *Social Compass* 49 (2): 213–24.

Ismail, R. (2006) 'Ramadan and Bussorah Street: The Spirit of Place', *GeoJournal*, 66: 243–56.

Ivakhiv, A. (2006) 'Toward a Geography of "Religion": Mapping the Distribution of an Unstable Signifier', *Annals of the Association of American Geographers*, 96 (1): 169–75.

Jazeel, T. and C. Brun (2009) 'Introduction: Spatial Politics and Postcolonial Sri Lanka', in T. Jazeel and C. Brun (eds), *Spatialising Politics: Culture and Geography in Postcolonial Sri Lanka*. New Delhi: Sage, 1–23.

Jenkins, P. (2007) *The Next Christendom: The Coming of Global Christianity*. Oxford: Oxford University Press.

Jerryson, M. (2010) 'Militarizing Buddhism: Violence in Southern Thailand', in M. K. Jerryson and M. Juergensmeyer (eds), *Buddhist Warfare*. Oxford: Oxford University Press, 179–209.

Jia, L., S. C. Karpen and E. R. Hirt (2011) 'Beyond Anti-Muslim Sentiment: Opposing the Ground Zero Mosque as a Means to Pursuing a Stronger America', *Psychological Science*, 22: 1327–35.

Josh, B. (2009) 'Conversions, Complicity and the State in Post-Independence India', in J. Bautista and F. G. L. Khek (eds), *Christianity and the State in Asia: Complicity and Conflict*. Oxon: Routledge, 97–114.

Juergensmeyer, M. (2007) 'Religious War, Terrorism, and Peace', in G. ter Haar and Y. Tsuruoka (eds), *Religion and Society: An Agenda for the 21st Century*. Leiden: Brill, 7–17.

Juergensmeyer, M. (2009) 'Religious Violence', in P. B. Clarke (ed.), *The Oxford Handbook of The Sociology of Religion*. Oxford: Oxford University Press, 890–908.

Kalra, V. S. (2000) *From Textiles Mills to Taxi Ranks*. Aldershot: Ashgate.

Kao, C.-Y. (2009) 'The Cultural Revolution and the Emergence of Pentecostal-Style Protestantism in China', *Journal of Contemporary Religion*, 24: 171–88.

Kemp, A. and R. Raijman (2003) 'Christian Zionists in the Holy Land: Evangelical Churches, Labor Migrants, and the Jewish State', *Identities: Global Studies in Power and Culture*, 10 (3): 295–318.

Keyes, C. (1993) 'Why the Thai Are Not Christians: Buddhist and Christian Conversion in Thailand', in R. Hefner (ed.), *Conversion to Christianity: Historical and Anthropological Perspectives on a Great Transformation*. Berkeley: University of California Press, 259–84.

Kilbourne, B. K. and J. T. Richardson (1982) 'Cults Versus Families: A Case of Misattribution of Cause?', *Marriage & Family Review* 4 (3–4): 81–100.

Kinney, J. (1995) 'Religion, Cyberspace and the Future', *Futures*, 27 (7): 763–76.

Kluver, R. and P. J. Cheong (2007) 'Technological Modernization, the Internet, and Religion in Singapore', *Journal of Computer-Mediated Communication*, 12 (3): article 18.

Knott, K. (2005a) 'Spatial Theory and Method for the Study of Religion', *Temenos*, 41 (2): 153–84.

Knott, K. (2005b) *The Location of Religion: A Spatial Analysis*. London: Sage.

Knott, K. (2010) 'Cutting through the Postsecular City: A Spatial Interrogation', in A. L. Molendijk, J. Beaumont and C. Jedan (eds), *Exploring the Postsecular: The Religious, the Political and the Urban*. Leiden: Brill, 19–38.

Knott, K. and S. Khokher (1993) 'Religion and Ethnic Identity Among Young Muslim Women in Bradford', *New Community*, 19: 81–107.

Knox, Z. (2003) 'The Symphonic Ideal: The Moscow Patriarchate's Post-Soviet Leadership', *Europe-Asia Studies*, 55 (4): 87–113.

Kong, L. (1993a) 'Ideological Hegemony and the Political Symbolism of Religious Buildings in Singapore', *Environment and Planning D: Society and Space*, 11: 23–45.

Kong, L. (1993b) 'Negotiating Conceptions of "Sacred Space": A Case Study of Religious Buildings in Singapore', *Transactions of the Institute of British Geographers*, 18: 342–58.

Kong, L. (2001a) 'Mapping "New" Geographies of Religion: Politics and Poetics in Modernity', *Progress in Human Geography*, 25 (2): 211–33.

Kong, L. (2001b) 'Religion and Technology: Refiguring Place, Space, Identity and Community', *Area*, 33 (4): 404–13.

Kong, L. (2002) 'In Search of Permanent Homes: Singapore's House Churches and the Politics of Space', *Urban Studies*, 39: 1573–86.

Kong, L. (2005a) 'Religious Schools: For Spirit, (F)or Nation', *Environment and Planning D: Society and Space,* 23 (4): 615–31.

Kong, L. (2005b) 'Religious Processions: Urban Politics and Poetics', *Temenos,* 41 (2): 225–49.

Kong, L. (2006) 'Religion and Spaces of Technology: Constructing and Contesting Nation, Transnation, and Place', *Environment and Planning A,* 38 (5): 903–18.

Kong, L. (2010) 'Global Shifts, Theoretical Shifts: Changing Geographies of Religion', *Progress in Human Geography,* 34: 755–76.

Kong, L. (2012) 'No Place, New Places: Death and Its Rituals in Urban Asia', *Urban Studies,* 49 (2): 415–33.

Kong, L. (2013) 'Christian Evangelizing Across National Boundaries: Technology, Cultural Capital, and the Intellectualization of Religion', in P. Hopkins, L. Kong and E. Olson (eds), *Religion and Place: Landscape, Politics and Piety.* Dordrecht: Springer, 21–38.

Kong, L., S. A. Low and J. Yip (1994) *Convent Chronicles: History of a Pioneer Mission School for Girls in Singapore.* Singapore: Armour.

Korf, B., S. Hasbullah, P. Hollenbach and B. Klem (2010) 'The Gift of Disaster: The Commodification of Good Intentions in Post-tsunami Sri Lanka', *Disasters, Special Issue: The Politicisation of Reconstructing Conflict-affected Countries,* 34 (1): 60–77.

Kramnick, I. and L. Moore (1997) 'Can the Church Save the Cities? Faith-Based Services and the Constitution', *American Prospect,* 35: 47–53.

Lane, B. (1988) *Landscapes of the Sacred: Geography and Narrative in American Spirituality.* Mahwah, NJ: Paulist Press.

Larsson, G. (2005) 'The Death of a Virtual Muslim Discussion Group: Issues and Methods in Analyzing Religion on the Net', *Online Heidelberg Journal of Religions on the Internet,* 1 (1): 1–7.

Lechner, F. and J. Boli (2003) 'Expanding World Culture: Pentecostalism as a Global Movement', in F. Lechner and J. Boli (eds), *The Globalization Reader.* Malden, MA: Blackwell, 387–91.

Leeds, M. (9 June 2006) 'Ruth Rales Jewish Family Service Prepares Pre-Enrollment Hurricane Emergency Care Contact List'. Press release by the Ruth Rales Jewish Family Service of South Palm Beach County.

Lefebvre, H. (1991) *The Production of Space.* Malden, MA: Blackwell.

Lehman, D. (2002) 'Religion and Globalisation', in L. Woodhead, P. Fletcher, H. Kawanami and D. Smith (eds), *Religions in the Modern World: Traditions and Transformations.* London: Routledge, 299–315.

Lemyre, L., M. Clement, W. Corneil, L. Craig, P. Boutette, M. Tyshenko et al. (2005) 'A Psychosocial Risk Assessment and Management Framework to Enhance Response to CBRN Terrorism Threats and Attacks', *Biosecurity and Bioterrorism: Biodefense Strategy, Practice and Science,* 3 (4): 316–30.

Leonard, M. (2007) 'Trapped in Space? Children's Accounts of Risky Environments', *Children and Society,* 21: 432–45.

Lev, M. (1989) *The Traveler's Key to Jerusalem: A Guide to the Sacred Places of Jerusalem*. New York: Knopf.

Levine, D. H. (1992) *Popular Voices in Latin American Catholicism*. Princeton, NJ: Princeton University Press.

Levitt, P. (2001a) 'Between God, Ethnicity and Country: An Approach to the Study of Transnational Religion'. Working Paper of the Transnational Communities Programme WPTC-01-13 <http://www.transcomm.ox.ac.uk/working%20papers/Levitt.pdf> (accessed 18 April 2012).

Levitt, P. (2001b) 'Transnational Migration: Taking Stock and Future Directions', *Global Networks*, 1 (3): 195–216.

Levitt, P. and N. Glick-Schiller (2004) 'Conceptualizing Simultaneity: A Transnational Social Field Perspective on Society', *International Migration Review*, 38 (4): 1002–39.

Lewis, P. (1994) *Islamic Britain*. London: I. B. Tauris.

Licklider, R. (1993) 'How Civil Wars End: Questions and Methods', in R. Licklider (ed.), *Stop the Killing: How Civil Wars End*. New York: New York University Press, 3–19.

Liederman, L. (2000) 'Pluralism in Education: The Display of Islamic Affiliation in French and British Schools', *Islam and Christian-Muslim Relations*, 11 (1): 105–17.

Lin, N., K. Cook and R. S. Burt (eds) (2001) *Social Capital: Theory and Research*. New York: Aldine de Gruyter.

Lincoln, B. (2003) *Holy Terrors: Thinking about Religion after September 11*. Chicago: University of Chicago Press.

Liow, J. C. (2007) 'Violence and The Long Road to Reconciliation in Southern Thailand', in L. E. Cady and S. W. Simon (eds), *Religion and Conflict in South and Southeast Asia: Disrupting Violence*. London and New York: Routledge, 154–73.

Liu, Q. (2009) 'A Close Look into an Immigrant Workers' Church in Beijing', *Nova Religio: The Journal of Alternative and Emergent Religions*, 12: 91–98.

Lofland, J. and R. Stark (1965) 'Becoming a World-Saver: A Theory of Conversion to a Deviant Perspective', *American Sociological Review*, 30 (6): 862–75.

McAlister, E. (1998) 'The Madonna of 115th Street Revisited: Vodou and Haitian Catholicism in the Age of Transnationalism', in S. Warner and J. Wittner (eds), *Gatherings in Diaspora: Religious Communities and the New Immigration*. Philadelphia, PA: Temple University Press, 123–60.

McAlister, E. (2005) 'Globalization and the Religious Production of Space', *Journal for the Scientific Study of Religion*, 44: 249–55.

McGregor, A. (2010) 'Geographies of Religion and Development: Rebuilding Sacred Spaces in Aceh, Indonesia, after the Tsunami', *Environment and Planning A*, 42: 729–46.

McLoughlin, S. (1998) 'The Mosque-Centre, Community-Mosque: Multi-Functions, Funding and the Reconstruction of Islam in Bradford', *Scottish Journal of Religious Studies*, 19 (2): 211–27.

McLoughlin, S. (2005) 'Mosques and the Public Space: Conflict and Cooperation in Bradford', *Journal of Ethnic and Migration Studies*, 31 (6): 1045–66.

Mahadev, N. (2014) 'Conversion and Anti-Conversion in Contemporary Sri Lanka: Pentecostal Christian Evangelism and Theravada Buddhist View on the Ethics of Religious Attraction', in J. Finucane and M. Feener (eds), *Proselytizing and the Limits of Religious Pluralism in Contemporary Asia*. Singapore: Springer, 211–35.

Mahoney, A., K. I. Pargament, A. Murray-Swank and N. Murray-Swank (2003) 'Religion and the Sanctification of Family Relationships', *Review of Religious Research*, 44: 220–36.

Mansor, E. and N. A. Ibrahim (2008) 'Muslim Organizations and Mosques as Social Service Providers', in A. E. Lai (ed.), *Religious Diversity in Singapore*. Singapore: Institute of Southeast Asian Studies, 459–88.

Marshall, K. (2005) 'Faith and Development: Re-Thinking Development Debates', World Bank, <http://web.worldbank.org/WBSITE/EXTERNAL/EXTABOUTUS/PARTNERS/EXTDEVDIALOGUE/0,,contentMDK:20478626~menuPK:64192472~pagePK:6419252 3~piPK:64192458~theSitePK:537298,00.html> (accessed 13 March 2015).

Martin, D. (1990) *Tongues of Fire: The Explosion of Protestantism in Latin America*. Oxford: Blackwell.

Martin, D. (2005) 'Issues Affecting the Study of Pentecostalism in Asia', in A. Anderson and E. Tang (eds), *Asian and Pentecostal: The Charismatic Face of Christianity in Asia*. Philippines: Regnum Books International, 27–36.

Massey, D. (1992) 'A Place Called Home?' *New Formations*, 17: 3–15.

Massey, D. (2005) *For Space*. London: Sage.

Mathews, M. (2008) 'Saving the City through Good Works: Christian Involvement in Social Services', in A. E. Lai (ed.), *Religious Diversity in Singapore*. Singapore: Institute of Southeast Asian Studies, 524–56.

Matthews, B. (2007) 'Christian Evangelical Conversions and the Politics of Sri Lanka', *Pacific Affairs*, 80 (3): 455–72.

Mauss, M. (1954) *The Gift: Forms and Functions of Exchange in Archaic Societies*. New York: W. W. Norton.

Mazumdar, S. and S. Mazumdar (1993) 'Sacred Space and Place Attachment', *Journal of Environmental Psychology*, 13: 231–42.

Megoran, N. (2004) 'Christianity and Political Geography: On Faith and Geopolitical Imagination', *The Brandywine Review of Faith and International Affairs*, 2: 40–5.

Menjivar, C. (1999) 'Religious Institutions and Transnationalism: A Case Study of Catholic and Evangelical Salvadoran Immigrants', *International Journal of Politics, Culture, and Society*, 12 (4): 589–611.

Metcalf, B. (1996) 'Introduction: Sacred Worlds, Sanctioned Practice, New Communities', in B. Metcalf (ed.), *Making Muslim Space in North America and Europe*. Berkeley: University of California Press, 1–27.

Mohammad, R. (2005) 'Negotiating the Spaces of the Home, the Education System, and the Labour Market', in G. W. Falah and C. Nagel (eds), *Geographies of Muslim Women: Gender, Religion and Space*. New York: Guildford, 178–202.

Molendijk, A., J. Beaumont and C. Jedan (eds) (2010) *Exploring the Postsecular: The Religious, the Political and the Urban*. Leiden: Brill.

Mullins, M. R. (2001) 'The Legal and Political Fallout of the "Aum Affair",
in R. J. Kisala and M. R. Mullins (eds), *Religion and Social Crisis in Japan:
Understanding Japanese Society through the Aum Affair*. Hampshire and New
York: Palgrave, 71–86.

Naylor, S. and J. R. Ryan (2002) 'The Mosque in the Suburbs: Negotiating Religion and
Ethnicity in South London', *Social and Cultural Geography*, 3: 39–59.

Nederveen Pieterse, J. (1992) *Christianity and Hegemony: Religion and Politics on the
Frontiers of Social Change*. New York and Oxford: Berg.

Nederveen Pieterse, J. (2004) *Globalization and Culture: Global Melange*. Lanham, MD:
Rowman and Littlefield.

Nielsen, J. (1992) *Muslims in Western Europe*. Edinburgh: Edinburgh University Press.

Norris, P. and R. Inglehart (2004) *Sacred and Secular: Religion and Politics Worldwide*.
Cambridge, NY: Cambridge University Press.

O'Riordan, T., C. L. Cooper, A. Jordan, S. Rayner, K. R. Richards, P. Runci and S. Yoffe
(1998) 'Institutional Frameworks for Political Action', in S. Rayner and E. Malone
(eds), *Human Choice and Climate Change. Volume 1. the Societal Framework*.
Washington, DC: Batelle Press, 345–439.

Olson, E., P. Hopkins, R. Pain and G. Vincett (2009) 'Youth, Religious Identity and
the Remaking of Post-Secular Scotland'. Unpublished manuscript, available upon
request from lead author.

Olson, L. R. (2007) 'Religious Affiliations, Political Preferences, and Ideological
Alignments', in J. A. Beckford and N. J. Demerath III (eds), *The SAGE Handbook of
the Sociology of Religion*. London: Sage, 438–58.

Oosterbaan, M. (2010) 'Virtual Re-Evangelization: Brazilian Churches, Media
and the Postsecular City', in A. Molendijk, J. Beaumont and C. Jedan (eds),
Exploring the Postsecular: The Religious, the Political, the Urban. Leiden: Brill,
281–308.

Orsi, R. (ed.) (1999) *Gods of the City: Religion and the American Urban Landscape*.
Bloomington: Indiana University Press.

Ostling, R. N. and J. K. Ostling (2000) *Mormon America*. New York: HarperCollins.

Owens, A. (2007) 'Using Legislation to Protect against Unethical Conversions in Sri
Lanka', *Journal of Law and Religion*, 22: 323–51.

Paerregaard, K. (2001) 'In the Footsteps of the Lord of Miracles: The Expatriation
of Religious Icons in the Peruvian Diaspora'. Working Paper Transnational
Communities Programme, WPTC-01-02 <http://www.transcomm.ox.ac.uk/
working%20papers/Paerregard.PDF> (accessed 9 July 2014).

Palmer, S. (2004) *Aliens Adored: Rael's UFO Religion*. New Brunswick, NJ: Rutgers
University Press.

Pannikar, K. N. (1991) 'A Historical Overview', in S. Gopal (ed.), *Anatomy of a
Confrontation: The Rise of Communal Politics in India*. London: Zed Books, 22–37.

Pargament, K. I. and K. I. Maton (2000) 'Religion in American Life: A Community
Psychology Perspective', in J. Rappaport and E. Seidman (eds), *Handbook of
Community Psychology*. New York: Kluwer Academic/Plenum, 495–522.

Park, C.-W. (2009) 'Christian Reactions to Government-Led Cremation in South Korea', in J. Bautista and F. G. L. Khek (eds), *Christianity and the State in Asia: Complicity and Conflict*. Oxon: Routledge, 155–65.

Parker, C. (1996) *Popular Religion and Modernization in Latin America*. New York: Orbis.

Parnini, S. N. (2013) 'The Crisis of the Rohingya as a Muslim Minority in Myanmar and Bilateral Relations with Bangladesh', *Journal of Muslim Minority Affairs*, 33 (2): 281–97.

Patterson, O., F. Weil and K. Patel (2010) 'The Role of Community in Disaster Response: Conceptual Models', *Population Research and Policy Review*, 29: 127–41.

Peterson, A., P. Williams and M. Vasquez (eds) (2001) *Christianity, Social Change and Globalization in the Americas*. New Brunswick, NJ: Rutgers University Press.

Petersen, G. D. (2009) 'Subject to Kings, Presidents, Rulers and Magistrates', in J. Bautista and F. G. L. Khek (eds), *Christianity and the State in Asia: Complicity and Conflict*. Oxon: Routledge, 166–83.

Phillips, D. (2009) 'Creating Home Spaces: Young British Muslim Women's Identity and Conceptualisations of Home', in P. Hopkins and R. Gale (eds), *Muslims in Britain: Race, Place and Identities*. Edinburgh: Edinburgh University Press, 23–36.

Phillips, D., C. Davis and P. Ratcliffe (2007) 'British Asian Narratives of Urban Space', *Transactions of the Institute of British Geographers*, 32: 217–34.

Pipa, T., T. Costanza, D. Thomas and M. Haley (3 November 2006) 'Research, Service Delivery Strategies, Best Practices: Disaster Mitigation'. Paper presented at 'Translating Research into Action: Nonprofits and the Renaissance of New Orleans', New Orleans.

Plüss, C. (2005) 'Constructing Globalized Ethnicity: Migrants from India in Hong Kong', *International Sociology*, 20 (2): 201–24.

Plüss, C. (2009) 'Migration and the Globalization of Religion', in P. B. Clarke (ed.), *The Oxford Handbook of The Sociology of Religion*. Oxford: Oxford University Press, 491–506.

Pollard, J. and M. Samers (2007) 'Islamic Banking and Finance: Postcolonial Political Economy and the Decentring of Econmic Geography', *Transactions of the Institute of British Geographers*, 32: 313–30.

Putnam, R. D. (2002) *Democracies in Flux: The Evolution of Social Capital in Contemporary Society*. New York: Oxford University Press.

Puwar, N. (2004) 'Fish in and Out of Water: A Theoretical Framework for Race and the Space of Academia', in I. Law, D. Phillips and I. Turney (eds), *Institutional Racism in Higher Education*. Stoke-on-Trent: Trentham Books, 49–58.

Quah, S. T. and C. K. Tong (1998) *Religion and Religious Revivalism in Singapore*. Singapore: Ministry of Community Development.

Rambo, L. R. (1989) 'Conversion: Toward a Holistic Model of Religious Change', *Pastoral Psychology*, 38 (1): 47–63.

Rambo, L. R. (1993) *Understanding Religious Conversion*. New Haven, CT: Yale University Press.

Rao, B. (2004) 'Religion, Law and Minorities in India: Problems with Judicial Regulation', in J. T. Richardson (ed.), *Regulating Religion: Case Studies from around the World*. New York: Kluwer Academic/Plenum, 381–413.

Reader, I. (1994) 'Japanese Religions', in J. Holm and J. Bowker (eds), *Sacred Place*. London: Frances Pinter, 187–202.

Rheingold, H. (1993) *The Virtual Community: Homesteading on the Electronic Frontier*. Reading, MA: Addison-Wesley.

Richardson, J. T. (1985) 'The Active vs. Passive Convert: Paradigm Conflict in Conversion/Recruitment Research', *Journal for the Scientific Study of Religion*, 24 (2): 163–79.

Richardson, J. T. and M. W. Stewart (2004) 'Medicalization and Regulation of Deviant Religions: An Application of Conrad and Schneider's Model', in J. T. Richardson (ed.), *Regulating Religion: Case Studies from Around the World*. New York: Kluwer Academic/Plenum, 507–34.

Robbins, T. (2003) 'Notes on the Contemporary Peril to Religious Freedom', in J. Beckford and J. Richardson (eds), *Challenging Religion: Essays in Honour of Eileen Barker*. London and New York: Routledge, 71–81.

Robbins, J. (2004) 'The Globalization of Pentecostal and Charismatic Christianity', *Annual Review of Anthropology*, 33: 117–43.

Robertson, R. (2009) 'Globalization, Theocratization, and Politicized Civil Religion', in P. B. Clarke (ed.), *The Oxford Handbook of The Sociology of Religion*. Oxford: Oxford University Press, 451–77.

Robertson, R. and J. Chirico (1985) 'Humanity, Globalization, and World-Wide Religious Resurgence: A Theoretical Exploration', *Sociological Analysis*, 46: 219–42.

Robinson, G. M. and D. A. Carson (2015) 'Resilient Communities: Transitions, Pathways and Resourcefulness', *The Geographical Journal*. DOI: 10.1111/geoj.12144.

Rorive, I. (2008) 'Religious Symbols in the Public Space: In Search of a European Answer', *Cardozo Law Review*, 30 (6): 2669–98.

Said, E. (1993) *Culture and Imperialism*. New York: Knopf.

Sampson, R. J., H. MacIndoe, D. McAdam and S. Weffer-Elizondo (2005) 'Civil Society Reconsidered: The Durable Nature and Community Structure of Collective Civic Action', *American Journal of Sociology*, 111 (3): 673–714.

Scheifinger, H. (2010) 'Hindu Embodiment and the Internet', *Online – Heidelberg Journal of Religions on the Internet*, 4 (1): 196–212.

Schober, J. (2007) 'Buddhism, Violence and The State in Burma (Myanmar) and Sri Lanka', in L. E. Cady and S. W. Simon (eds), *Religion and Conflict in South and Southeast Asia: Disrupting Violence*. London and New York: Routledge, 51–69.

Shaikh, A. M. (1992) 'A Muslim Response to the Education Reform Act 1988', *British Journal of Religious Education*, 14 (2): 74–98.

Shamir, R. (2005) 'Without Borders? Notes on Globalization as a Mobility Regime', *Sociological Theory*, 23 (2): 197–217.

Shaw, A. (1988) *A Pakistani Community in Britain*. Oxford: Basil Blackwell.

Shupe, A. (1991) 'Globalization versus Religious Nativism: Japan's Soka Gakkai in the World Arena', in R. Robertson and W. R. Garrett (eds), *Religion and the Global Order*. New York: Paragon House, 183–99.

Sider, R. J. and H. R. Unruh (2001) 'Evangelism and Church-State Partnerships', *Journal of Church & State*, 43 (2): 267–95.

Smilde, D. (2007) *Reason to Believe: Cultural Agency in Latin American Evangelism*. Berkeley: University of California Press.

Smit, B. and J. Wandel (2006) 'Adaptation, Adaptive Capacity and Vulnerability', *Global Environmental Change – Human and Policy Dimensions*, 16 (3): 282–92.

Smith, A. D. (1986) *The Ethnic Origins of Nations*. Oxford: Blackwell.

Smith, J. Z. (1978) 'The Wobbling Pivot', in J. Z. Smith (ed.), *Map Is Not Territory: Studies in the History of Religions*. Leiden: Brill, 88–103.

Springer, S. (2011) 'Violence Sits in Places? Cultural Practice, Neoliberal Rationalism, and Virulent Imaginative Geographies', *Political Geography*, 30: 90–8.

Stark, R. and W. S. Bainbridge (1996) *A Theory of Religion*. New Brunswick, NJ: Rutgers University Press.

Stoll, D. and D. Levine (1997) 'Bridging the Gap between Empowerment and Power in Latin America', in S. H. Rudolph and J. Piscatori (eds), *Transnational Religion and Fading States*. Boulder, CO: Westview Press, 63–103.

Stump, R. W. (2008) *The Geography of Religion: Faith, Place and Space*. New York: Rowman and Littlefield.

Sultan, M. (1999) 'Choosing Islam: A Study of Swedish Converts', *Social Compass*, 46 (3): 325–35.

Talmon, Y. (1962) 'Pursuit of the Millennium: The Relation between Religion and Social Change', *Archives Europeennes de Sociologie*, 3: 125–48.

Tambiah, S. (1986) *Sri Lanka: Ethnic Fratricide and the Dismantling of Democracy*. Chicago: University of Chicago Press.

Tan, C. (2008) 'From Moral Values to Citizenship Education: The Teaching of Religion in Singapore Schools', in A. E. Lai (ed.), *Religious Diversity in Singapore*. Singapore: Institute of Southeast Asian Studies, 321–41.

Tan, E. K. B. (2008) 'Keeping God in Place: The Management of Religion in Singapore', in A. E. Lai (ed.), *Religious Diversity in Singapore*. Singapore: Institute of Southeast Asian Studies, 55–82.

Taylor, C. (2007) *A Secular Age*. Cambridge, MA: Belknap Press of Harvard University Press,

Taylor, M. C. (2001) *The Moment of Complexity: Emerging Network Culture*. Chicago: University of Chicago Press.

Taylor, R., J. S. Jackson and L. Chatters (1997) *Family Life in Black America*. Thousand Oaks: Sage.

Tong, C. K. (2007) *Rationalizing Religion: Religious Conversion, Revivalism and Competition in Singapore Society*. The Netherlands: Brill.

Tong, C. K. and L. Kong (2000) 'Religion and Modernity: Ritual Transformations and the Reconstruction of Space and Time', *Social & Cultural Geography*, 1 (1): 29–44.

Tsing, A. (2000) 'The Global Situation', *Current Anthropology*, 15 (3): 327–60.

Tweed, T. (1999) *Our Lady of Exile*. New York: Oxford University Press.

Tweed, T. (2006) *Crossing and Dwelling: A Theory of Religion*. Cambridge, MA: Harvard University Press.

US Department of State (1999) 'Annual Report on International Religious Freedom for 1999: Israel'. <http://www.state.gov/www/global/human_rights/irf/irf_rpt/1999/irf_israel99.html> (accessed 21 May 2015).

US State Department (2010) '2010 International Religious Freedom Report'. <http://www.state.gov/j/drl/rls/irf/2010_5/index.htm> (accessed 26 March 2012).

Valentine, S. R. (2008) *Islam and the Ahmadiyya jama'at: History, Belief, Practice*. London: Hurst.

Valins, O. (2003) 'Defending Identities or Segregating Communities? Faith-Based Schooling and the UK Jewish Community', *Geoforum*, 34: 235–47.

van den Berghe, P. L. (1967) *Race and Racism: A Comparative Perspective*. New York: Wiley.

van der Veer, P. (ed.) (1996) *Conversion to Modernities: The Globalization of Christianity*. London: Routledge.

van der Veer, P. (2001) *Imperial Encounters: Religion and Modernity in India and Britain*. Princeton, NJ: Princeton University Press.

Vasquez, M. A. (2008) 'Studying Religion in Motion: A Networks Approach', *Method and Theory in the Study of Religion*, 20: 151–84.

Vasquez, M. A. and M. F. Marquardt (2000) 'Globalizing the Rainbow Madonna: Old Time Religion in the Present Age', *Theory, Culture & Society*, 17 (4): 119–43.

Vasquez, M., M. Marquardt and I. Gomez (2001) 'Saving Souls Transnationally: Pentecostalism and Gangs in El Salvador and the United States', in A. Peterson, P. Williams and M. Vasquez (eds), *Christianity, Social Change and Globalization in the Americas*. New Brunswick, NJ: Rutgers University Press.

Vasquez, M. A. and M. F. Marquardt (2003) *Globalizing the Sacred: Religion across the Americas*. New Brunswick, NJ: Rutgers University Press.

Vertovec, S. (1999) 'Conceiving and Researching Transnationalism', *Ethnic and Racial Studies*, 22: 447–62.

Vertovec, S. (2000) 'Religion and Diaspora: New Landscapes of Religion in the West, Oxford'. Working Paper of the Transnational Communities Programme WPTC-01-01, <http://www.transcomm.ox.ac.uk/working%20papers/Vertovec01.PDF> (accessed 18 April 2012).

Viswanathan, G. (1998) *Outside the Fold: Conversion, Modernity, and Belief*. Princeton, NJ: Princeton University Press.

Vryonis, S. (2005) *The Mechanism of Catastrophe: The Turkish Pogrom of December 6–7, 1955, and the Destruction of the Greek Community of Istanbul*. New York: Greekworks.

Walker, B., L. Gunderson and A. Kinzig (2006) 'A Handful of Heuristics and Some Propositions for Understanding Resilience in Social-Ecological System', *Ecology and Society*, 11 (1): 13.

Wallace, I. (2006) 'Territory, Typology, Theology: Geopolitics and the Christian Scriptures', *Geopolitics*, 11 (2): 209–30.

Wanner, C. (2004) 'Missionaries of Faith and Culture: Evangelical Encounters in Ukraine', *Slavic Review*, 63 (4): 732–55.

Watanabe, M. (2001) 'Opposition to Aum and the Rise of the "Anti-Cult" Movement in Japan', in R. J. Kisala and M. R. Mullins (eds), *Religion and Social Crisis in Japan: Understanding Japanese Society Through the Aum Affair*. Hampshire and New York: Palgrave, 87–106.

Weber, M. (1956) *The Sociology of Religion*. Translated by Ephraim Fischoff. Boston, MA: Beacon Press.

Weichselgartner, J. and I. Kelman (2015) 'Geographies of Resilience: Challenges and Opportunities of a Descriptive Concept', *Progress in Human Geography*, 39 (3): 249–67.

Werbner, P. (1991) 'Factionalism and Violence in British Pakistani Communal Politics', in H. Donnan and P. Werbner (eds), *Economy and Culture in Pakistan*. London: Macmillan, 188–215.

Werbner, P. (1996) 'Stamping the Earth with the Name of Allah: *Zikr* and the Sacralizing of Space Among British Muslims', *Cultural Anthropology*, 11 (3): 309–38.

West, J. (2006) 'Religion as Dissident Geopolitics? Geopolitical Discussions within the Recent Publications of Fethullah Gülen', *Geopolitics*, 11 (2): 280–99.

Wielander, G. (2009) 'Bridging the Gap? an Investigation of Beijing Intellectual House Church Activities and Their Implications for China's Democratization', *Journal of Contemporary China*, 18: 849–64.

Wiley, A., H. Warren and D. S. Montanelli (2002) 'Shelter in a Time of Storm: Parenting in Two Poor, Rural Africa American Communities', *Family Relations*, 51: 265–73.

Wilford, J. (2010) 'Sacred Archipelagos: Geographies of Secularization', *Progress in Human Geography*, 34: 328–48.

Winter, G. (1961) *The Suburban Captivity of the Churches: An Analysis of Protestant Responsibility in the Expanding Metropolis*. New York: Doubleday.

Wisner, B., Gaillard, J. C. and Kelman, I. (eds) (2012) *Handbook of Hazards and Disaster Risk Reduction*. Abingdon: Routledge.

Wohlrab-Sahr, M. (1999) 'Conversion to Islam: Between Syncretism and Symbolic Battle', *Social Compass*, 46 (3): 351–62.

Woods, O. (2012a) 'The Geographies of Religious Conversion', *Progress in Human Geography*, 36 (4): 440–56.

Woods, O. (2012b) 'Sri Lanka's Informal Religious Economy: Evangelical Competitiveness and Buddhist Hegemony in Perspective', *Journal for the Scientific Study of Religion*, 51 (2): 203–19.

Woods, O. (2013a) 'The Spatial Modalities of Evangelical Christian Growth in Sri Lanka: Evangelism, Social Ministry and the Structural Mosaic', *Transactions of the Institute of British Geographers*, 38 (4): 652–64.

Woods, O. (2013b) 'Converting Houses into Churches: The Mobility, Fission, and Sacred Networks of Evangelical House Churches in Sri Lanka', *Environment and Planning D: Society and Space*, 31: 1062–75.

Woodward, M. (2007) 'Religious Conflict and the Globalization of Knowledge in Indonesian History', in L. E. Cady and S. W. Simon (eds), *Religion and Conflict in South and Southeast Asia: Disrupting Violence*. London and New York: Routledge, 85–104.

Wright, T. (2008) 'Indonesia's Mega Churches', *Asia Weekly* 2 (37) (September): 12–22.

Yang, F. (1998) 'Chinese Conversion to Evangelical Christianity: The Importance of Social and Cultural Contexts', *Sociology of Religion*, 59 (3): 237–57.

Yang, F. (2005) 'Lost in the Market, Saved at McDonald's: Conversion to Christianity in Urban China', *Journal for the Scientific Study of Religion*, 44: 423–41.

Yang, F. (2006) 'The Red, Black and Gray Markets of Religion in China', *Sociological Quarterly*, 47 (1): 93–122.

Yoshihide, S. (2010) 'Geopolitical Mission Strategy: The Case of the Unification Church in Japan and Korea', *Japanese Journal of Religious Studies*, 37 (2): 317–34.

Zaleski, J. (1997) *The Soul of Cyberspace: How New Technology Is Changing Our Spiritual Lives*. San Francisco, CA: Harper.

News Articles

ABC News Australia, 'Iraq Crisis: Could an ISIS Caliphate Ever Govern the Entire Muslim World?', 3 July 2014.

ABC Radio Australia, 'East Timor Looks to New Agreement with Vatican', 17 October 2008.

Agence France-Presse, 'Bavarian Catholics Angered by Muezzin's Call', 23 July 1997.

All Africa, 'Muslims Ordered to Pull Out of Catholic Schools', 24 October 2009.

BBC Monitoring Caucasus, 'Hijab Banned at University in Russia's Pyatigorsk – Rebel Website', 24 December 2010.

BBC News, 'Indian Prime Minister Shot Dead', 31 October 1984.

BBC News, 'Violence Follows Gandhi Killing', 1 November 1984.

BBC News, 'Danish Muslims in Cartoon Protest', 15 February 2008.

BBC News, 'Timeline: Ayodhya Holy Site Crisis', 30 September 2010.

BBC News, 'Berlin House of One: The First Church-Mosque-Synagogue?', 21 June 2014.

BBC News, 'Sudan Death Row Case: US Works for Meriam Ibrahim Exit', 24 June 2014.

Channel NewsAsia, 'Fire Safety Concerns Affect Lunar New Year Celebrations in Thailand', 15 January 2009.

Channel NewsAsia, 'Government Won't Interfere in AWARE Sage', 26 April 2009.

Daily Mail, 'Berlusconi's Allies Demand Ban on Building New Mosques, Fearing Advent of "Eurabia"', 16 September 2008.

Daily Mail, 'Mosque's Plan to Broadcast Call to Prayer from Loudspeaker "Will Create Muslim Ghetto"', 14 January 2008.

Daily News & Analysis, 'Forward March', 3 July 2009.

Exeter Express & Echo, 'Catholic MP Steps into Row Over Adoption Agency Rules', 30 January 2007.

Financial Times, 'Satanic Verses Lifts the Lid on Long-Standing Racial Tension: The Wider Issues Arising from the Rushdie Affair', 24 June 1989.

Financial Times, 'Promise of Peace Still Not Fulfilled', 3 February 1998.

Gulf News, 'Letter from Lahore: Curb on Misuse of Loudspeakers', 11 June 2001.

Hindustan Times, 'VHP Body Threatens Stir over Prayer Ban at Mosque', 14 December 2000.

Hindustan Times, 'A Heavy Cross to Bear', 27 June 2007.

India Today, 'Babri Masjid Bloody Aftermath', 5 December 2011.

Irish Times, 'Wearing the Hijab at School', 4 June 2008.

Irish Times, 'Hijab Symbolises Rift between Islamic and European Values', 15 September 2009.

Jerusalem Post, 'Efrat Preparing "Zionist Response" to Synagogue Desecration', 29 October 2000.

Kent News, 'Religious Leaders React to Community-Crushing Riots', 20 August 2011.

Legally India, 'Katju's Latest Essay: Freedom of Speech to Avoid Insulting Religion: Jesus Gay OK; Lit Prizes "a Mystery", Midnight's Children "Unreadable"', 30 January 2012.

Los Angeles Times, 'Disputed Tomb of the Patriarchs; Arabs, Jews, Pray Under Same Roof, Under Guard', 29 March 1986.

MSNBC, 'Red Mosque Cleric Predicts "Islamic Revolution"', 7 December 2007.

National Secular Society, 'Government Resists Calls to Regulate Madrassas', 26 January 2012 <http://www.secularism.org.uk/news/2012/01/government-resists-calls-to-regulate-madrassas>.

New Straits Times, 'Ban Religious Processions', 18 February 2010.

New Straits Times, 'Guan Eng Blamed for Call to Ban Religious Procession', 19 February 2010.

New York Times, 'Sikhs, in Rally, Press the Army to Quit Temple', 3 September 1984.

New York Times, 'Gunman Slays 20 at Site of Mosque', 25 February 1994.

New York Times, 'Call to Prayer in Michigan Causes Tension', 5 May 2004.

New York Times, 'Judge Bars "Intelligent Design" from Pa. Classes', 20 December 2005.

New York Times, 'Germans Split Over a Mosque and the Role of Islam', 5 July 2007.

New York Times, 'Across Nation, Mosque Projects Meet Opposition', 7 August 2010.

New York Times, 'US Actions in Iraq Fueled Rise of a Rebel: Baghdadi of ISIS Pushes an Islamist Crusade', 10 August 2014.

Pakistan Press International Information Services, 'Ban on Bringing Out Religious Processions, Rallies in Quettato Continue: Governor Balochistan', 10 April 2004.

Straits Times, 'Bigger Does Not Mean Better', 9 October 1997.

Straits Times, GRCs: 20 years on, 2 August 2008.

Straits Times, 'Thaipusam Rules Not New: Shanmugam', 15 January 2011.

Sunday Herald Sun, 'World in Brief', 21 March 2004.

Sydney Morning Herald, 'Web of Disbelief: Religion Has Staked a Big Claim in Cyberspace, but Has It Done a Faustian Deal?', 23 December 2000.

The Dartmouth Review, 'Religious Hypocrisy', 29 February 2012.

The Economist, 'Taken Unawares: Liberals Rally to Take on the Christian Right', 7 May 2009.

The Economist, 'Myanmar's Shame', 20 May 2015.

The Guardian, 'Opposition to Satanic Verses – Director of Islamic Foundation of Leicester', 14 February 1990.

The Guardian, 'Ground Zero Mosque Plans "Fuelling Anti-Muslim Protests across US"', 12 August 2010.

The Guardian, 'Catholic Church Steps Up Gay Marriage Campaign', 11 March 2012.

The Guardian, 'Verdict on UK Riots: People Need a "Stake in Society", Says Report', 28 March 2012.

The Guardian, 'Nigerian Man Is Locked Up after Saying He Is an Atheist', 25 June 2014.

The Independent, 'Life Under ISIS: The Everyday Reality of Living in the Islamic "Caliphate" with Its 7th Century Laws, Very Modern Methods and Merciless Violence', 15 March 2015.

The Sunday Times, 'Religion Not Clearly Defined in Bill on Forcible Conversion', 8 February 2009.

The Telegraph, 'Benjamin Netanyahu Backs Ban on Mosques Using Loudspeakers', 12 December 2011.

The Times of India, 'No Loopholes in ASI Evidence', 2 October 2010.

The Times of India, 'Death Mars Puri Rath Yatra', 3 July 2011.

The Washington Times, 'Ban Koran-Burning?; If Islam Becomes a Protected Faith, Free Expression Will Be No More', 8 April 2011.

Today, '"Still Our No 1 Security Concern"; Terrorism, JI and Self-Radicalised Lone Wolves Are Real Threat Today, Says DPM Teo', 10 September 2011.

Toronto Sun, 'Montreal Borough Votes To Ban Religious Processions', 6 April 2012.

USA Today, 'At Conservative Church, Once-Shunned Gays Fuel Growth', 19 October 2011.

Washington Post, 'Put Kindness Back into Public Policy, Coalitions Urge', 10 June 1993.

Washington Post, 'Here's Some Good News, America', 26 March 1994.

Xinhua News Agency, 'China Focus: China's Burial Traditions Under Fire after Joss Paper Burning Kills 2', 5 April 2011.

Index

Lightning Source UK Ltd.
Milton Keynes UK
UKOW01f1918100817
307039UK00001B/55/P